T0323864

ANCIENT PHILOSOPHICAL POETICS

What is poetry? Why do human beings produce and consume it? What effects does it have on them? Can it give them insight into truth, or is it dangerously misleading? This book is a wide-ranging study of the very varied answers which ancient philosophers gave to such questions. An extended discussion of Plato's *Republic* shows how the two discussions of poetry are integrated with each other, and with the dialogue's central themes. Aristotle's *Poetics* is read in the context of his understanding of poetry as a natural human behaviour and an intrinsically valuable component of a good human life. Two chapters trace the development of the later Platonist tradition from Plutarch to Plotinus, Longinus and Porphyry, exploring its intellectual debts to Epicurean, allegorical and Stoic approaches to poetry. The book will be essential reading for classicists as well as ancient philosophers and modern philosophers of art and aesthetics.

Key Themes in Ancient Philosophy provides concise books, written by major scholars and accessible to non-specialists, on important themes in ancient philosophy which remain of philosophical interest today.

MALCOLM HEATH is Professor of Greek Language and Literature at the University of Leeds. He has also taught at the Universities of Oxford and St Andrews. His publications include *The Poetics of Greek Tragedy* (1987), *Political Comedy in Aristophanes* (1987), *Unity in Greek Poetics* (1989), *Hermogenes* On Issues: *Strategies of Argument in Later Greek Rhetoric* (1995), *Interpreting Classical Texts* (2002) and *Menander: A Rhetor in Context* (2004), as well as many journal articles. He has translated Aristotle's *Poetics* for Penguin Classics (1996), and is currently working on a book on Aristotle and the anthropology of poetry.

KEY THEMES IN ANCIENT PHILOSOPHY

SERIES EDITORS

Catherine Osborne

Reader in Philosophy, University of East Anglia

G. R. F. Ferrari

Professor of Classics, University of California, Berkeley

Each book in this new series offers a concise and accessible treatment by a single author of a topic of major philosophical importance in the ancient Greek and Roman world. The emphasis is on a discussion of those debates of real philosophical interest, placed within their historical context. Future volumes will consider topics such as virtue, knowledge, psychology, cosmology, society, love and friendship, cause and explanation and persuasion and argument. The books are designed for use in a teaching context, where they will bridge a gap between general introductions to individual philosophers or periods and specialist monographs. They will also appeal to anyone interested in the enduring influence and significance of ancient philosophy.

ANCIENT PHILOSOPHICAL POETICS

MALCOLM HEATH

CAMBRIDGE
UNIVERSITY PRESS

CAMBRIDGE
UNIVERSITY PRESS

University Printing House, Cambridge CB2 8BS, United Kingdom

One Liberty Plaza, 20th Floor, New York, NY 10006, USA

477 Williamstown Road, Port Melbourne, VIC 3207, Australia

314-321, 3rd Floor, Plot 3, Splendor Forum, Jasola District Centre, New Delhi - 110025, India

103 Penang Road, #05-06/07, Visioncrest Commercial, Singapore 238467

Cambridge University Press is part of the University of Cambridge.

It furthers the University's mission by disseminating knowledge in the pursuit of
education, learning and research at the highest international levels of excellence.

www.cambridge.org
Information on this title: www.cambridge.org/9780521168687

© Malcolm Heath 2013

First published 2013

A catalogue record for this publication is available from the British Library

Library of Congress Cataloging in Publication data
Heath, Malcolm.
Ancient philosophical poetics / Malcolm Heath.
p.   cm. – (Key themes in ancient philosophy)
Includes bibliographical references and index.
ISBN 978-0-521-19879-0 (hardback) – ISBN 978-0-521-16868-7 (paperback)
1. Poetics–History–To 1500.   2. Philosophy, Ancient, in literature.   3. Language and
languages–Philosophy.   4. Plato. Republic.   I. Title.
PN1040.H43 2012
808.1–dc23
2012023161

ISBN 978-0-521-19879-0 Hardback
ISBN 978-0-521-16868-7 Paperback

Contents

Preface

My first debt is to the series editors, John Ferrari and Catherine Osborne, for inviting me to write this book. My second, and most important, is to the students on my course 'Should We Ban Homer?' in 2009/10: without their engaged and intelligent contributions, developing the material would have been much harder, and much less enjoyable. An anonymous reader for Cambridge University Press provided insightful commentary on the initial outline proposal. Without that stimulus, Chapter 4 would have had even less to say about the Epicureans than it does, and I might have persisted (with however bad a conscience) in my pretexts for not engaging with Plotinus: the resulting change of plan has had beneficial consequences, direct and indirect, throughout Chapters 4 and 5. Chapter 5 also benefited from Timothy Costelloe's timely invitation to contribute to an edited collection on the history of the sublime (Heath 2012). Some of the ideas in Chapter 2 were refined in the light of discussion of *Republic* 2–3 and 10 at two meetings of the Yorkshire Ancient Philosophy Network in 2010/11. The editors put me further in their debt by making extremely helpful comments on a draft, as did my colleague Regine May.

Chapter 3 draws in part on work undertaken for an ongoing project on Aristotle and the anthropology of poetry (Heath 2008; 2009c; 2009d; 2011); the approach outlined here will in due course be worked out in more detail in a monograph, provisionally entitled *Poetical Animals*. I am grateful to the Arts Humanities Research Council and the Leverhulme Trust for their financial support for this project.

Introduction

This is a book about ancient philosophical poetics. It is not concerned with ancient literary theory, criticism or scholarship in general. Those are interesting topics with important implications for our understanding of ancient poetry.[1] Here, however, our concern is with ancient attempts to answer specifically philosophical questions about poetry.

Specifically philosophical questions? That is not a well-defined or stable class. But I take it to include, for example, such questions as these. *What* is poetry? How is it related to, and differentiated from, other human practices and products? *Why* is poetry? What motivates its production and consumption? If it is a universal human behaviour, common to cultures all over the world, how is it rooted in human nature? What does poetry contribute to human life? What is the point of it? In what ways may it be of value? Are we doing it properly? Eating is a natural human behaviour, but people are prone to eat things that are bad for them. Is the consumption of junk poetry harmful? How could we tell if our taste for poetry is leading us astray? If poetry is potentially dangerous, should society protect us by regulating its production or dissemination? Should there be laws to promote its true purpose? If we live in a society without such laws, how can we organise our own lives to ensure that we, and those for whose well-being we care, have a healthy diet, whether of food, or of poetry? These questions take us far beyond technical aspects of poetics, and beyond aesthetics narrowly defined. There are broader issues in, most obviously, ethics and politics, but also in psychology and anthropology. These in turn lead us on to theology; to questions about the fundamental structures of reality, the sources of knowledge, and the grounds of value; and also, of course, to differing conceptions of philosophy itself.

---

[1] Heath 2002: 99–134.

Such an expansive agenda demands selectivity. Plato and Aristotle select themselves. Plato, an elusive ventriloquist, resists systematisation. The *Republic*, which is the main focus of Chapter 2, by no means exhausts his engagement with poetry (some other strands will make their appearance in later chapters); but it provides an opportunity to follow the development of a sustained argument about poetry in the context of larger concerns. Aristotle, by contrast, is systematic, in the sense that he is constantly alert to connections between different parts of a hugely ambitious, though always provisional and evolving, philosophical project. Chapter 3 therefore takes the *Poetics*, which is primarily technical in its concerns, as a starting-point from which to work outwards to other texts so as to clarify philosophical premises left unstated in the *Poetics* itself.

By the criterion of philosophical stature, Plotinus would be our third selection; but he does not have an extensively articulated poetics. Proclus, who brought the later Platonist synthesis to a peak of sophistication, is too complex to be dealt with adequately in short compass. My approach to later Platonist poetics therefore examines the dynamics of a philosophical tradition rather than the thought of a single dominant figure. Chapter 4 exhibits an important transition in Platonist thinking about poetry, and explores the background to it. The conclusions to which that transition led are likely to strike modern readers as implausible and, when proposed by philosophers who present themselves as followers of Plato, paradoxical. Chapter 5 confronts this paradox, surveying the Platonic resources which motivated and made possible the later Platonist approach, and illustrating some of its variants. Plotinus provides one of three case studies; the others are Maximus of Tyre and Longinus. These selections may seem odd: Maximus would not figure on any list of the greatest philosophers of antiquity, and the attribution of the treatise *On Sublimity* to Longinus is disputed. But the case against Longinus' authorship is, in my view, inconclusive, and Maximus proves to have more substance – as a representative figure, at least – than may appear on superficial acquaintance.

Maximus' orations and the treatise *On Sublimity* have at least the merit of survival. I have chosen in this book to concentrate mainly on extant works because it is hard to determine what philosophical positions were developed, and how they were argued, in texts that cannot be read *in extenso*. That is my excuse for giving only brief attention to Epicurean poetics, which must be precariously reconstructed from fragmentary (and often tendentious) evidence. The Stoics, too, are under-represented, figuring only insofar as their modifications of certain traditional conceptions of poetry were reabsorbed (with further modifications) into later Platonism. Selectivity, as I have said, has been unavoidable.

But let us begin at the beginning: how did poetry become an issue for philosophy?

CHAPTER ONE

Poetry: the roots of a problem

I ARCHAIC POETRY

One of the earliest surviving Greek poems describes the poet's encounter with the Muses. While Hesiod was tending his sheep on the slopes of Mount Helicon, the goddesses 'taught him beautiful song', gave him a staff (the characteristic accoutrement of the poetic performers known as rhapsodes), breathed a divine voice into him, and commissioned him 'to hymn the race of blessed immortals'. In the course of this encounter, the Muses say (*Theogony* 26–8):

Shepherd bumpkins! Utter disgraces! No more than bellies! We know how to tell many falsehoods resembling real truths, and we know, when we choose, how to sing true things.

These puzzling words, by turns mocking and cryptic, are commonly understood as endorsing the truthfulness of Hesiod's poem. But why, in that case, would Hesiod have advertised his patrons' deceptive potential? One possibility is that he needed to explain discrepancies between his own and others' poems. If so, there is no attribution of authority to poetry in general: Hesiod claims a special (though not necessarily unique) authority for his own poetry. But this claim to authority depends on three premises which there is no reason to grant: that Hesiod is telling the truth about his encounter with the Muses; that he correctly understood the Muses' words as a promise to tell him the truth; and that the Muses made that promise truthfully. The first two premises are unsupported; the Muses' own words undermine the third. An audience might reasonably view the content of Hesiod's poetry agnostically, therefore. So might Hesiod himself. In attributing these words to his Muses he acknowledges the uncertainty inherent in any human attempt to account for the origins of the universe and the history of the gods. These are matters beyond direct human knowledge, exceeding our capacity to distinguish truth from plausible falsehood. We are dependent on insights that come from outside

4

us, and cannot confidently pass judgement on the authenticity of what we receive.[1]

The Muses' deceitfulness should not surprise us. Archaic poetry takes it for granted that gods are deceptive. In epic narrative, mortals are unaware of the divine determinants of their experience. Priam's confidence that Hector's piety protected his body in death, even though it did not save his life (*Il.* 24.425–8), is true as far as it goes. But sacrifices will not save Troy from destruction: Zeus has given greater weight to the wishes of Hera, who is motivated by an intense personal hatred (4.1–68). Priam does not know this, and the limitations of his insight are not corrected when Hermes, the god with whom he is unwittingly conversing, finally abandons his disguise (24.459–69). Moreover, Homer's gods are capable of deceiving humans into self-destructive wrongdoing. Athene disguises her identity when – on Zeus's instructions – she induces Pandarus to break a truce (4.69–104). Even when its divine origin is revealed to the recipient, advice may be deceptive: Agamemnon's dream, though truly sent by Zeus, is untruthful (2.1–40).

The narrator of the *Iliad* makes clear his (and our) dependence on the Muses for information about matters beyond our reliable knowledge. When he invokes the Muses, he contrasts their eye-witness knowledge with human ignorance: only the renown of past deeds has reached our ears (*Il.* 2.484–92). The poet's song will be reliable if the Muses respond positively to his request. But the transmission of the 'renowns of men' is recognised by poet and characters alike as a function of epic (*Il.* 6.358; 9.189, 526; *Od.* 3.203–4; 8.72–4, 580; 24.296–8). If poetry is a vector of renown, and renown is not a reliable source of knowledge, then poetry cannot be consistently reliable. Perhaps not all poetry is inspired by the Muses; perhaps, as in Hesiod, the Muses do not always tell the truth.

The *Odyssey*, too, expresses an awareness that poets are purveyors of falsehood. Odysseus, a notably untruthful story-teller, is repeatedly compared to a bard. When Alcinous pays him this compliment (*Od.* 11.363–9), it is not the manner of Odysseus' story-telling that carries the conviction of truth (Alcinous says explicitly that falsehood cannot reliably be discerned from the way people speak) but his physical appearance (which Athene has altered: 8.18–22). Eumaeus' use of the comparison is even more telling (17.513–21): he is warning Penelope not to trust the stranger, whose skilful stories he rightly disbelieves (14.166–9, 363–5, 378–89).

---

[1] Hesiod is more assertive in *Works and Days* 10: 'I shall speak real truths to Perses.' Here his theme, ethics and farming, falls within the bounds of human experience.

Archaic audiences would not have found this puzzling. Poetry did not transmit stories in fixed canonical versions; fluid traditions gave rise to multiple conflicting variants. Adaptation and innovation can be detected in the Homeric poems themselves, and Hesiod corrects the *Theogony*'s account of Strife (225–6) by distinguishing two kinds of strife in *Works and Days* (11–26). His Muses had misled him on this point, at least.

It does not, however, follow that archaic poets had no influence over their audiences' beliefs. A common framework underpinned the polyphony of conflicting detail, and the tradition's repeated rehearsal of a shared pattern of cultural, ethical and religious assumptions would have had a powerful cumulative effect in reinforcing and transmitting certain patterns of thought. Audiences do not need to think about ideas made familiar by repetition. Indeed, poetry may actually inhibit the ability to think critically about its content, or to exercise reflective control over the effect its content has on them. In archaic and classical sources there is a sustained emphasis on the intensely, bewitchingly pleasurable nature of poetry. Its sound, rhythm and other formal qualities astound and seduce, as does the imaginatively compelling impact of its narrative content. Hesiod's Muses were born to be 'forgetfulness of ills and relief from cares' (*Th.* 55). In the *Odyssey*, when a singer's performance goes well the audience listens with silent, rapt attention (1.325–6). This effect is compared to enchantment (1.337, 17.518–21).[2]

2 PHILOSOPHICAL CRITIQUE

Poetry, then, is a medium which cannot guarantee the truth of the things it tells us. Nor can we reliably assess their truth, both because they are beyond human knowledge and because poetry's bewitching psychological power puts us into a state of mind that inhibits reflection. For that very reason, poetry's rehearsal of a familiar worldview is likely to influence our beliefs, values and behavioural tendencies at a level so deep that we are unaware of what is happening to us, and unable to control it. In this sense, it may be correct to say that 'from the beginning all have learned from Homer' (Xenophanes B10) or that 'most people's teacher is Hesiod' (Heraclitus B57). Here we glimpse the beginnings of critical scrutiny of poetry early in the history of Greek philosophy.[3]

---

[2] This section draws on Heath 1985: 258–62. Other views of the *Theogony* proem: e.g. Bowie 1993, 8–23; Finkelberg 1998: 131–60. Early poetics: Walsh 1984: 3–36.
[3] Introduction to presocratic philosophy: Warren 2007; see further Long 1999; Curd and Graham 2008. General discussions of the issues touched on in this section include Most 1999; Morgan 2000: 46–88.

The fragments of Xenophanes' poems give some idea of the grounds on which he developed his wide-ranging critique of traditional poets.[4] Homer and Hesiod are condemned for attributing immoral behaviour ('stealing, adultery, and mutual deception') to gods (B11–12). He describes stories of gods fighting Titans and Giants as useless fictions (B1.21–3), and rejects stories of the birth of gods (B14). Hesiod's *Theogony* included both kinds of story, as did other early poetry. But Xenophanes' revisionary account of the world and the gods went deeper. Everything that has traditionally been believed about the gods is wrong: 'there is one god, greatest among gods and men, not at all like mortals in body, nor in mind' (B23). We do not learn this from the Muses, but must search for the truth for ourselves: 'the gods did not disclose everything to mortals from the beginning, but mortals in time by searching improve their discoveries' (B18). No one has, or will ever have, clear knowledge of gods: even if someone happens to say exactly what is the case, it is only opinion (B34). But some opinions should be credited: 'let these things be believed, as being like real truths [*eoikota tois etumoisi*]' (B35). That last phrase, though not identical to Hesiod's 'resembling real truths [*etumoisi homoia*]', is close enough to suggest a deliberate echo and a pointed challenge.

What is the nature of that challenge, and how radical an innovation was involved? Early Greek poets, I have argued, had a subtler self-awareness than is often recognised.[5] The seeming modesty of the claim which Xenophanes makes for himself looks questionable in this light. The traditional poet can be genuinely modest about his poetry's claim to truth. Adopting a heteronomous pose, he has no need to authorise the content of his poetry himself; its authority depends on the Muses, who (we are reminded) need not tell the truth. By contrast, the philosopher's bid for epistemic autonomy means that he must be *self*-authorising. This is so even where the truth-claim is qualified. Though he disclaims access to truth as such, Xenophanes is nevertheless confident that he has achieved something sufficiently like the truth that it has a claim on our acceptance; and he is confident that he has through his own powers succeeded in discovering enough about truth to enable him to distinguish authentic from deceptive likeness to the truth. Why should we believe him?

---

[4] Commentary: Lesher 1992. See also Granger 2007a.

[5] Contrast e.g. Most 1999: 343: 'Homer and Hesiod claim that … the only validation of their poetry is that it tells the truth, conforming veridically to a real past or present state of affairs. The epic Muse guarantees a superhuman knowledge of matters distant in time and space or otherwise remote from ordinary human knowledge.'

Why, for that matter, should we believe Parmenides?[6] Like Hesiod, he claims dependence on divinity; his goddess, like Hesiod's Muses, speaks both truth and falsehood. She, however, tells us which is which, contrasting 'the unshaken heart of truth' with 'the beliefs of mortals, in which there is no true conviction' (B1.29–30). Whatever we may or may not conjecture about Parmenides' ecstatic experiences,[7] the only reasonable grounds for assent is the force of the goddess's arguments: she herself urges him to judge what she has said by reason (*logos*, B7.5–6). This is good advice: we cannot do better when we need to make up our minds about truth and falsehood than to follow the arguments that seem best to their conclusions.

But philosophers notoriously disagree with one another. Heraclitus derided not only Hesiod, but also Xenophanes, Pythagoras and Hecataeus (B40).[8] If philosophers cannot agree among themselves on which philosopher's arguments are best and which conclusions should be accepted, how can we trust what any of them says? This point is philosophically serious: philosophical disagreement (*diaphōnia*) was used by ancient sceptics as a reason for suspending judgement.[9] That does not let the poets off the hook; but it puts the philosophers on a hook of their own. They cannot question poetry from a standpoint that is beyond question. How, then, will they convince us that they have good reason for saying the things they do about poetry, and about the worldview expressed in poetry? Within a traditional culture, the familiarity of basic assumptions may pre-empt the question of their truth. Philosophical critique removes that complacency; at the same time, it prompts questions about the philosophers' counter-traditional claims that will not be easy to answer.

[6] Commentary: Coxon 2009; Palmer 2009 provides a demanding analysis. See also Granger 2008.
[7] Gemelli Marciano 2008.
[8] See Granger 2004. Commentary: Robinson 1987.
[9] S.E. *P.* 1.165 (cf. 1.88–9); Cic. *Ac.* 2.117–47. See Barnes 1995a: 1–35.

CHAPTER TWO

A radical solution: Plato's Republic

According to early Greek poets, poetry bewitches us (§1.1). The state of mind it puts us into inhibits us from thinking critically about what it is saying. It may shape our thoughts, imaginations and actions at a level too deep for us to be aware of or control. That psychological power was still felt in the fifth and fourth centuries. Gorgias speaks of poetry's over-powering emotional impact: 'its hearers shudder with terror, shed tears of pity, and yearn with sad longing; the soul, affected by the words, feels as its own an emotion aroused by the good and bad fortunes of other people's actions and lives' (B11.9). In Plato's *Ion* a rhapsode describes how the recital of dramatic or pathetic scenes from the *Iliad* and *Odyssey* grips the emotions of performer and audience alike (535b–e). In the *Republic*, Socrates acknowledges how intensely we enjoy sharing the emotions of characters in epic or tragedy (10, 605c–d). He strongly disapproves: our enjoyment of this emotional stimulus is morally dangerous. Socrates also maintains, as Xenophanes did (§1.2), that poetry's theological falsehoods pose a threat to our moral integrity (2, 337d–383c). The critique of poetry in the *Republic* is the primary focus of this chapter. Sporadic reference will be made to other works, but there will be no attempt to produce a synthesis of Plato's views on poetry.[1] Since Plato is an implicit back-ground or explicit source to most subsequent discussions of poetry, there will be opportunities to fill in some of the gaps in later chapters (espe-cially, but not only, §5.1). Here we will take the opportunity to examine in some detail the philosophical critique of the poetic tradition in its most

---

[1] Good brief accounts of Plato on poetry: Asmis 1992; Ferrari 1989; Moss 2007. More extended treatments: Burnyeat 1999; Halliwell 2002: 1–147; Halliwell 2011: 155–207; Janaway 1995. Collections of papers: Moravcsik and Temko 1982; Destrée and Herrmann 2011; Boys-Stones and Haubold 2009 (focusing on Hesiod). Mason 2010 provides a short introduction to Plato; see further: Benson 2006; Kraut 1992; Fine 2008. Introductions to the *Republic*: Pappas 2003; Ferrari 2007. For a broader perspective on Plato's political philosophy (including *Laws*) see Schofield 2006.

sophisticated and radical form – a complex but (I shall contend) coherent argument about poetry, developed in the context of broader issues.

I DOES PLATO MEAN WHAT HE SAYS?

To speak of Socrates' critique of poetry may give a misleading impression. There is not (as is sometimes carelessly supposed) a wholesale rejection of poetry as such. Socrates takes it for granted that poetry has a place in human life, and conducts a searching enquiry into which *kinds* of poetry can safely be retained. The outcome is radical, even so: Homer and tragedy are banned. But this proposal should not be taken out of context. Radicalism pervades Plato's responses to culture and society across the board. If Socrates is right, says an opponent in another dialogue, human life will be completely overturned (*Grg.* 481c); Socrates would not demur (*Crito* 49d). Existing societies are so comprehensively defective that they do not provide a starting-point for reform. A clean slate is needed. The existing civic order must be erased before constructive work begins: philosophers must come to power, and everyone over the age of ten must be sent out of the city into the countryside (*Rep.* 7, 540d–1b). 'This', as Socrates dryly acknowledges, 'is not very easy' (6, 501a).

The radicalism of Plato's proposals may prompt us to wonder whether he really means what he says. A prior question is: does he really say it? Here is how the *Republic* begins (1, 327a):

I went down to the Piraeus yesterday with Glaucon, the son of Ariston, to offer my prayers to the goddess, but also because I wanted to see how they would manage the festival, this being the first time it was held.

The 'I' is not Plato, but Socrates. The *Republic* is a report of what happened when Socrates visited the Piraeus the previous day, and Socrates is the only speaker. What he reports is a conversation, and he tells us what he and various other people said in the course of the discussion. But Plato never speaks in his own voice: he says nothing on his own account about poetry, or about any of the other issues discussed in the *Republic*.[2]

Given the historical Socrates' significance to Plato, it is possible that his fictive counterpart serves as an authoritative spokesperson, to whose conclusions Plato is fully committed – though Socrates' elusive ironies and disclaimers of knowledge make him an unlikely candidate for such a role.

---

[2] Plato's use of the dialogue form: Kosman 1992; Frede 1992; Kahn 1998; Rowe 2006; McCabe 2008; Gill 2009.

It is also possible that Plato adopted the dialogue form precisely so that he was not committed to the fictive Socrates' conclusions – though the significance of the historical Socrates to Plato makes him an equally unlikely choice for achieving radical distance. Intermediate positions are many and various. For the rest of the chapter, I shall proceed non-committally, attributing the arguments and their conclusions to the fictive Socrates. For present purposes, the question may not matter. Philosophy is more than doxography. We are not here to catalogue philosophers' opinions, but to engage with and assess their arguments, in the hope of coming to a better understanding of the issues they address. Plato's views on the arguments put forward in the dialogues may be of interest for many reasons, but would not (if we could discover them) absolve us of the responsibility to assess the arguments for ourselves. What if Plato fully endorsed the argument and its conclusions? Perhaps he overlooked its weaknesses. What if he had (and hinted at) reservations? Perhaps a residual infirmity prevented this disillusioned lover of poetry from appreciating the full force of the grounds for rejection (cf. 10, 607e–8b). Either way, what we should be doing if we are reading Plato philosophically is thinking about the arguments and their implications for the substantive issues.[3]

That, at least, is what Plato's Socrates would tell us: 'it makes no difference to me … whether you believe this or not: it's the argument [*logos*] I'm putting to the test' (*Prt.* 333c); 'what is to be examined is by no means who said it, but whether it is true or not' (*Chrm.* 168b). For what it is worth, there is reason to think that Plato would agree, too, and that the dialogues were designed precisely to encourage us to think in this way. In *Phaedrus* Socrates locates genuine philosophy in live discussion (275d–7a). Plato's works are (or, as in the case of *Republic*, report) *dialogues* for this reason. Though they are not substitutes for live discussion, they are a reminder of it. To read them as doctrinal statements is therefore to misread them. The point is reinforced by Socrates' habit of professing ignorance or uncertainty. The critique of poetry in *Republic* itself ends by inviting poetry's supporters to mount a defence, flagging its own provisional status (10, 607b–8a). Whether Plato had much confidence in the likelihood of such a defence succeeding is uncertain and, again, beside the point. The invitation in itself is a reminder of something that we ought in any

---

[3] Cf. Cic. *ND* 1.10: 'Those who ask to know my own opinion on each point display more curiosity than is necessary. It is not authority that should be looked for in discussion so much as the force of reason. In fact, those who wish to learn are generally hindered by those who profess to teach: they cease to employ their own judgement, and take as settled whatever conclusion they see their chosen teacher has reached.'

case to understand about philosophy: it exists in the process of reflection and enquiry, not in the accumulation of a horde of answers.

Provisionality does not in any way diminish the significance of Socrates' critique, however, or remove the challenge which is the other side of Socrates' invitation to poetry's defenders. It is a plausible supposition that a well-ordered society needs to exercise control over media which, if uncontrolled, would destroy its order. On that supposition, if we are unable to refute the critique and meet the challenge, can we avoid acknowledging the need for a radical political solution to the problem of poetry (if not Socrates' proposed solution, then some other)? If implementing such a solution proves impractical, do we not need urgently to consider the implications for the lives we live in societies which have failed to solve the problem?

2 *REPUBLIC*: WHY POETRY?

Certain kinds of poetry, Socrates argues, pose a problem that must be solved to achieve a good society. This is, admittedly, only one of many problems in existing societies; but it is a serious one, and *must* be solved. But why does poetry ever become an issue in the *Republic*?

When Socrates went down to the Piraeus with Plato's brother Glaucon, they met some friends who insisted on their staying to watch a horseback torch race in the evening. They go to Polemarchus' house to wait, and Socrates falls into conversation with Polemarchus' elderly father, Cephalus. If you are as wealthy as Cephalus, Socrates suggests, it is easy to be contented in old age. Cephalus admits that wealth helps, but insists that it is not enough: a good conscience is also needed. As death approaches, stories of how wrongdoing is punished after death begin to be disturbing. But if you have money and use it well, you have no need to worry: you do not need to cheat or steal, you can discharge your debts, you can sacrifice to all the gods. The conversation has thus brought us to the basic question of the *Republic*: what does it mean to be *dikaios*? That word is conventionally translated as 'just'; alternatives to 'justice' include 'doing right' and 'morality'. As the discussion develops, the focus shifts: the question is not only what counts as behaving justly, but also what inner quality makes you behave like that; so 'integrity' comes into play. But translation is not the crucial point. Socrates and his friends can use the *word*; what they find difficult is giving an account of the *thing itself*. That is what the dialogue explores.

When Socrates begins to press this question, Cephalus extricates himself by pleading a prior engagement. Polemarchus offers a conventional but superficial answer, and Socrates easily ties him up in a series of knots. That prompts an aggressive intervention by Thrasymachus, who rejects conventional morality, maintaining that it is a fiction which helps people in power exploit those they have power over; it is better, more advantageous, to ignore the constraints of morality – if you can get away with it. Socrates ties Thrasymachus up in knots, too. Their shared inability to defend their opinions in the face of Socrates' questioning suggests that neither Polemarchus, complacent and conventional, nor Thrasymachus, aggressively critical of conventional views, has any real understanding of what justice is.

Socrates maintains in the *Apology* that his wisdom consists in not thinking that he knows what he does not know. Others are ignorant without realising it, and Socrates' questioning of people with a reputation for wisdom has exposed their inability to give a coherent and consistent account of the things they are reputed to know (*Ap.* 21b–d). The same applies here. Though Socrates has shown that Polemarchus and Thrasymachus do not understand what justice is, he does not claim to understand what justice is himself. Indeed, after his apparent triumph over Thrasymachus, he realises that he has allowed himself to get side-tracked. He has been arguing about whether justice is good or bad: but how can he be sure of that, when he still does not know what justice *is* (1, 354b–c)?

To make matters worse, Glaucon finds Socrates' argument unsatisfactory (2, 357a–362c). Though he does not agree with Thrasymachus' challenge, he has the intellectual honesty to insist on a convincing response. His main point is that people in general do not think that morality is valuable in itself: they pay attention to it only because of its consequences. They accept moral conventions because they do not want to be exploited by others, but would willingly exploit others if they could do so with impunity. Moral conventions provide a protection against ill-treatment that people would like to enjoy, while themselves remaining free to treat others badly. If, for example, they were able to make themselves invisible, so that they could steal with no fear of being caught, they would do so. They would see no point in respecting other people's rights if they got no benefit from it. Furthermore, most of the benefits come, not from being just, but from having a reputation for being just. Can Socrates show that there is a reason to go on behaving justly, even if the consequence is a bad reputation and maltreatment?

Glaucon's brother Adeimantus joins in (362d–7e). Opinion-formers promote morality by focusing on its consequences: rewards for behaving well, or for having a reputation for behaving well, and punishments for being caught in wrongdoing. These consequences include the punishments after death that made Cephalus anxious.[4] Moreover, everyone says that being good is difficult and disagreeable; being bad is easier, and more fun. That is why punishments are required to keep people in line. But if the appearance of being good is enough, the benefits can be decoupled from their disagreeable concomitants. Morality's advocates do not help their case by invoking the gods as back-up: there are stories of gods inflicting misfortune on people who have done no wrong; there are rituals that allow wrongdoers to expiate their guilt and avoid divine punishment; and if you want to secure yourself against punishment in the underworld, mystery cults promise their initiates a happy afterlife.

Glaucon argued that people do not really believe that being just is a good thing in itself: they are concerned only with the benefits that come from being, or appearing to be, just. Adeimantus has argued that the benefits do not make being good worthwhile: being good is difficult, and it is possible to get the benefits of wrongdoing without its potential detriments. Though they do not agree with these opinions, the two brothers maintain that Socrates will not have answered Thrasymachus convincingly unless he can meet this challenge. To do that, Socrates must answer the question which he lost sight of in his debate with Thrasymachus: what is justice? Now he suggests a way to approach the problem (368c–9a). Since it is easier to see something on a large than on a small scale, they should first find out what it means for a whole city to be just, and then look for the likeness of the larger in the smaller in order to determine what it means for an individual to be just. This is the idea that sets Socrates off on the project of describing an ideal society.

This project may take up most of the rest of the *Republic*, or it may take up only a few pages. On the latter view, the ideal society is briefly introduced, and then spoiled; everything that follows is an attempt to put the damage right. Socrates' first sketch of an ideal society (369b–372d) constructs a small community that can meet all, but only, its most basic needs. Its social order is based on a principle of specialisation: each of the inhabitants concentrates on a single role (369e–370c). This principle will later turn out to be the large-scale image of justice in the individual that they were looking for (4, 443b–4a). But the route to that discovery is

---

[4] Traditional thinking about *post mortem* punishments: Saunders 1991: 52–61.

temporarily blocked by Glaucon's protest that Socrates has been describing a city fit for pigs (2, 372d). So Socrates must make the community larger, more complex, more elaborate. He agrees to this demand, on the grounds that thinking about such a city will throw light on the origins of both justice and injustice. But he says quite clearly that the first city he described is the true and healthy city; the second, more elaborate one is 'fevered' (372e).

In the rest of the *Republic* Socrates shows how to keep that fever under control, describing the social structures that are necessary if a complex society is to avoid becoming horribly feverish and diseased. He clearly thinks that he succeeds. The third, no longer feverish, city is 'good and correct' (5, 449a), even 'perfectly good' (4, 427e) and 'best' (6, 497b); it is a model to aspire to (10, 592b). In one passage (7, 527c) he calls this imaginary community Callipolis ('Fine City'). So he thinks that this is a good, well-ordered society. Can he really believe that the City of Pigs represents a purer ideal?[5] The main worry is not the one that Glaucon voices – that it is too basic. Rather, the City of Pigs appears to have no room for philosophy. By contrast, philosophy is central to Callipolis: the city is ruled by philosophers. Can Plato's Socrates take a non-philosophical community seriously as an ideal? But in Callipolis philosophy manages the unruly desires that broke out in the fevered city, without eliminating them. In the City of Pigs, there were no unruly desires. If people spontaneously live in accordance with justice and moderation, then (it might be argued) they have no more need of philosophers than of doctors. The question is, perhaps, an idle one: we all live in fevered communities, from which there is no way back to contentment in a City of Pigs – none achievable, at any rate, by even the most radical social reform.

When the City of Pigs is made feverish, it admits a host of new arrivals (373a–d): perfumers, prostitutes, pastry-cooks, huntsmen, beauticians, wet-nurses, nannies, hairdressers, barbers, experts in preparing and cooking meat, livestock farmers, and (inevitably, with such an unhealthy lifestyle) doctors. The fevered city does not yet see a need for philosophers. But among the new arrivals are visual artists and musicians, the latter including poets, rhapsodes, actors, chorus members, and theatrical producers. Socrates calls all these people 'imitators' (373b). It is at this point, then, that poetry appears on the scene. Professional soldiers must also be added to the population (373d–4e). The city's newly elaborate requirements entail territorial expansion, and it will need to defend itself against

---

[5] A good discussion of the issues in Morrison 2007: 250–4.

aggressors; so the fevered city needs an army. That creates a problem (375a–6c): how do we ensure that these soldiers ('Guardians') do not turn against the people they are meant to protect? They must be brought up in a regime that shapes their character and opinions in such a way that, while they are courageous and aggressive towards the city's enemies, they can be relied on to respect the rights of their fellow-citizens and to obey the city's laws.

Education, then, is the foundation of a well-ordered city. It is not hard to appreciate the sense of this, but modern readers may be bewildered by how quickly poetry enters into the discussion of education, and how prominently it figures. Its role in education was one of the many ways in which poetry was more central to classical culture than to ours. Among the people Socrates meets at the start of the *Republic* is Niceratus, son of the famous general Nicias (327c). He never speaks, but in Xenophon's *Symposium* he says (3.5):

My father, who took care that I should grow up to be a good man, made me learn all of Homer; even now I would be able to repeat the whole *Iliad* and *Odyssey* by heart.

Although Nicias went to an unusual extreme, memorising poetry for moral benefit was a normal educational practice. In a long speech about moral education which Plato puts into the mouth of Protagoras we read (*Prt.* 325d–6a):

Later, when they [i.e. fathers] send them to school, they instruct the teachers to take more care over the children's good behaviour than literacy or playing a musical instrument. The teachers do take care of this, and when they have learned to read and are in a position to understand the written as well as the spoken word, they put before them on their desks the works of good poets and make them learn them by heart – poems containing many admonitions, many descriptions, praises, and encomia of good men of old, so that the child will be inspired to imitate them and will long to be like them.

Reading poetry was therefore educationally important because it was seen as shaping young people's moral character: they will be inspired to emulate the great men the poets portray.

The first one-and-a-half books of the *Republic* provide ample evidence that the influence of poetry was thought to extend into adulthood, too.[6] Cephalus quotes Pindar (1, 331a). Polemarchus introduces his idea of justice with an appeal to another lyric poet, Simonides (331d–e). Socrates

---

[6] See Halliwell 2000.

makes a show of being impressed by Simonides' wisdom, before demonstrating that what he says makes no sense – or (as Socrates puts it) he was speaking poetically, in riddles, so that it is hard to make out what he meant (332b). A little later Socrates teasingly pretends that Polemarchus thinks that justice is being good at stealing, and that he got the idea from Homer and Simonides (334a–b): 'was that what you meant?' 'Certainly not – though I'm no longer sure what I did mean.' Adeimantus' intervention in book 2 has a good deal to say about poets. The opinion-formers he refers to include fathers, who want their children to be good. They encourage them to be good, not by praising morality itself, but by talking about its rewards and the rewards of having a good reputation. But so do Homer and Hesiod (363a–b). Hesiod also tells us how hard it is to be good (364c–d, quoting *WD* 287–9), and Homer says that wrongdoers can placate the gods with prayers and sacrifices (364d–e, quoting *Il.* 9.497–501). If the gods do not exist or take no interest in human affairs, we need not worry about them; but if they do exist, and do take an interest in us, then our information about them comes mainly from the poets, who are the very people who assure us that gods can be won over (365d–6a).[7] In sum: Xenophanes (§1.2) was right to say that 'all have learned from Homer' (B10). People are influenced by Homer and other poets, and that influence is morally destructive. The poets are responsible, or partly responsible, for the attitudes towards morality and justice that lead ultimately to Thrasymachus' repudiation of morality.

These, then, are the broad cultural and specific contextual reasons why poetry becomes an issue in the *Republic*. We may now begin to trace the course of Socrates' critique. This comes in two stages. The first, in books 2–3, which itself has two parts, will be examined in the next two sections (§3.3–4). We will then survey some themes from the intervening books (§3.5); these will prove to be important when Socrates returns to the subject of poetry in book 10 (§3.6). Finally, we will consider how the two stages of the critique are related to each other (§3.7), and the implications of Socrates' arguments for the place of poetry both in the ideal community (§3.8) and in the imperfect communities in which we live (§3.9).

---

[7] These three theological errors reappear in *Laws* as the source of all impieties (10, 885b); believing in gods who can be appeased is worse than not believing, or believing in gods who take no interest (12, 948c–d). The defence that these things have been heard from the best poets, orators, seers, priests and others is anticipated (885c–d; cf. 12, 941b–c). See Saunders 1991: 301–18; Mayhew 2008.

3 *REPUBLIC* 2–3: WHAT POETS MAY SAY

Socrates shares the common assumption that reading the poets shapes moral character, but argues that existing poets, especially Homer, distort it. Homer's heroes (and those of tragedy, too) are not the kind of people that Guardians in a well-ordered society should take as their role-models. This argument, though it is introduced in the context of the education of young Guardians, applies to the cultural environment of all the citizens of Socrates' city. The good effects of keeping bad role-models hidden from children will be undermined if, when eventually they encounter them as adults, they are impressed and aspire to be like them. Early on in the discussion Socrates says that we will not 'carelessly allow our children to hear any old stories ... and to take into their souls beliefs which are, for the most part, inconsistent with those we think they should have when they are grown up' (2, 377b). Adult Guardians must be protected from corrupting influences of poets, too (378c–d, 380c; 3, 387b). And the restrictions cannot apply only to Guardians: if corrupting poetry is allowed in the city at all, it will be impossible to keep the Guardians away from it. There must be a consistent message.

Socrates starts, nevertheless, with small children. The first stories they hear are ones told by their mothers and nurses. Socrates insists that even those nursery tales will have to be brought under control, since that is a child's most impressionable age (2, 377a–c), but he does not discuss them in detail. He jumps ahead to Hesiod, Homer and other poets, on the assumption that when they have decided how to regulate those, the same principles can be applied to nursery tales (377d–e). Again, Socrates is interested in ensuring that a consistent message is delivered at every stage.

He begins the discussion by flagging the question of truth: should we start children off with true stories or false ones? The question takes Adeimantus by surprise (376e–7a), but the kinds of stories typically told to children are not (literally) true, and stories that are (literally) false may convey a deeper truth. Winnie-the-Pooh, though fictitious and a poor guide to comparative ethology, may show us something about friendship, loyalty, courage, and the dangers of over-eating. There is truth *in* the untrue stories we tell to children (377a). Socrates will later acknowledge that falsehood is sometimes positively useful (382c–d): for example, when you are deceiving an enemy, or trying to talk a friend out of doing something that would be harmful. When we tell stories about the remote past, and do not know the truth, we can make a false story *resemble* the truth, and ensure that it is useful. Later on again, Socrates suggests creating a myth about the city's origins that will reinforce the solidarity of the citizens and their respect for their roles in the city's social structure (3, 414b–5d). This 'noble falsehood' is not only false in fact: it describes things that could not actually happen (the original population was formed underground, and then sent up by Mother Earth to the country they inhabit). But it is a useful falsehood, and therefore a good one, because it will help keep the city in a healthy state. Falsehood can be a useful medicine – though the medicine must be prescribed by properly qualified people: only the rulers may decide what falsehoods to permit (3, 389b–d; cf. 5, 459c–d).

Socrates' immediate concern, therefore, is not with the truth or falsehood of stories, but with their consequences.[8] That is important, because in the course of this discussion Socrates makes large but unsubstantiated claims about what is and is not true. Consider what he says about the gods. God should be described as he really is (379a); and god is good (379b); so he cannot be the source of any harm or evil (as distinct from deserved and beneficial punishments: 380a–b); this means that god is not responsible for most of what happens in the world (379c); god also cannot change (380d–1c); therefore god cannot appear to humans in disguise (381d–e); nor will god deceive humans – none of the limitations which sometimes make falsehoods useful to humans apply to god (382a–3c). As Socrates points out, these principles conflict with what is found in many passages from poetry: Hesiod's Succession Myth (an account of the struggle in which the supreme god Uranus is overthrown by his son Cronos, and Cronos in turn is overthrown by his son Zeus); Zeus throwing Hephaestus out of Olympus; fights between gods, or between gods and giants, or between gods and heroes; Athene inciting Pandarus to break the truce; gods appearing in human form; and so on.

When Adeimantus posed his challenge to Socrates, he said that the poets were our main source of knowledge about the gods (365d–e). Socrates clearly disagrees: he does not deny that beliefs about the gods are influenced by the poets, but in asserting a theology so much at odds with the poetic tradition he implicitly claims to have access to a source of knowledge about them independent of, and more reliable than, the poets. Adeimantus concedes Socrates' claims unquestioningly (evidently, then, he did not really believe what he said before). Yet Socrates simply helps himself to his counter-traditional theology. He does argue in support

---

[8] Truth and falsehood: Woolf 2009; Schofield 2007; Schofield 2006: 284–309; Belfiore 1985.

of his denial of divine change, disguise and deception; but the arguments presuppose the initial premise that god is good, which he makes no attempt to defend. Is Socrates cheating? Perhaps not. If he is to show that justice is good in itself, and not only because of its beneficial consequences, his argument must be one that would work even if the gods could not be relied upon to reward justice (367e). His chosen strategy is to examine justice in a community. A just community must have an educational system that inculcates beliefs conducive to justice. Even if the traditional stories about the gods were true, therefore, Socrates would have to reach the same conclusion: stories that will have a bad effect on the moral outlook of the citizens should not be allowed in the city, regardless of their truth. At this stage, therefore, Socrates does not need to justify his optimistic beliefs about the gods: his conclusion about the regulation of poetry follows regardless.[9]

Hesiod, Homer and other poets tell stories about gods and heroes that are, Socrates believes, untrue, and should be criticised for this because these are untruths that are not spoken 'well' (377d–e). What is crucial is whether the stories promote virtue (378e), and the poets' gods fail on that criterion: people who have been told that gods quarrel with each other are likely to conclude that they may quarrel with each other, too (378b–c).[10] Such stories must therefore be suppressed. With regard to the Succession Myth, Socrates says: 'even if these stories were true, I would not think that they should be told so casually to people lacking in discrimination and maturity; it is best to keep silent, or if there is some reason why it is necessary to tell them, they should be heard as esoteric secrets by as few people as possible' (378a).

Socrates rounds off this section as follows: 'As regards the gods, then, these are the kinds of stories which it seems they should and should not hear, right from childhood, if they are going to honour the gods and their parents, and not make light of their friendship with each other' (3, 386a). Adeimantus agrees; and Socrates goes on: 'What if they are to be brave? Shouldn't they be told these things, and the kind of thing that will tend to make them fear death as little as possible?' (386a). He proceeds to

---

[9] In the *Laws*, poets must show that just people are happy and unjust people are miserable, irrespective of external goods (2, 660d–661d, 662b–c). This doctrine is so beneficial that it should be inculcated even if it were untrue (663d–4a).

[10] Euthyphro, prosecuting his father for homicide, complains that people disapprove of his action even though they believe that Zeus bound his father (*Euthphr.* 5e–6c); he accepts the truth of 'even more amazing things than these, which most people don't know' (6b–c), and infers that gods disagree on ethical judgements (7d–8b). On Euthyphro see Furley 1985; Kahn 1997; Edwards 2000.

eliminate frightening stories about the underworld (386b–c), even though people enjoy the poets' scary descriptions (387b). The same principle applies to stories in which famous men behave as if death were a terrible thing. Poets must not show heroes mourning (387d–8d). Nor should they show heroes setting a poor example to the Guardians by laughing uncontrollably (388e–9a), or telling lies (389b–d), or being insubordinate to their superiors (389d–90a), or lacking in self-control with regard to food, drink and sex (390a–d), or being acquisitive and taking bribes (390d–e), or being disrespectful towards the gods (391a–c), or committing serious crimes (391c–e).

In this first part of the discussion, therefore, Socrates has looked at the content of poetry: stories about gods and heroes must be purged of anything that would set a bad example to the citizens of his city. Socrates is confident that this means purging the stories of falsehoods, but that is not his immediate concern. Rather, he is concerned with the stories' moral effects. Falsehoods that are beneficial are allowed (provided that suitably qualified people are in charge of deciding which ones they are); truths that might have a bad effect should be suppressed.

4 *REPUBLIC* 3: HOW POETS MAY SAY IT

Socrates turns next from the content of poetry to the way it is presented. All myth and poetry is narrative (*diēgēsis*): it tells us what has happened, is happening, or will happen (392d). There are three ways in which a poet can narrate (392d–4c). In simple narrative, the poet reports what happens. If the report is interspersed with passages of direct speech, in which the poet impersonates a character in the sense that he makes his own words resemble the character's words, the poet is using both simple narrative and narrative through imitation (*mimēsis*). The opening of the *Iliad* illustrates the point. Homer uses simple narrative to report Chryses' arrival at the Greek camp, but switches to narrative through imitation when he gives us Chryses' speech. By changing direct to indirect speech Socrates recasts the passage as simple narrative. If the passages in which the poet tells the story in his own voice are removed, so that only the direct speech of characters remains (as in drama), this is narrative through imitation alone.

Socrates then poses a question (*Question 1*): which of these modes should poets be allowed to use? Adeimantus assumes that the implied question is whether tragedy and comedy should be allowed (394d), but Socrates answers evasively: 'Perhaps … or perhaps even more than that.

For my own part, I don't yet know; but wherever the argument carries us, like a wind, that's where we must go.' He then poses another question (*Question 2*): should the Guardians be 'imitative' or not (394e)? The answer to Question 1, about what poets should be allowed to do, will depend on the answer to Question 2, about the Guardians. Though the discussion has moved on to embrace poetic form as well as content, therefore, Socrates' primary concern is still with the relationship between poetry and moral character. In the first part of the discussion, the character the Guardians should have determined *what* the poets should be allowed to say; here, it determines *how* the poets should be allowed to say it.

What exactly is the force of Question 2? Many interpreters assume that asking whether the Guardians should be 'imitative' (*mimētikos*) is the same as asking whether the Guardians should imitate. But that cannot be what Socrates means.[11] When he argues that the Guardians should not be 'imitative', he evokes the principle that one person should (in real life) have a single role: it is not possible for one person to do many different jobs well (395a). This is the principle of specialisation which Socrates introduced in setting up the City of Pigs (2, 369e–370c). Here, Socrates extends the principle: it is not possible for one person to imitate many things well, either (3, 395a–b). A further step is that there should be no divergence between what one imitates and one's real-life role. Imitation is habit-forming (395d). If the Guardians are expected to devote themselves exclusively to being defenders of the city's freedom and good order, they should not pretend that they are some other kind of person in their spare time (395b–6a). It does not follow that Guardians are not to imitate at all: only that they should not imitate non-Guardians. 'Being imitative' therefore means being the kind of person who will act out many different roles, regardless of whether they are appropriate to their one real-life role. This defines the force of Question 2, and clarifies Socrates' negative answer: the Guardians must not be imitative, in the sense that they must not be prone to indiscriminate imitation. But that is consistent with their imitating people who are like themselves, or (if they are young) like what they should become.

This answer to Question 2 yields a partial answer to Question 1: poets may be allowed to imitate, within the limits set by the ban on indiscriminate 'imitativeness'. The next step is to define these limits. Socrates now introduces a distinction between two kinds of narrative (396b–c). The first is the way a good man will tell a story (396c–e). A good man will

---

[11] See especially Belfiore 1984.

have no qualms about imitating good men. He will throw himself into the role of a good man doing good things or saying good things; but he will not do this with things that are inappropriate to a good man. For example, he would not want to speak the insulting, insubordinate words which Achilles addresses to Agamemnon in *Iliad* 1, but he would be happy to speak the words of Diomedes when he rebukes his companion for answering back to Agamemnon in *Iliad* 4 (cf. 389e–390a). The good man will therefore use both simple narrative and narrative through imitation, like Homer (396e), but his use of imitation will be more limited than Homer's, both in its extent and in the range of different characters imitated. The second kind of narrative is the bad man's (397a–b), which is indiscriminate in the range of different characters imitated, and therefore makes much more extensive use of imitation; simple narrative will be very restricted.

Socrates has given two different ways of classifying narrative, and it is important not to confuse them. The initial classification divided narrative in three: simple narrative; narrative through imitation; and narrative that makes use of both. The second classification divides narrative in two: the good man's, and the bad man's. These two kinds are distinguished by whether the range of imitation is restricted or indiscriminate, and (therefore) whether the use of imitation is limited or extensive. This second classification answers Question 1 by making a distinction within the original category of poetry that combines simple narrative with narrative through imitation. Poets may imitate *up to a point*. Therefore, they may combine simple narrative with narrative through imitation, but only within very restrictive limits.

Socrates acknowledges a consideration that might make us hesitate to accept this restriction: the bad man's imitation is more varied and interesting than the good man's (397b–c). So he modifies the second classification by adding a mixed kind (397c), and poses a further question (*Question 3*): 'Shall we admit all these into the city? Or one of the unmixed ones? Or the mixed one?' (397d). This threefold classification does not signal a return to Question 1, to which we already know the answer: this is a different threefold classification. Yet Question 3 is peculiar: should we allow the good man's narrative, or the bad man's narrative, or a mixture of the good man's and the bad man's narrative? Surely it is obvious that the bad man's narrative cannot be allowed, even as part of a mixture. But that is precisely Socrates' point. His worry is that the good man's narrative will seem dull, because it lacks variety (397d–e). So there is a strong temptation to enliven it by mixing in a moderate amount of indiscriminate

imitation. Socrates has good reason to check whether Adeimantus is willing to abide by the conclusions they have reached, or whether he will be
tempted by the compromise.

Adeimantus resists temptation, and Socrates brings this discussion
of poetry to a close by saying farewell to the indiscriminate imitator
(398a–b):

> So it seems that if a man who was clever enough to turn himself into every kind
> of person, and could imitate everything, should arrive in our city and want to
> give a display of his poems, we would treat him with reverence, as someone holy,
> wonderful and pleasing – but we would say that there is no one like that in our
> city, and it is not lawful for such a person to come among us; and we would send
> him off to another city, pouring myrrh on his head and crowning him with a
> garland of wool; but we ourselves would employ the more austere and less pleas-
> ing poet and story-teller, for our benefit – someone who would imitate the way
> a good man speaks, and keep what he says within the guidelines which we laid
> down originally, when we were trying to educate the soldiers.

Socrates hinted earlier that something greater than tragedy and comedy
might be at stake (394d). Now we know what he meant. Though Homer
is not openly named in this passage (the truth will only be brought fully
into the open when Socrates returns to the question of poetry in book
10), there is no doubt that he is the versatile man who is excluded from
the city. This conclusion was not unprecedented. Heraclitus said bluntly:
'Homer deserves to be thrown out of the contests and given a beating'
(B42). Heraclitus' comment evokes a festival competition between poets:
the stewards, equipped with sticks to keep order, will treat Homer as a
disruptive influence, and drive him out with a beating. Socrates is gentler: 'we would send him off to another city, pouring myrrh on his head
and crowning him with a garland of wool' (3, 398a). But in a culture
which held Homer in such high regard, this proposal is no less radical
and provocative.

Is it needlessly radical? Why has a question about what poets should be
allowed to do been made to depend on a question about the Guardians?
There is no suggestion that Guardians will themselves be rhapsodes or
actors, indiscriminately imitating as they perform a poet's compositions.
It is sometimes suggested that reading poems aloud in school would have
the same effect.[12] But the expulsion of the versatile performer shows that
Socrates' concern is still with the influence of exposure to poetry performed by others. Why, then, should it matter how much imitation there

---

[12] E.g. Halliwell 2002: 52.

is in performances the young Guardians watch or listen to? Two reasons
are implicit in Socrates' argument. First, an indiscriminate imitator is,
as such, a bad role-model. If he is admired (as Homer is), people may get
the impression that performing multiple roles is acceptable. Secondly, the
indiscriminate imitator is, necessarily, a bad man; he will therefore not be
able to imitate good men well, and will give a misleading impression of
what good men are like. A third reason will be introduced when Socrates
returns to poetry in book 10: the damaging psychological effects that
indiscriminately imitative performances have on their audiences (§2.6).

5 *REPUBLIC* 4–7: EXTENDING THE FRAMEWORK

At the beginning of book 10, Socrates remarks: 'There are many features
of our city which make me think we were absolutely right in the way
we founded it – and I'm thinking not least of poetry when I say that'
(10, 595a). This launches a further lengthy discussion of poetry. Why does
Socrates come back to poetry in book 10? Presumably, he now has more to
say. The conversation has ranged widely since he and Adeimantus reached
agreement on the principles governing poetry in the middle of book 3;
some of the conclusions confirm and deepen the understanding of poetry
reached earlier. Before we proceed, then, we must have some idea of what
is said in the intervening books. A detailed exposition of these complex and much-debated books is impossible here: instead, a (necessarily
impressionistic) outline of three key points that are presupposed in book
10 must suffice. These are, first, that human beings are psychologically
complex, and potentially conflicted: they are subject to different kinds of
motivation which, without careful education, will be directed to inappropriate goals and will be at odds with each other. Secondly, there is a distinction between the world as it is experienced through the senses, and
the underlying reality which is accessible only to understanding. Thirdly,
the majority of people, failing to grasp that distinction, inhabit an illusory world: their moral opinions are confused and misleading; they are
ignorant even of their own ignorance.

To determine whether justice is a good thing in itself, Socrates must
establish what justice is (§2.2). His strategy of starting on a large scale,
identifying justice in a whole community before looking for justice in
the individual, motivates an attempt to describe a well-ordered city. The
city's population comprises three parts. Socrates initially distinguishes the
productive majority of the citizens from the Guardians who will protect
them. The Guardians' education is designed to ensure that they will be

fierce enough to be good defenders, but sufficiently well-behaved not to turn against the people they are defending. But Socrates goes on to make a distinction within the Guardians: some will be selected to be the city's Rulers; these are the Guardians proper, while the fighters are renamed Auxiliaries (3, 414b). At this point Socrates switches from his large-scale model back to the individual (4, 434d–e): does the individual soul have the same three-part structure as the city (435b–c)?

Socrates' argument for psychological complexity (4, 434d–441c) is based on the existence of different kinds of motivation, potentially conflicting with each other.[13] He is not interested in superficial conflicts of motivation, such as the difficulty one might have in choosing between two favourites on a restaurant menu, but in more radical conflicts: I want to eat the cake (the cream and chocolate look delicious), and want not to eat it (I know it is unhealthy). This conflict is between different kinds of motivation: appetitive desire based on appearances is at odds with an aversion based on a reasoned judgement (439c) about what is really good for me. Perhaps, as I hesitate, with appetite and reason in the balance, I become self-conscious: I do not want my companions to think that I lack self-control. An appetite for things that look pleasant, or an aversion to what will be painful or unpleasant, may be resisted by a sense of shame, or by other impulses like anger or love. These passionate responses can support my reasoned judgement about what is good, as when I am ashamed to eat the cake which I know would be bad for me, but they are distinct from reasoned judgement (441b–c). Small children, who do not yet have the capacity for reasoning, do have analogous impulses (thwarted desires may evoke anger), as do nonhuman animals (an animal's desire to avoid a predator may be outweighed by the instinct to protect its young). Socrates concludes that the soul does have a three-part structure: appetite; the 'spirited' part that drives passionate responses; and reason.

Though all human beings have appetites, passionate impulses and rational judgements about what is good, they do not all have the same appetites, impulses or judgements. Individuals vary in the particular things that motivate them, and in the extent to which their motivations are mutually consistent and responsive to reason's direction. What is crucial is how we have been brought up, and how experience has shaped our appetites, passions and thinking. Some people's experience has given them thoroughly perverse desires. Socrates mentions Leontius, who got a thrill out of looking at the corpses of executed criminals (439a–440b).

---

[13] Helpful discussions in Lorenz 2006; Moss 2008.

He knew it was wrong, and hated the fact that he was drawn to this. His appetite, which had come to associate looking at corpses with pleasure, was in conflict with his spirited part and reason, but the perverted appetite was too strong to be restrained.

Imagine someone who has been taught to believe that what is good is simply what is pleasant: a good life is a life devoted to satisfying one's appetites for food, drink, sex, and (as it may be) looking at corpses or inflicting pain. This man is in a worse state than Leontius: it is not only his appetite, but also his reason, that has been perverted. It has been demoted to the role of a servant of the appetites. Instead of using his reason to discover what is really good, and subordinating passion and appetite to that, he will devote his reasoning powers to finding the most effective way to achieve whatever seems good to his appetites.[14] That, in Socrates' view, is not a good thing.

After dividing the soul, Socrates finds the discussion again being hijacked by his friends, who think he has not said enough about the ideal community and ask him to go into more detail. The detail is provocative. Socrates argues that the Guardians (both Auxiliaries and Rulers) will include men and women, treated on an equal basis: they will have the same education and duties. He argues, secondly, that marriage and families will be abolished in the Guardian class: they must be a single, united group, not fragmented into potentially competing families. Thirdly, he argues that the city's Rulers must be philosophers. But what does it mean to be a philosopher? Socrates first suggests that the distinguishing feature of philosophers is a love of learning (5, 475c). But, as Glaucon points out (475d), this description applies to 'sightseers',[15] people who run about looking at the sights, seeing shows, and so on. Socrates must distinguish these sightseers from philosophers.

Ordinary sightseers like to look at beautiful things. But do they know what beauty really is? Beauty manifests itself in many different ways. Helen of Troy is beautiful, but so was Penelope. What makes them both beautiful, despite their different looks? Perhaps Helen was a beautiful baby: but the beauty of a beautiful baby is not the same as that of a beautiful woman; both beauties are different from the beauty of beautiful music. Moreover, beauty manifests itself imperfectly. Beautiful as she was, Helen was not beautiful in every respect: her adulterous character

---

[14] There are instructive case studies in disruptive interactions between reason, spirit and appetite in books 8–9 (e.g. 8, 549c–550b, 553b–d, 558c–60c; 9, 571a–3b).

[15] I borrow Waterfield's felicitous rendering of *philotheamones*, 'lovers of looking'.

was positively ugly, despite her beautiful face. And will she still be beautiful when she's old and grey? Any instance of beauty that we encounter will be beautiful in a particular, limited way; will not be perfectly beautiful; will not be beautiful forever. What is the one thing that all instances of beauty have a share in, that makes them beautiful (to whatever extent they are so)?

The 'sightseers', then, are people whose horizons are entirely bounded by the world of their experience – the things they see, hear, touch. They come across things and think 'oh, that's beautiful!' They have beliefs about beautiful things, but do not ask themselves what beauty itself is. They are content with appearances. But philosophers look beyond the world as they experience it and seek to understand what beauty is, what justice is, and so on (479a, 479e–480a). They are concerned with reality. They are 'sightseers of the truth' (475e).

The distinction Socrates has made between the many things that happen to be (more or less) beautiful and beauty itself is an expression of what is conventionally known as Plato's 'Theory of Forms'. The Form of Beauty is what beauty really is, beauty itself. The idea is eloquently expressed in the *Symposium* (210e–211b):

First of all, it is for ever. It neither comes into being nor passes away, neither waxes nor wanes. Then it is not beautiful in one way and ugly in another; nor beautiful at one time and ugly at another; nor beautiful in relation to one thing and ugly in relation to another; nor beautiful here and ugly there, as being beautiful to some people and ugly to others. Nor again will beauty appear to him in the form of a face or hands or anything else that belongs to the body, or any thought or piece of knowledge, nor as existing in something other than itself, whether in an animal or the earth or the sky or anything else at all, but as itself in itself by itself, having a single form for ever, and all other beautiful things as participating in it in such a way that, while these other things come into being and pass away, it does not undergo any increase or diminution, and suffers no change whatsoever.

This beauty is not part of our experience – not something that we can see or hear or touch. It can only be grasped by understanding. The things that we see or hear or touch, and that seem beautiful to us, are beautiful to the extent that they share in or are images of this Beauty.

Only those who understand what beauty really is can reliably judge how far something in the world as we experience it shares in or faithfully reflects Beauty. Others can only say what *appears* beautiful to them, what they think is beautiful. They may be wrong. When Socrates says that the city's Rulers must be philosophers, he is saying that the city must be governed by those who look beyond appearances and opinions and can get to the truth about what is right and what is wrong. This will only ever be a small minority of people (6, 503b–d). So Socrates' city is one in which most people do what they think is good, with no deep understanding of what goodness really is. It is nevertheless essential that their opinions about what is right and wrong are a reasonable approximation to the truth. That is why education is crucial, and why it is necessary to regulate young people's exposure to poetry. Poetry will shape their imaginations and form their opinions about what is right and wrong. Exposure to Homer would give them the impression that it is right to be insubordinate, to lack self-control, to mourn dead comrades extravagantly, to play many different roles that are unsuited to their function in society. Exposure to the purified poetry that Socrates recommended in books 2–3 will produce better results.

The education described in books 2–3 is therefore not enough to produce philosophers. It will shape appetites and passions correctly, and ensure their subordination to reason (4, 441e–2a), and it will furnish reasoning with sound and stable opinions (4, 429e–430b); but it will not yield understanding (7, 522a). What more is needed to get the rulers beyond that stage? The question about the education of the Guardians posed in books 2–3 required far-reaching revisions to the existing pattern of education, but these were still variations on a familiar theme. The education of philosopher-rulers is radically new. Later, Socrates will make concrete suggestions about the course of studies that trainee philosophers must undergo. But before we can appreciate what this will involve, we must undergo a profound reorientation. We must stop thinking like sightseers, whose horizons are bounded by the world as we experience it. To help his companions towards this, Socrates produces a series of images designed to give some imaginative purchase on what is involved in understanding beauty itself, justice itself, and so on.

First, the Sun (6, 506d–9b). To see things that are visible, we need the power of sight, but also light; and the source of light is the Sun. What do we need to understand things that are intelligible? Socrates suggests that, just as the Sun makes things visible to those who can see, the Form of Good makes things intelligible to those who can understand. Think of the challenge posed to Socrates about justice: is justice a good thing in itself, or is it only the consequences of justice that are good? To answer the question, we must know what makes things good. If justice is a good thing, we cannot fully understand what it is without understanding goodness. Similarly, to make any serious decision about our lives we need to know whether that would be a good thing to do (504d–5b); so we need to understand what goodness is. Goodness makes sense of everything else. Socrates goes further (509b): the Sun does not only make things visible: it is also the source of growth and life. In the same way, the Form of Good does not only make things intelligible: it makes them what they are. In other words, the world is the way it is because it is good that it is that way. That principle cannot, admittedly, be applied to all the messy details of the world of our experience. The point is that the fundamental structures of reality are the way they are because it is good that they are so. The Form of Good is the key to understanding them because goodness is the reason why things are as they are.[16]

The second image, the 'divided line' (6, 509d–511e), develops further the contrast between the visible world and the intelligible world, and the possibility of cognitive ascent from one to the other. In the visible world, there are things, and there are shadows and reflections of those things. Often we are not well acquainted with things in the visible world. My knowledge of plants is so vague, ill-informed and wildly inaccurate that it is as if I had only ever seen shadows or reflections or pictures of plants, and never come across the things themselves. My mother, a keen gardener, has a confident grasp of plants based on a lifetime's direct experience of tending them. Yet this experience is still acquaintance with things that can be seen and touched. Is it possible to progress from the visible world to the intelligible world? In geometry, we may use drawings as an aid to thinking, but the drawings are not what we are thinking about. The geometer's square is not something that can be drawn. Geometrical diagrams are approximations. They are like shadows or reflections of the geometrical reality, which is something that must be grasped by understanding, not by sight. In the same way, visible things have images – shadows, reflections, paintings; but they are themselves images of intelligible reality. Geometry therefore provides a model of how we might proceed from instances of beauty to an understanding of beauty itself. The trainee philosophers will spend a long time studying geometry and other mathematical disciplines (7, 521b–531d), but that is only a preparatory stage for what Socrates calls 'dialectic' (531d–5a). He does not describe this in any detail, but the ultimate goal is to leave perceptible aids behind, and to do without the assumptions we have taken as starting-points for thinking on the basis of our experience. Once we have grasped the Form of Good, we

---

[16] God, Socrates insisted in book 2, is good, and a source of good. We now, retrospectively, see the thinking that underlies this theology.

no longer need such assumptions, because (as the image of the Sun suggested) the Form of Good makes sense of everything else.

The third image is a Cave (7, 514a–518b). There are prisoners in the Cave, who have spent all their lives there, immobilised so that they can only look at the Cave's rear wall. Behind them is a screen; behind that people parade up and down, holding up models of men, animals and so forth; behind that, a fire is burning. The firelight casts shadows of the models on the Cave wall, where the prisoners can see them. The prisoners are trapped, not only in the Cave, but also in profound ignorance. They mistake the things they see on the Cave wall for reality, unaware that they are only shadows of other things. Yet those other things are themselves only effigies. To see the real things, the prisoners must leave the Cave. But they would be dazzled if they turned to face the fire; the light of the Sun would be even more dazzling. A long process of gradual adjustment to the light will be needed before they are able to see reality as well as they could see the shadows on the wall of the Cave.

The Sun is, again, the Form of Good (cf. 532a–d; 533c–4a). The real things outside the Cave are the Forms: just as the Sun makes things outside the Cave visible (once the cave-dweller's eyes have adjusted), so the Form of Good makes the other Forms intelligible (once we have undergone the long philosophical training needed to understand what goodness itself really is). The models in the Cave are things in the world as we experience it: as we said earlier, visible things may themselves be images of an intelligible reality. What are the shadows on the Cave wall? Think of my ideas about plants, so vague, ill-informed and wildly inaccurate that it is as if I had only ever seen shadows or reflections or pictures of plants.

Socrates introduces the Cave as an image of 'our nature', and applies it to human beings in general (514a). It seems absurd to say that my ignorance of plants is typical of the human condition. My mother provides an immediate counterexample: she has genuinely well-founded confidence about plants. But Socrates' concern is with our beliefs about what is right and wrong, about justice, beauty, goodness. In the *Apology* (21b–2e) Socrates concedes that craftsmen have genuine understanding of things within their craft, but they proved to be as confused as the politicians and poets when they claimed to understand ethical matters – just as Polemarchus' apparently confident grasp of justice was exposed as ignorance in book 1. Where do our beliefs about those things come from? We have been influenced by the way we were brought up, by opinion-formers in the society we live in, and by our peers. Unfortunately, if we do not live in Socrates' fine city, these sources are all thoroughly untrustworthy guides to what is right and wrong. As long as we think that the world of our experience is all there is, we might suppose that we have a confident grasp of right and wrong in the way my mother has a confident grasp of plants. But if Socrates is correct, and there is more to reality than that, we are deluding ourselves. What we think is a confident grasp of right and wrong is a bunch of illusions, like the shadows on the Cave wall. Ignorant of our own ignorance, we are its prisoners.

6 REPUBLIC 10: IMITATION REVISITED

Book 10 begins with Socrates' claim that the intervening books have reinforced the conclusions about poetry reached in books 2–3, especially 'not on any account admitting any of it that is imitative. That it is absolutely not to be admitted is now even clearer, in my view, since we have distinguished the separate aspects of the soul' (10, 595a). Socrates goes on to speak of 'imitative' poets, and the harm they do (595b). This creates a presumption that the first of the three key points from the intervening books (§2.5) has given further reason for excluding imitative poetry as defined in book 3, where 'imitative' (*mimētikos*) described the kind of poet who 'was clever enough to turn himself into every kind of person, and could imitate everything' (3, 398a, cf. §2.4). His poetry makes indiscriminate use of narrative through imitation (*mimēsis*), in which the poet takes on the role of good men and bad men alike. Yet Socrates launches the argument of book 10 by posing a question about 'imitation in general' (10, 595e). Does that imply that he is now concerned with imitation in a broader sense? Is his argument about imitation in general inconsistent with the arguments of books 2–3, as many interpreters have concluded? I shall argue in the next section that Socrates' two discussions of poetry have a consistent and integrated agenda; in this section, I trace the course of this book's complex and sometimes difficult argument, identifying seven key points as way markers.

To answer his question about imitation in general, Socrates invokes the second of the three key points from the intervening books: the distinction between Forms and their instances in the world of our experience. Here his illustrations – couches and tables (595e–6b) – are more down to earth, and easier to grasp.[17] The distinction between reality and

---

[17] Worries about Forms of artefacts (on which see e.g. Broadie 2007) are therefore a distraction from the illustrative point. Similarly, we need not be troubled by the statement that god makes the Forms (597b–d). The contextually crucial point is negative: if no one *other* than god makes them, they have objective priority over any human thought or action.

its particular instances remains. Looking at couches will not tell you what makes something a good couch if you do not know what a couch *is*. That does not need advanced dialectical study: an adequate grasp of the nature of functional artefacts can be gathered from the experience of using such artefacts. Couch-makers, then, do not make what a couch ought to be; they make particular couches, taking account of what a couch ought to be.

There are people who make couches, people who make tables, and so on: but what would you call someone who can make everything (596c)? Glaucon says he would be amazingly clever, a genius. But suppose you carry a mirror round with you: then it would be easy to make everything (596d–e). Or what about a painter (596e)? Glaucon insists that the man with a mirror and the painter do not make real things, only things that look like them (596e). But, as Socrates points out (597a), the craftsman does not make reality, either. Just as the Form of Beauty has objective priority over particular beautiful things, what a couch ought to be has objective priority over particular couches; and this is not something that anyone makes, but follows from the couch's function. We can now say what an imitator is (*Point 1*): an imitator makes neither the reality of X (the Form of X, or what X ought to be) nor real instances of X, but only things that look like instances of X (596e). So imitators, whether they are painters or tragic poets (597e), are two steps away from reality or truth.

The next stage of the argument takes up the point that the painter produces something that looks like a couch, but is not a couch. Imitation therefore does not relate to what something is, only to the way it appears (598a–b). Here we seem to have reached the general account of imitation that Socrates has been looking for. The reason why imitation can make everything is that it needs only a superficial acquaintance with each of the things it imitates (598b). In fact, it only needs to be acquainted with its image (*eidōlon*).[18] For example, when a painter paints a picture of a carpenter, he needs to know what a carpenter looks like, but does not need to be a carpenter himself: that is, he does not need to have the specialist knowledge that makes a carpenter a carpenter (598b–c). If understanding what makes a carpenter what he is were necessary for a painter to paint pictures of carpenters, and so on with every other kind of person, it would

---

[18] *Eidōlon* is also used of the shadows in the Cave (7, 532b–c), and of the tyrant's illusory pleasures (9, 586b–c). But the word is not always so pejorative: the principle of specialisation is a genuinely useful *eidōlon* of justice, even though (being external rather than internal) it is not what justice truly is (4, 443c–d).

be genuinely amazing if any painter could paint a wide range of people. So (*Point 2*) imitation is imitation of appearances, not of reality. That is why imitators can produce images of anything: they can dispense with understanding what each thing is, and need only know what it appears to be.

In reality, the idea of a universal genius who understands everything is silly. Anyone who imagines that he has come across one has been taken in by a kind of conjuring trick: what he has encountered is an imitator who can make it look as if he understands everything – a trap you are likely to fall into if you cannot tell the difference between knowledge, ignorance and imitation (598c–d; cf. *Sophist* 233d–5a). But there are people who do say that about poets, especially Homer (598d–e). Some maintain that the poets understand all crafts, and all human morality, and everything about the gods. Their premise is that a good poet cannot produce good poetry if he does not know what he is doing. Taking it (presumably) as a datum of experience that Homer is an exceptionally good poet, their argument is: he could not be a good poet if he were ignorant of the things he writes about; so he must understand the things he writes about. Socrates must now consider whether they are right, or whether the general account of imitation he has just worked out applies to the poets, too (598e–9a). Note that he does not automatically transfer his conclusions about painting to poetry. The comparison with painting is a heuristic device, not a proof. Thinking about painting generates ideas which may be applicable to poetry as well, but Socrates must verify that the application to poetry works independently of the comparison.

So he poses a further question (599a): if someone were able to make both an object that could be imitated and an image of it, would he devote his life to making images? To Socrates, it is obvious that he would not: he would rather do fine things than imitate them, since it is better to be praised for doing fine things oneself than to sing other people's praises for the fine things they have done (599b). Apply this test to Homer. Was he a doctor? That is, did he cure people, or train other doctors? Or did he do no more than imitate the way doctors talk (599b–c; cf. *Ion* 538b–c)? Socrates poses the question, but prefers to focus on more important matters: military leadership, running a city, education (599c–d). If Homer had any knowledge of what makes people better or worse, whether in the public or in the private sphere (even if that knowledge fell short of understanding: 599d), it should be possible to identify cities which chose him as a legislator, wars won under his leadership (cf. *Ion* 541b–2a), innovations he made in areas of technical expertise, people who associated with him because they admired his way of life and wanted to learn from him. There is no evidence of any of these things (599d–600c). But if Homer or Hesiod had been able to teach people, and make them better, they would have done so: they would not just have made imitations (600c–e).[19] So (*Point 3*) Homer and other poets cannot have understood the things they portrayed: if they had, they would not have been content *only* to produce imitations of other people doing fine things, but would have done fine things themselves.

The conclusion (600e–601a) is that Homer and all poets are imitators of images of virtue, and are not in contact with the truth. The analogy with painting has passed the test. Just as a painter produces something that looks like a craftsman without understanding the craft that makes the craftsman what he is, so the poet produces what seems like a good man without understanding the virtue that makes the good man what he is. The fact that he does this using poetic language, rhythm and music helps him work the conjuring trick: these things produce 'enchantment' (cf. §1.1). If we stripped it down to bare prose, it would be easier to see through the illusion (601a–b).

The next stage of the argument reinforces the conclusion that the imitator, who makes an image, is not acquainted with what something really is, but only with its appearance (601b–c). This further argument relies on the difference between the person who uses an object, the person who makes it, and the painter who makes a picture of it (601c–2a). Earlier Socrates used examples like couches and tables. These would be less helpful here: the couch- or table-maker is probably also a user of couches and tables. Socrates' new example, a horse's bridle, works better: horse-riding was the preserve of the wealthy in classical Athens, so the craftsman who makes the bridle would be unlikely to use it. But what Socrates said about couches and tables is still relevant. What a couch or other artefact ought to be is determined by its function, which the user understands (cf. *Crat.* 389a–390d). The craftsman who makes a bridle must take account of the bridle's function, which the horse-rider, who uses bridles, understands. Riders tell bridle-makers what they require; bridle-makers must then

---

[19] In Plato's day many *claimed* to have learned from Homer, but the question is whether they were right to think so. Socrates' argument is that the priorities manifested in Homer's life make it doubtful whether he was the kind of person who could be relied upon as an educator. Contrast Solon, whose achievements as a legislator are recognised at 599d–e (cf. *Smp.* 209d), and who wrote poetry. According to the fictional scenario of *Timaeus*, he planned to turn the story of ancient Athens' war against Atlantis into an epic poem. Had he done so, he would have been immune to Socrates' challenge to Homer; but he gave priority to political activity (21b–d).

work out how to meet that requirement. Riders know what a bridle ought to be; bridle-makers need to have a true belief about what the bridle ought to be, which they can get from the rider. But the painter does not need either knowledge or true belief about what bridles ought to be: he only needs to know what bridles look like, and he does not need to talk to riders or bridle-makers to find that out (601c–2a). Indeed, the painter's task is easier still. Most people who look at his pictures are not horse-riders or bridle-makers; they, too, do not know what a bridle ought to be. So the painter only needs to imitate what a bridle looks like to people who do not know anything about bridles (602b). So (*Point 4*): users understand the things they use, and craftsmen have true beliefs about the things they make; but imitators need neither understanding nor true beliefs about the things they imitate, since they have only to produce something that looks convincing to people who have neither understanding nor true beliefs about those things.

Here we make contact with the third key point from the intervening books (§2.5). The user–maker–imitator distinction maps onto the images of the Divided Line and Cave. Most people do not have either knowledge or true beliefs about what a bridle should be or (more importantly) what justice or virtue really are. They have opinions about these things, but these opinions are unreliable, since they are not derived from people who understand justice or virtue. Most people's opinions are derived from what seems to be just or virtuous. Like painters, poets who dramatise just or virtuous acts (602b) need only produce something that corresponds to how those things appear to ignorant people. We are trapped in a situation in which most people have unreliable opinions about what is right and wrong that are reinforced by being reproduced in the stories poets tell.

Next Socrates takes up his initial claim that the exclusion of imitative poetry has been confirmed by the division of the soul (595a). In relation to which part of a human being does imitation have the effect which it does have (602c)? Glaucon is understandably confused, so Socrates explains by referring to visual illusions (602c–d) – both natural illusions (as when something looks large close up but small from a distance, or a straight stick in water looks bent), and artificial illusions, such as paintings that use shading to create a three-dimensional illusion (*skiagraphia*)[20] and conjuring tricks (cf. 598d). Things may have a deceptive appearance, and there are ways to counter these illusions, such

---

[20] On *skiagraphia* see Pemberton 1976. The tyrant's illusory pleasures are described as *skiagraphia* as well as *eidōla* (9, 586b, see n.18); cf. 2, 365c; 9, 583b; *Phd.* 69a–b.

as measurement (602d–e). But experience shows that the corrective may not change the appearance. (Though I know that the two lines in the Mueller-Lyer illusion are the same length, they still *look* different.) In book 4, the tripartition of the soul was established by the co-presence of radically conflicting motivations. In the same way, the co-existence of illusory appearance and correct judgement shows that two parts of the soul are in conflict. The correct judgement is the product of the reasoning part of the soul: the illusory appearance must belong to one of the non-rational parts. The non-rational parts of the soul are inferior to reason: so painting, and imitative art in general, is far removed not only from the truth (as was established earlier), but also from intelligence: it associates with the inferior parts of the soul (603a–b). So (*Point 5*) imitation appeals to non-rational parts of the soul.

The argument for that conclusion relied on visual illusions, but Socrates is again careful to ensure that the application to poetry is independently confirmed (603b). We might expect him to focus on the audiences of poetry, since they provide the obvious parallel to people looking at a visual illusion. But Socrates takes an indirect approach, focusing initially on the characters *in* the poems. Imitative poetry imitates people doing things (603c): they perform actions either under compulsion or voluntarily; they think that as a result of their action they are faring well or badly; and consequently they are either distressed or pleased. Socrates goes on to argue that these people have a conflict in their soul, just as the victims of visual illusions are subject to a conflict between a thing's appearance to the non-rational parts of the soul and their rational judgement about what it really is (603c–d). A good (*epieikēs*) man will feel grief if his son dies, or someone else to whom he is very close; but his grief will be 'measured' (603e: not coincidentally, this is the same word used for reason's corrective to visual illusions; cf. 387d–e). When he is in company, he will be more restrained in expressing his grief; he will express his grief more freely when he is alone (604a). He desires to express grief, but believes that the expression of grief should be restrained. Appetitive desire pushes him towards extravagant expressions of emotion, but reason resists (604a–d). (The fact that he is ashamed to do this in public suggests that spirit is supporting reason.)

Will a poet show the man taking the loss calmly, or expressing his grief in an intensely emotional way? Obviously, the latter (604d–e). There is more to imitate, because there is more variety in the man's behaviour. The behaviour of the man who reacts in a calm, rational way is stable, uniform, and dull to watch. (In 3, 397b–c the bad man's indiscriminate imitation had greater variety and interest than the good man's restricted use of narrative through imitation.) Moreover, it is not easy to convey calm, rational behaviour to a large and miscellaneous audience: because they would not react calmly themselves, they will not be able to make sense of the good man's reaction ('Doesn't he *care*?'). Socrates' unexpectedly indirect route has thus circled back to the audience. An audience consisting mostly of people who do not exercise rational control over their own emotions and desires will want to see characters expressing their feelings in extravagant ways – and if the imitative poet wants to be a success, he must give the audience what they want (605a).[21] So (*Point 6*) to be successful with a large audience that does not have its appetites and emotions under rational control, imitative poetry must portray people behaving in ways that are not under rational control. Hence imitative poetry has the effect it does have on audiences (cf. 602c) by appealing to the non-rational parts of the soul, and the conclusions drawn from the analysis of painting and visual illusion do apply to poetry: neither has a sound relationship to the truth, and neither operates in relation to the best part of the soul (605a).

By 'imaging images' (*eidōla eidōlopoiounta*) the imitative poet, removed from the truth, gratifies the non-rational parts of the soul, which cannot tell what things really are. In doing so he stimulates and strengthens it, subverting our capacity for rationality, and thus replicates in the individual soul the bad effects that follow when the wrong people get power in a city (605b–c).[22] When Socrates concludes that the imitative poet cannot be received into a city that is supposed to be well-ordered (605b) there is an unmistakable echo of the farewell to the imitative poet in book 3 (398a–b). As promised at the start of book 10, Socrates has confirmed the earlier conclusion by drawing especially (in this phase of the argument) on the division of the soul. So we might think that, having proved what he set out to prove, he has reached the end of his argument about imitative poetry. In fact, 'we have not yet made the most serious allegation against it' (605c).

---

[21] Sophists, artists, musicians, poets and politicians are constrained to conform to the demands of mass audiences: 6, 492b–3d; cf. *Grg.* 501d–2e, 51a–c; *Laws* 3, 700e–1b. Role of the audience: Harte 2010.

[22] The image of the inner city and its constitution returns at 608b, echoing 9, 591e. Books 8–9, which explore connections between distorted political constitutions and distorted psychological conditions (8, 544d–5a), are rich in such imagery (8, 553c–d, 559e–61c; 9, 572e–3b, 574d–5a). A child's education should establish a Callipolis-style inner constitution (9, 590e–1a); the theoretical city, though it cannot be realised in practice, is a 'paradigm in heaven' that can be realised within the individual (9, 592b).

Socrates has been talking about poetry's appeal to, and effects on, a large and miscellaneous audience of people lacking in rational control. He now moves on to a more serious problem: it also has a damaging effect on good people, who do have a fair degree of rational control. 'The fact that it is capable of harming even good (*epieikēs*) people, with very few exceptions, is quite terrifying.' The discussion of poetry started in book 2 with its place in education (§2.3): childhood, when people are most impressionable, is a crucial stage. But people remain vulnerable, even if their moral character and moral beliefs appear to have been properly established by their good upbringing. Exposure to the wrong kind of poetry can still undermine their character and moral beliefs in adulthood (605c–d):

Even the best of us, when we hear Homer or any other of the tragic poets imitating one of the heroes in a state of grief and making a lengthy speech in his lamentations, or even singing and beating his breast, you know that we enjoy it, and that surrendering ourselves and being carried along, sharing his suffering and taking it seriously, we praise as a good poet whoever most puts us in this state.

That response may seem out of character. The good man, who would be ashamed to make an extravagant display of his own grief (605d–e; cf. 604a), should find it repellent when a hero is shown doing that in poetry. Instead, he watches with approval and enjoyment. What explains this seemingly inconsistent reaction (606a–b)?[23] Socrates focuses on errors of judgement that arise when the non-rational part of the soul that desires and gains satisfaction from emotional indulgence interacts with rational soul in someone who has been well, but imperfectly, trained. With regard to the individual's own sufferings, the rational part of the soul would impose restraint on the desire for emotional indulgence. But in the case of another's sufferings, it relaxes its guard and lifts the restraint. It does not see anything to be ashamed of in pitying in someone else what would be shameful in oneself, and it counts the pleasure as a gain which it would be reluctant to surrender by taking a disdainful view of the poem as a whole.[24] Only a very few people, Socrates claims (606b, cf. 605e), are able to reason their way to an understanding of the damage which is done (*Point 7*): our response to other people's sufferings influences our response to our own, so that tolerating emotional extravagance in others stimulates and strengthens the non-rational parts of the soul, making it harder to maintain rational control over our own emotions in real-life situations.

---

[23] This passage is discussed in Belfiore 1983; Scott 1999.
[24] Cf. *Phd.* 83d on the power of pleasures and pains to make the soul believe that the truth is what the body says it is. Pleasure and illusion in poetry: Moss 2006.

That is the effect of tragedy (and Homer). Comedy has a similar effect. The catalogue of things that poets must not attribute to heroes in book 3 included uncontrolled laughter (3, 388e–9a) as well as mourning (387d–8d). When we take pleasure in jokes (whether in comic performance or in social situations) that we would be ashamed to tell ourselves, we strengthen what we normally hold in restraint (10, 606c). So Socrates here revisits things said in his first discussion of poetry, but makes a deeper point. His argument in book 3 was that it sets a bad example to young people to show heroes mourning and laughing, getting angry, lacking self-control with regard to food and sex, and so on (387d–391e). Here he argues that imitation of all these things in poetry (10, 606c) has a direct, disruptive impact on the psychological stability even of mature, well-brought up members of the audience.

We have now reached the end of the argument: all that remains is for Socrates to sum up the conclusions. First (606e–7a), if Homer's admirers say that his poetry is educational, we must politely disagree: he is out-standingly poetic, and showed the way for tragedy; but the only poetry permissible in the city is hymns to the gods and encomia of good men. Any poetry more entertaining than those will lead to the city being dominated by pleasure and distress rather than reason. And yet, secondly (607b–e), if someone can provide a successful argument in favour of keep-ing poetry and imitation that aims at pleasure in the well-ordered city, we will happily readmit it: we too feel the enchantment of that kind of poetry, especially when listening to Homer. If the friends of poetry suc-ceed in showing that this kind of poetry is beneficial to the city, as well as enjoyable, we will have gained. But, thirdly (607e–8b), in the absence of a successful defence, we must act like a disillusioned lover who forces him-self to break off a relationship that he knows is bad for him. We still feel attracted to this kind of poetry, and would be delighted to discover that it is after all acceptable: but we must keep reminding ourselves of why we cannot take it seriously and why we must treat it with caution. As Socrates points out, the stakes are as high as they possibly could be (608b).

7 INTEGRATING THE CRITIQUE

In books 2–3, Socrates said that all poetry is *narrative*, and distinguished simple narrative from narrative *through imitation*, in which the poet impersonates the people in the story. He also introduced the idea of being *imitative*: an imitative poet is one who is *indiscriminate* in his use of imi-tation, impersonating bad characters as well as good characters. Narrative through imitation is not objectionable as such: Socrates objects to poets who are indiscriminately imitative – poets who imitate *many things*. When he begins book 10 by reaffirming the exclusion of imitative poetry, the initial presumption must be that he means what he meant in book 3: he is only excluding poetry that makes indiscriminate use of narrative through imitation. The fact that in book 10 Socrates talks primarily about Homer and tragedy is consistent with that presumption. Moreover, Socrates does not argue that all poetry should be banned. It is customary to speak of Plato's attack on poetry, but this convenient shorthand is misleading. Socrates explicitly allows hymns to the gods and encomia of good men to be kept in the well-ordered city (607a).[25] In the ancient world it was conventional to celebrate a god by giving an account of the god's great deeds; so hymns often included narrative. It was also possible to celebrate a great man by narrating his deeds. When Socrates, contending that Homer and other poets did not understand the things they wrote about, says that it is better to be praised than to sing other people's praises, the word he uses is 'encomium' (599b): it is better to be the subject than the singer of encomia. Homeric poetry is thus conceived as encomiastic: his narrative of (for example) Diomedes' great deeds in battle is a way of celebrating the hero's greatness.[26] The hymns and encomia of good men that Socrates licenses therefore fall within his definition of poetry as narrative.

In Socrates' city, the poet is allowed to celebrate gods and good men. There is no need to specify hymns of good *gods*, since it is axiomatic that gods are good. Homer's poetry is criticised in book 2 for conflicting with that axiom. Its portrayal of heroes also disqualifies it as encomium. To continue with the example of Diomedes, Socrates commends his self-disciplined response to Agamemnon's insulting remarks in *Iliad* 4, by contrast with Achilles' lack of discipline in book 1 (2, 389e). But he could hardly commend Diomedes' aggression towards Aphrodite, Apollo and Ares in *Iliad* 5. The hero backs off from the confrontation with Apollo, but should not even have thought of fighting a god; and while it is true that he has Athene's support against Aphrodite and Ares, showing gods in conflict with each other, or as vulnerable to wounds, offends against the theological axioms. Homer's encomiastic narratives would not be

---

[25] Hymns were sung in the City of Pigs (2, 372b). Does the addition of encomia here reflect the greater need for social regulation in the inferior, more complex, and therefore less stable, community of Callipolis?

[26] In *Tim.* 19c–d Socrates describes the narrative of the ideal city's wars that he would like to hear as an encomium (cf. §5.4). Critias' narrative of ancient Athens' war with Atlantis, which will supply Socrates' desideratum, is a hymn and encomium of the goddess Athene (21a, see n.19).

among the encomia allowed in Socrates' city. But that would be true even if Homer had used simple narrative exclusively: a story of gods fighting each other, or being wounded by a mortal, would be unacceptable even if it were told without any impersonation. So this objection depends on Socrates' restrictions on what a poet may say, independently of the argument about how a poet may say it. Some poetry must be banned regardless of whether it uses imitation in the sense introduced in book 3. Conversely, the argument in book 3 does not ban all poetry that uses imitation: Socrates bans poetry that is indiscriminately imitative, but raises no objection to poetry that imitates good men.

Does Socrates change his mind in book 10? The hymns and encomia that Socrates allows would contain narratives of the great deeds of gods and good men: but what form would the narrative take? If Socrates now insists on their using simple narrative, without any narrative through imitation, book 10 is more restrictive than book 3. If he would still allow poets to imitate good men, book 10 seeks a deeper understanding of why the conclusion reached in book 3 was right, but does not argue for a more restrictive conclusion.

Some considerations do seem to suggest that Socrates is arguing for a more restrictive conclusion in book 10, or (if he is not) that he ought to be. The argument is concerned with the nature of imitation *in general* (595e): that implies a wider target, and it is hard to see why Socrates would invest so much time and energy in exposing the inadequacies of imitation *as such* if the use of narrative through imitation by poets remains unobjectionable. Moreover, when Socrates introduces 'imitation' as a quasi-technical term in book 3, he describes narrative which gives the character's direct speech as making oneself like another person in respect of voice or appearance (393c). Making one thing resemble something else is the point of the comparison with painting in book 10: painting produces an object which looks like something it is not. So the analogy with painting ought to apply to any use of narrative through imitation, not just the indiscriminate kind. In short: if Socrates has not been arguing for a more restrictive conclusion in book 10, the long argument about imitation in general seems pointless.

On the other hand, there are many reasons to deny that Socrates is more restrictive in book 10. First, the opening reference to the earlier conclusions about 'imitative poetry' implies that the target is the same as it was in book 3. Secondly, there is no explicit declaration of a more restrictive policy. Thirdly, the poet who was sent away from the city in book 3 was the kind of poet who 'could make himself into anything by his own skill, and could imitate everything' (398a). That concern is echoed in book 10, when Socrates introduces the person who can imitate everything, with a mirror or by painting (596c, 598b). Fourthly, the poets most insistently referred to in book 10 are Homer and the tragedians, who are indiscriminate imitators. Fifth, some of Socrates' arguments only apply to indiscriminate imitation. That is true especially of his worries about the psychological impact of extravagant displays of emotion. If the poet imitates a good man, there will be no extravagant displays of emotion; if the poet simply describes a bad man's grief in simple narrative, it will not have the same psychological impact on the audience. The extravagant emotional displays on which the most serious allegation is based (605c–d) clearly involve indiscriminate use of narrative through imitation (so, too, 603b–c, on the plausible assumption that the characters do not keep their opinions about their good or bad fortune to themselves). Sixth, in trying to understand poetic imitation, Socrates uses painting as a comparison. If the critique of imitation counts against all uses of imitation in poetry, we would have to ban all non-abstract visual art, too, as well as instrumental music that imitates virtuous character and action (3, 399a–c; 400a). But these have all been given a central role in education (3, 401a–2a; cf. 411e–2a; 7, 522a–b). It is hard to believe that all these earlier conclusions could be overturned without explicit comment. Finally, an unrestricted rejection of imitation would be crazy. Are young Guardians not to imitate the behaviour of the good men celebrated in encomia? Does Socrates retract his exhortation to imitate the harmonious and reasoned order of the heavens (6, 500b–c)?

In approaching this problem, it may not be fruitful to focus on the word 'imitation'.[27] Plato does not always use that word in the same way. Consider a passage in book 2 (382b–c), where Socrates says that speech is an imitation (*mimēma*) of what is in the soul. Noises coming out of my mouth are not the same thing as the belief I hold; but the noises I make may be like my belief, in the sense (at least) that the meaning they express is the same as what I believe.[28] If all speech is an imitation of what is in the soul, all poetry must be imitation in this sense of 'imitation'; but since a total ban on imitation in this sense would reduce us to silence, poetry's being imitation in this sense cannot constitute grounds for exclusion. Plato's use of the word 'imitation' and its cognates is therefore flexible.

---

[27] Good discussions of 'imitation' in Belfiore 1984; Moss 2007; Richardson Lear 2011.
[28] Language as imitation: cf. *Crat.* 430b; *Critias* 107b. Bodily deportment as imitation of character: *Rep.* 3, 401a.

Fixating on a word with a variable range of application is likely to give rise to confusion and uncertainty. For example, at 2, 373b poets in general are introduced as 'imitators'. Consistently with that, at 2, 388c 'imitation' is applied to a passage in the *Iliad* in which Zeus speaks: but the concept of 'narrative through imitation' (which has not yet been introduced) is irrelevant to the point of the criticism, since a simple narrative of Zeus lamenting would be equally objectionable. And yet, though all poets are in this broad sense imitators, some poetry (including some poetry that makes use of imitation in the narrower sense) is preserved in the face of the critique of 'imitation in general' in book 10. It will be more fruitful, therefore, if we can identify Plato's key concerns in the two discussions of poetry and understand how those concerns connect to each other.

The discussion in books 2–3 has two main stages, concerned with what the poets may say and with how the poets may say it. It is in the latter stage that the distinction between simple narrative and narrative through imitation is made. But it would be a mistake to think that the second stage treats poetic form independently of content. Portraying supposedly good men behaving badly (like Homer's heroes) would be an error of content; but what would be an error in poetic form? We cannot say 'narrative through imitation', since Socrates allows a limited use of narrative through imitation. What he disallows is using narrative through imitation to present what a bad man says or does. It is therefore a certain *combination* of form (imitation) and content (bad speech or action) that Socrates condemns as indiscriminately imitative. That content is acceptable in simple narrative: the poet can tell us that bad men behave badly. That form is acceptable if it is used to present a different content – a good man behaving well. Only the combination is problematic.

According to books 2–3, then, there is content that cannot be allowed in poetry at all: for example, accounts of good men behaving badly. There is content that is allowed, and which poets are allowed to present using narrative through imitation: good men behaving well. There is also content that is allowed, but in simple narrative only: poets are not allowed to present bad men behaving badly by means of narrative through imitation. The obvious conclusion to draw from this is that there is something particularly dangerous about imitation (in the sense: producing something that looks or sounds like something it is not). Because it is potentially dangerous (dangerous when combined with the wrong content), its use must be limited.

Suppose that this is the underlying question that Socrates is concerned with at the beginning of book 10: what is it about producing something

that looks or sounds like something it is not that makes it so dangerous
that its indiscriminate use cannot be allowed? Book 10 argues that imitation is possible even if one is ignorant of the truth. Since imitation is of
appearances, it is not necessary to understand (or even to have true beliefs
about) what something really is to produce an imitation of it. That is why
it is possible to imitate many things. If imitation required understanding,
imitators would have to be specialists; an indiscriminate imitator is necessarily an ignorant imitator. That is especially true if an imitator depends
on the approval of a large, miscellaneous audience: then all he needs to
know is how the thing appears to people who are themselves ignorant. An
indiscriminate imitator who depends on the approval of a large, miscellaneous audience is necessarily working with two layers of ignorance – his
own and his audience's.

It will not matter very much if your grossly inaccurate painting of a
geranium elicits admiration of your artistry and botanical expertise from
me, a grossly ignorant observer of geraniums. But if you write poetry that
portrays human actions, good and bad, it matters a great deal if you get
it wrong: you will produce false beliefs in me about what is good and
bad, or reinforce my existing false beliefs. Moreover, because you do not
know what is good and bad in human behaviour, you do not realise that
people should maintain rational control over their non-rational appetites
and emotions. So you will expose your audience to portrayals of people
acting without that control (for example, by displaying their emotions
extravagantly). That will stimulate and strengthen the non-rational parts
of the audience's souls. Even good people, who in real life do have their
appetites and emotions under rational control, will be affected by this;
you will be stimulating and strengthening the non-rational parts of their
souls, too.

The basic point, then, is that imitation by its nature creates the possibility of imitating in ignorance of the truth. That ignorance links all the
aspects of Socrates' discussions of poetry. First, it is what leads to the errors
of content in the first stage of the discussion in books 2–3: poets tell bad
stories about gods and heroes because they do not realise they are false.
Ignorance on this level has an effect even when poets restrict themselves
to simple narrative. But, secondly, if poets use narrative through imitation, ignorance leads them into indiscriminate imitation: poets indulge
in indiscriminate imitation because they do not realise that this sets a
bad example to the audience. Thirdly, ignorance leads poets to portray
things that stimulate and strengthen the non-rational part of the audience's souls: poets exhibit extravagant emotional displays because they

(and the audiences who enjoy them) do not realise the damage it does to them. The audience's ignorance is complicit in this, since it produces the demand for indiscriminate and emotionally indulgent imitation that corrals poets into these errors.

We can now see a further reason why it is not fruitful to focus on the meaning of 'imitation'. 'Imitation' is not Socrates' fundamental concern. It is a conceptual tool that he uses to dig down to deeper issues. The fundamental issue is ignorance: imitation is dangerous because it *can* be done ignorantly, and thereby can – and in existing societies typically *does* – potently amplify the effects of shared ignorance on the population. By its nature, therefore, imitation will tend to become indiscriminate imitation when it is not regulated by philosopher-rulers – which means, in effect, that imitation always tends to become indiscriminate. Examining imitation in general in book 10, therefore, has allowed Socrates to achieve a deeper understanding of the problems identified in books 2–3. He has found the single underlying explanation of those problems, has discovered the additional problem of poetry's psychological impact, and has grounded all this in the central ideas of the *Republic* as a whole.

8 POETRY IN WELL-ORDERED CITIES

Socrates has proposed a ban on the poetry of Homer and the tragedians, but not a ban on all poetry: some poetry is retained in his well-ordered city. This poetry will be free of the content errors prescribed in book 2; it will not engage in indiscriminate imitation, although it may include narrative through imitation, subject to the limitations prescribed in book 3; and it will refrain from stimulating and reinforcing inappropriate emotions identified in book 10 as the most dangerous aspect of imitative poetry. These negative points explain why some poetry is permissible, but not why it is worth keeping. What positive value will it have in the city? How will poetry be managed there? Who will write the poems? Although Socrates does not answer all these questions, it may be instructive to try to work out the implications of what he says for ourselves.

Socrates introduced poetry at the start of his discussion of the education of the Guardians. These are the city's defenders, later renamed Auxiliaries (3, 412d–e, 414b): 'Guardians' is now restricted to those selected from the Auxiliaries for philosophical training. Presumably, then, the primary reason why poetry is allowed to remain in the city is that – properly purged – it will help to educate Auxiliaries and potential Guardians. In particular, it will educate them morally: it will give them the right beliefs about the virtues, and provide them with images of virtuous action on which to pattern their own lives.

Who will the poets be? In the classical period, professional poets and performers travelled widely. When Socrates meets the rhapsode Ion, he has just won a competition in Epidaurus and has come to Athens to compete at the Panathenaea (*Ion* 530a–b). This is why the 'man who could make himself into anything by his own skill, and could imitate everything' arrives from outside the city (*Rep.* 3, 398a–b), and why Socrates speaks of Homer and Hesiod as going from place to place to perform (10, 600d). But only those who have been through the city's educational programme can be relied upon to have the right beliefs about virtue. Anyone from outside will be an ignorant imitator of the kind Socrates criticises in book 10: the images of virtuous action they produce are *false* images. So we might suppose that the poets must be drawn from the city's own population. Since Socrates has no discernible plan for educating the productive majority of the citizens, it may seem to follow that poets would have to be drawn from the Auxiliaries or Guardians. Let us begin by exploring that inference.

Why would any Auxiliary/Guardian be a poet? It is not enough to say that they will be performing a valuable function by writing poetry that helps to make the citizens better. Shoemakers and chefs perform valuable functions in the city, but no Auxiliary/Guardian will be a shoemaker or chef. That would contravene Socrates' principle that people should specialise in a single role. A stronger justification is needed, and there are some prima facie objections. When Socrates rejects the view that Homer and the other poets must have understood the things they wrote about he proposes a test: people who can do something will do it, not just imitate it, because doing fine things gains more honour than merely imitating them (10, 599a–b). That does not count decisively against Auxiliary/Guardian poets. The test is not whether a person produces imitations, but whether a person is devoted exclusively to producing imitations. The poets in Socrates' city would do fine things as well as imitating them. But that raises a further objection. An Auxiliary/Guardian who is also a specialist imitator appears to have two distinct roles, contravening the principle of specialisation. To answer this objection, we need to find a way in which being an imitator may be part of the role of an Auxiliary or Guardian, not separate from it. For example, an Auxiliary serving in the cavalry must be an expert rider, but that is part of his or her (5, 452a, 457a–b) role as an Auxiliary.

Imitating as a form of learning is not alien to being an Auxiliary: the imitation of good men is not only allowed, but required. Young Guardians should imitate virtuous role-models (3, 395b–d), since modelling their behaviour on the kind of person they are supposed to become will help form their character correctly. What of imitating as a form of teaching? Consider a modern analogy. Trainee doctors learn in part by watching qualified doctors doing their job, and modelling themselves on these exemplars. But demonstrations do not always use live patients: resuscitation techniques can be demonstrated on dummies, and volunteers may play the role of casualties. Moreover, training videos may provide useful images of doctors doing their job, even if the people in the videos are actors, not real doctors. For the videos to be reliable as training materials the actors' roles would have to be scripted by people with medical expertise. A doctor who writes such scripts does so as a doctor, unlike a doctor who writes scripts for a TV hospital drama as a lucrative sideline to medical practice. (Socrates would predict – correctly – that dependence on a mass audience's approval for success in the latter enterprise will create a pressure to give sensationalised and misleading images of doctoring.) As it happens, when Socrates challenges Homer's claims to universal expertise, his first example is expertise as a doctor: did Homer just imitate doctors' talk, without understanding? Socrates is willing to accept two kinds of evidence of understanding (10, 599c): did Homer cure anyone? Did he teach anyone else to be a doctor? So making other people into doctors is an authentic exercise of a doctor's expertise. Similarly we may assume that Socrates would regard making other people virtuous as an authentic exercise of virtue. This is why he turns his attention to whether Homer made people better, in the public or private sphere (599d).

The objection to members of the Auxiliary/Guardian class being poets therefore seems to fail. Their poetry will not be an example of ignorant imitation, since in imitating virtuous agents they will imitate what they are and what they know from their own experience; they will achieve a public good by the educational effect of their poetry; and in producing imitations that make people more virtuous they are not taking on a role that is separate from their role as Auxiliary or Guardian, since making people virtuous is an authentic exercise of their own virtue. If their poetry helps to preserve the city's moral order, they will be acting within their role as 'craftsmen of freedom' (3, 395b–c).

Can we be more precise? Will the poets be Auxiliaries, or Guardians? The crucial difference is that the Auxiliaries' education forms their character and inculcates correct opinions about virtue; but they do not *understand* the virtues. For that, the philosophical training of the Guardians is needed. The Auxiliaries have true beliefs about virtue. For example, in a threatening situation they will be able to identify the courageous thing to do and, being of good character, will do it. But they would not be able to explain why that is courageous in terms of what courage itself is. They are familiar with the many instances of courage, but do not have an understanding of the Form of courage. They would probably be unable to give satisfactory answers if Socrates started questioning them about courage.[29] Should we then conclude that the poets must be Guardians? They are the ones whose philosophical training has endowed them with understanding. Moreover, their role is to rule and guide the city; that includes moulding the characters of the citizens, for which poetry is an appropriate tool. On the other hand, they might exercise this function indirectly. Perhaps, instead of being front-line teachers, they set the curriculum. Properly educated Auxiliaries writing poetry within parameters specified by the Guardians would not produce false images of virtue.

Poets would thus be required to work under the direction of philosopher-rulers. Recall Socrates' distinction between the user, maker and imitator of an object such as a horse's bridle (10, 601b–2b). The user has a genuine understanding of what a bridle ought to be; the maker only needs true beliefs about what a bridle ought to be, which can be imparted by the user; the imitator needs neither understanding nor true beliefs, but only needs to know what a bridle looks like. How does this apply to the place of poetry in the well-ordered city? The user corresponds to the Guardians, whose intellectual grasp of the virtues corresponds to the user's empirical grasp of the design-requirements for a bridle. The bridle-maker, who has true beliefs about bridles because the users give him the design-specification, corresponds to the Auxiliaries, who have true beliefs (but not understanding) as a result of the education which the Guardians have prescribed. And the imitator is … ? On the hypothesis we have been considering, imitation has disappeared as a separate role: because ignorant imitators have been banned, the imitators will be either Guardians, who understand (like users), or Auxiliaries, who have true beliefs (like makers). As we saw above, in imitating they will not be doing something separate from their role as Guardians or Auxiliaries.

But if poets are craftsmen working under the direction of philosopher-rulers, we need to reconsider the initial inference that poets

---

[29] This is why their souls' stable order would be at risk from premature exposure to dialectic (7, 538c–9d). Moreover, these Auxiliaries might be less reliable in coping with novel opportunities and challenges in unfamiliar contexts: consider the unfortunate posthumous choice made by someone who had lived in a well-ordered city, but whose virtue was habitual rather than philosophical, described in 10, 619b–c.

must be Guardians or Auxiliaries. Since Socrates makes no attempt to provide a comprehensive account of the city's social and legislative structures, it is risky to draw conclusions from his silences: the impression that there are no educational arrangements for the rest of the citizens may be an illusion. They will, at a minimum, benefit from living in a well-ordered city, which excludes bad influences and shapes the environment to be formative of good moral character (3, 401a–d). Moreover, it is hard to see how the movement between classes which Socrates envisages (3, 415a–c) would be possible if there were no opportunities to observe children of the third class responding to education. Since this class includes everyone who is not a soldier or philosophically trained ruler,[30] some at least will need to be trained in crafts or other forms of professional expertise. That might include training in the technical aspects of poetic composition, which is not part of the educational programme for Auxiliaries or Guardians. So why should this class not provide the city's poets, musicians and visual artists? They may not equal the Auxiliaries in the stability of their moral opinions and character. But this would not pose a risk to public morality if they are required to compose within the guidelines laid down by the rulers (2, 379a), and to submit their compositions for approval before they are made public. The skilled embroiderers who embroider robes for the image of a goddess would not (one imagines) be a squad of Auxiliaries; but they would have to follow guidelines that would ban the portrayal of gods fighting giants (2, 378c).[31]

The kind of legislative detail that the *Republic* lacks can be found in the *Laws*. This second-best city (5, 739a–e) is not a precise analogy to Callipolis. It does not have a tripartite citizen body, and there are many differences in its way of life. In particular, the Athenian Stranger who is the main speaker in the *Laws* is not as restrictive as the *Republic*'s Socrates with regard to permissible kinds of poetry. There will, of course, be hymns and encomia to gods, heroes, and dead citizens of distinction, though not to anyone still living (7, 801d–2a), but invectives are also allowed (12, 957c–d). So is comedy, on the grounds that people cannot understand what is serious if they are not exposed to the ridiculous. But only slaves and foreign professionals may perform comedy: citizens are barred from active participation, since ridiculous behaviour is inconsistent with virtue (7, 816d–e). It is absolutely forbidden to satirise

---

[30] See Vasiliou 2008, 232–46.
[31] Socrates is alluding to a customary part of the decoration of the robe the Athenians gave their patron goddess at the Panathenaea; cf. *Euthphr.* 6b–c; Xenophanes B1.21–3 (§1.2). See Barber 1992.

(*kōmōidein*) a citizen, whether in comedy, iambic invective or lyric, but the non-citizens who perform comedy may satirise each other, provided the satire is jocular, and not done angrily or in earnest (11, 935d–6b). Official approval is required before any comedy can be performed. Since comic scripts would have been approved in advance, the rule that breaches of the ban on mockery of citizens are punishable by expulsion from the city's territory (11, 935e–6a) must be directed at in-performance improvisation by the non-citizen performers. The only reference to tragedy also refers to visiting poets or performers. If they request permission to enter the city and perform (one recalls the arrival of versatile imitator in *Rep.* 3, 3398a–b), their repertoire must first be approved by the authorities; a licence will only be granted if it is consistent with the city's values (7, 817a–d). The terms in which their performances are described do not suggest that they are likely to pass this test ('haranguing children and women and the whole mob', 7, 817c; cf. *Grg.* 502c–d; 2, 658b–d is only a little less disparaging about the tragic audience: 'youths, educated women, and more or less the whole mass of the population').

In the *Laws* it is a fundamental principle that poets must conform to the city's standards. Since it is assumed that poets are incapable of reliably discriminating good from bad, they are required to submit their work to the authorities for approval before making it public (7, 801b–d; cf. 2, 656c, 659c–661d on choral poetry). Existing songs and dances must also be rigorously assessed before they are approved for use (7, 802a–d). The one partial exception (an exception also to the ban on encomia of living citizens) relates to encomia and invectives performed at the monthly festivals at which 'imitation' combats provide military training (8, 829a–c). Since the content of these encomia is contingent on the outcome of the combats, the poems themselves could not be pre-approved. Weakened control over the poems is compensated by enhanced stringency in selecting poets: they must be at least fifty years old, virtuous, and honoured for their fine achievements – but their compositions need not have artistic merit (829c–d). No one else may perform a poem that has not had prior approval, regardless of its artistic merit (829d–e). These regulations, taken as a whole, reflect complete confidence that a rigorous regime of licensing and censorship will be effective enough in enforcing ideological correctness that even non-citizens can be accepted as poets. If applied to Callipolis, there would be no objection to poets drawn from the third class, except in contexts which require improvisation; then the poets must be citizens honoured for their fine achievements – which is likely to limit eligibility to Auxiliaries, though there is no assumption that they would have the technical skills to compose poems with any merit other than ideological reliability.

Socrates' well-ordered city does not exist. It is unlikely ever to exist: even Socrates' suggestion of expelling everyone over the age of ten from the city (*Rep.* 7, 540d–1b) would leave a population tainted by bad influences at their most impressionable age. If it did come into existence, it would not be indefinitely sustainable (8, 546a–7a). In reality, then, we find ourselves living in irreformably corrupt societies. If we are philosophically minded, we will follow Socrates' advice to stay out of politics and concentrate on ensuring that our own souls have the good constitutional order that is lacking in the external environment (9, 591b–2b; cf. *Ap.* 31c–2e). That environment includes the kinds of poetry Socrates condemns as corrupting, such as Homer and tragedy (to say nothing of computer games, novels, films, TV dramas, opera, comics, songs, raps ...). We have been warned that they pose a threat even to good people like ourselves (10, 605c–6d). So we need to use prophylactic measures to keep our souls in a healthy state. Our knowledge of the harmful nature of imitative poetry is like a medicine to protect us against its effects (595b); Socrates' arguments may be used as people might use a magical incantation (*epōidē*) to protect themselves from harm (608a).

Such prophylaxis will not be widely practised. In a pessimistic discussion of the possibility of the philosophical character in a corrupt society, Socrates declares that the masses cannot be philosophical (6, 494a); there will be only a small remnant of true philosophers (496a–e). Philosophy is primarily an activity of the leisured wealthy elite (*Ap.* 23c), but that constituency is already corrupted, and therefore resistant. Moreover, as Socrates observes when he dismisses allegorical interpretation as a defence against his critique of poetic theology, poetry will have an effect on those who are too young (or too ignorant and foolish) to deploy sophisticated interpretative techniques to disarm its potential harmfulness (2, 378d–e: cf. §4.3). So the problem of poetry could only be fully solved by political control. Individual prophylaxis is not an adequate substitute for a political solution, since few people will be able (and, in a corrupt society, fewer still willing) to engage in philosophy. But it is the best that can be done.

Prophylaxis is especially important for those philosophically inclined people who *like* poetry. Socrates admits that he is 'enchanted' by it, and invites Glaucon to make the same admission – especially in Homer's case;

that is why they would welcome a successful defence of poetry against his criticisms (10, 607c–d). Since Plato demonstrably has a deep knowledge of the poets, and his engagement with poetry is close, sensitive and subtle,[32] this is one case where it seems safe to apply what is said by the fictive Socrates to Plato himself. But Socrates' image of the disillusioned lover, attracted to someone although aware that the relationship risks distorting one's life and character (607e–8b), illustrates the danger this presents. The continuing attraction may make us too ready to accept a defence. We must be on our guard.

Will the philosopher be a poet? The dilemma is summarised by Socrates in *Gorgias* (501e–2c): the poet must either indulge the mass desire for gratification, in the manner of existing choral song and tragedy, or say what is beneficial whether it is pleasant or not. Clearly, the philosopher cannot succeed as a poet before a mass audience in the fevered city without unacceptable compromise. Existing poetry is a form of flattery addressed to a large and motley audience, 'children and women and men, slaves as well as free' (*Grg.* 502c–d; cf. *Laws* 7, 817c). Existing politics, too, is a form of flattery, gratifying the people without regard to their improvement (*Grg.* 502d). But that is to say that existing politics is the pseudo-politics of the fevered city: in keeping out of this kind of politics (*Ap.* 31c–e), Socrates was Athens' only practitioner of *genuine* politics (*Grg.* 521d). Might the philosopher be, by analogy, a genuine poet? Socrates himself, according to *Phaedo* (60d–61b), took up poetry in the last days of his life, in obedience to a dream. After an experimental hymn he turned to narrative poetry, drawing on Aesop's fables for material: this was poetry of the kind that is literally false, but a vehicle of truth.

Plato was not a poet in the sense in which he defines the term, since he does not use verse. The point is not trivial: poetic form produces an enchantment that makes poetry more potent (*Rep.* 10, 601a–b). But Plato's prose has a bewitching literary artistry of its own. Does he respect the principles laid down in the *Republic*? He was not writing for the gratification of a mass audience. His narratives, though a pleasure to read, are certainly meant to be beneficial; though fictional (we cannot suppose that *Republic* is a report of a real conversation), they were intended to be vehicles of truth, or of a search for truth. His use of narrative through imitation is extensive: the *Republic* imitates one character throughout, and that character's speech is almost all imitation of others. Was this extensive imitation also indiscriminate? It might be thought that Thrasymachus (in

---

[32] Exemplary discussions in Pender 2007; 2009.

Republic 1) or Callicles (in *Gorgias*) are characters that a good man should be ashamed to make himself resemble (*Rep.* 3, 396c–e). There is an escape clause: the good man will not imitate unworthy characters seriously, though he might do so for amusement. It might be argued that Plato's dialogues are covered by this exemption, since all written discourse, according to Socrates in *Phaedrus* (276c–e), is not serious but for amusement. But this argument is too potent. It would give too much licence to visual art and music, all of which are described as amusements (*Statesman* 288c; *Laws* 10, 889d); and things that are not (and do not deserve to be) taken seriously may give rise to serious harm (*Rep.* 4, 424d–e; 10, 602b). The force of the escape clause is therefore elusive. Perhaps, then, we should conclude that *Gorgias* and *Republic* 1 would be inappropriate texts for shaping the character of the ruling class in an ideal society. In our fevered societies, on the other hand, engaging in debate with such opposition, and staging such debates in written 'reminders', might be a therapeutic aid – not so much to the interlocutors, who are impervious, but to the few who are open to persuasion that their way of thinking is misguided, and want to understand how they should think instead. The fact that the dialogues invite a different kind of cognitive and emotional engagement from imitative poetry could also be urged as a defence: the point is to not to stimulate intense emotion, but to encourage critical thought.

Plato's use of myth is not objectionable in principle: recall that Socrates licenses a 'noble falsehood' as the founding myth of his city. The mention of Socrates' poetic retelling of Aesop's fables (*muthoi*) is followed almost at once by a reference to story-telling (*muthologein*) about life after death (61d–e) – a legitimation in advance for the eschatological myth with which *Phaedo* concludes. What is crucial is that the surface meaning of a myth should not be harmful (as the Succession Myth is harmful), and that it should convey beneficial truths. In the *Republic*, the assessment and licensing of falsehoods is in the hands of qualified authorities – the philosopher-rulers, who have grasped the Form of Good. But Socrates disclaims this knowledge (6, 506b–e), and Plato makes no claim to it (he has not gone through the training necessary to produce philosopher-rulers). Plato has neither the philosophical authority to license falsehoods on his own account, nor access to the guidance of those qualified to do so. Outside the ideal city, it could not be otherwise. But this raises again the problem of philosophical self-authorisation (§1.2).

At the end of the myth in *Phaedo*, Socrates acknowledges that he cannot insist on the truth of his mythical eschatology; but he thinks that accepting that it (or something like it) is the truth is a 'noble risk', if the soul's immortality is granted (114d). Much more than immortality is needed to secure Socrates' conclusions, however, including a theology that is non-negotiable (63b–c), though it is not established by argument (in the *Republic*, too, the theology is presented only through the image of the Sun).[33] Earlier in *Phaedo* (77d–8a) the incantations to assuage our fears of the soul's dispersal are Socrates' arguments; in *Republic* 10, too, it is Socrates' argument (*logos*) against imitative poetry that is recommended as an incantation (*epōidē*) to protect us from the seductions of poetic pleasure (608a). Here, however, in *Phaedo* it is a myth that has been elaborated for use as an incantation (114d). In the *Laws*, songs are incantations that influence the child's soul towards virtue (2, 659d–e, 671a); the stories children hear from nurses and mothers are incantations, too (10, 887d), and the persuasive 'incantations' of myth are a substitute for compulsion by argument (903a–b).[34] Plato's spell-binding artistry affects us in similarly non-rational ways; it takes effort for the reader to remember that literary artistry does not make arguments any more sound, or conclusions any more likely to be true. Should readers not be concerned that Plato feels licensed to induce us by non-rational means towards positions the truth of which he is, on his own admission, in no position to guarantee? Unless we have decided to trust him on other grounds, we should resist the effect of his artistry – especially when we recall that human life will be completely overturned if he is right (§2.1). There is a striking tension between the radicalism of the conclusion to which Plato's arguments lead and their acknowledged provisionality (e.g. *Rep.* 6, 506b–e; 533a). Can the authorisation problem be solved by writing promissory notes on philosophical insights as yet unattained?

---

[33] There is a sustained defence in *Laws* 10. See Mayhew 2008.

[34] The laws themselves are equipped with preambles to make the listener better disposed and easier to teach (4, 722b–3b), since legislators need to make citizens easily persuaded to virtue (718c–d; cf. 5, 730b). See Stalley 1994.

CHAPTER THREE

The natural history of poetry: Aristotle

Aristotle brings changes in substance and in style. Consider this quotation from the *Poetics* (25, 1460b35–61a1):

> If it is neither true nor as it ought to be, one might reply that this is what people say; e.g. stories about the gods: it may be that talking like that is neither an idealisation nor the truth, and perhaps Xenophanes was right; but at any rate, that is what people say.

The compression of this passage is characteristic. Aristotle often presents a key concept, argument or conclusion without full explanation, leaving the reader to unpack the meaning and its unstated rationale. In the present instance, once the meaning is unpacked, the passage appears to take a stance radically opposed to that of Plato. The context is an overview of 'problems' in poetry, and the kinds of solution available. Fourth-century intellectuals had subjected the Homeric poems to minute scrutiny, revealing many features that were, at first sight, odd or objectionable.[1] These included apparent implausibilities in the narrative. For example, why does Helen not notice her brothers' absence from the Greek army until the ninth year of the war (*Il.* 3.236–42)? Why does the Phaeacian crew that takes Odysseus home to Ithaca not wake him up, but leave him asleep on the shore (*Od.* 13.116–25)? Other passages were objectionable on moral or theological grounds: for example, Achilles' insulting outburst against Agamemnon (*Il.* 1.225–44) or the gods fighting each other (*Il.* 21.385–513). Moral and theological objections of this kind are familiar from *Republic* 2 (§2.3), but Aristotle here looks back to Plato's predecessor, Xenophanes (§1.2).

Aristotle agrees that the poets' stories about the gods are not true, but denies that this is a genuine problem: in poetry, consistency with popular belief is a sufficient defence. To appreciate the significance of this claim, imagine how the discussion in *Republic* 2 might have proceeded

---

[1] Heath 2009a examines the contribution of Aristotle's contemporary, Heraclides of Pontus.

if Aristotle had been present. Socrates says: 'As for saying that god, who is good, causes bad things to happen to anyone, we must oppose in every way anyone saying that in his own city, or hearing it ... since it would not be pious if someone should say that, nor in our best interest, nor self-consistent' (380b–c). Adeimantus' acquiescent reply is forestalled by Aristotle's proposed solution: 'But, Socrates, that's what people say.' We might imagine Socrates responding: 'Exactly! You've put your finger on the problem. We can't allow poetry that encourages people to say things like that.' It is inconceivable that he would say: 'Good point! I withdraw my objection.' Aristotle's approach to poetry seems, at least in this respect, to be radically different from Plato's.

That does not mean that we should read the *Poetics* as a direct reply to Plato. Aristotle knew Plato's works very well, and would undoubtedly have been aware of their points of disagreement. But, though he engages in direct controversy with a variety of unnamed opponents in the *Poetics* (13, 1453a12–13, 23–6, 30–2; 26, 1462a2–6), none of them is Plato. Aristotle reaches different conclusions because he has different starting-points and a different agenda. Allowing Plato to set our agenda for reading the *Poetics* can only lead to misunderstanding.

One important aspect of the agenda of the *Poetics* is its restricted remit. It is concerned with the technicalities of poetry as a form of productive expertise – *tekhnē*, in Greek. Conventional translations are not entirely satisfactory. 'Art' risks confusion with the modern notion of 'the arts': the scope of *tekhnē* includes, for example, medicine and building. 'Skill' fails to capture the dimension of explicit understanding: the goal of an Aristotelian *tekhnē* is to articulate the implicit rationale of what skilful practitioners do. Each *tekhnē* is in some measure autonomous, in the sense that it has its own starting-points, goals and procedures. But this autonomy is limited. There is a hierarchy of disciplines in which politics is 'architectonic', determining which other activities are to be permitted in a community, subject to what limitations (*NE* 1.2, 1094a26–b2). The contrast between Plato and Aristotle might therefore turn out to be less radical than our initial quotation makes it seem. In principle, something that is unobjectionable within the limited technical remit of the *Poetics* (such as theological error) might properly be subject to restrictive political regulation. But, if so, that decision lies beyond the task Aristotle sets himself in the *Poetics*. For this reason, though this chapter must start from the *Poetics*, it cannot end there.[2]

---

[2] Brief accounts of Aristotle on poetry: Ferrari 1999; Heath 1996: vii–lxvii. More extended treatments: Halliwell 1986; Halliwell 2002: 151–259; Halliwell 2011: 208–65; Else 1986; Belfiore 1992.

I   WHAT IS POETRY?

Consistently with its remit, most of the *Poetics* is taken up with technical analyses of the main kinds of poetry. The analyses of tragedy and epic have survived; there was probably a continuation, now lost, which dealt with comedy.[3] In these analyses Aristotle is trying to discover what features make an epic a *good* epic, or a tragedy a *good* tragedy. Questions that arise include (for example): what is the best kind of tragic plot (§3.6)? The ground is prepared for these technical analyses by two tranches of introductory material. Chapters 1–3 determine what poetry is, and identify the main axes on which kinds of poetry are differentiated. Chapters 4–5 are largely concerned with an outline history of Greek poetry, showing how epic, tragedy and comedy developed from primitive beginnings. The bridge between the abstract opening analysis and the historical outline is provided by a brief account of how poetry is rooted in human nature – what we might call (though the terminology is not Aristotle's) the anthropology of poetry.

Aristotle begins on what seems familiar territory to those who have read *Republic*: poetry is a kind of imitation (1, 1447a13–16). It is differentiated from other kinds of imitation, such as the visual arts, instrumental music and dance, by its *medium*: poetry is imitation in language, enhanced by rhythm with or without melody (1447a21–b23). Differences in the combination and distribution of rhythmic and melodic enhancement provide one way in which kinds of poetry are differentiated (1447b24–8). Epic uses rhythm alone: it is in verse, but not sung. Lyric poetry uses rhythm and melody together. Drama uses rhythm throughout, but melody only in parts: the acts, which are predominantly spoken (though with some solo song), are interspersed with choral lyric.

Kinds of poetry can also be differentiated with reference to the *object* that is imitated. All poetry imitates people doing things (2, 1448a1; cf. *Rep.* 10, 603c), but there is a distinction in the kinds of people involved: epic and tragedy are concerned with people who behave well; characters in comedy behave in absurd and disgraceful ways (2, 1448a16–18; cf. 5, 1449a32–7).

Collections of papers: Rorty 1992; Andersen and Haarberg 2001. Anagnostopoulos 2009 is an outstanding guide to Aristotle; see also Barnes 1995b (though the treatment of the *Poetics* is weak).
[3] Janko 1984 argues that the Tractatus Coislinianus preserves a summary of this continuation: this thesis is highly controversial. On Aristotle and comedy: Heath 1989a; Janko 2001; Halliwell 2008: 307–31.

A final difference between poetic kinds is *mode*. The three modes of imitation which Aristotle distinguishes correspond to Plato's division of poetry into simple narrative, narrative through imitation, and narrative using both of those forms (*Rep.* 3, 392d–4c: cf. §2.4). But a change in terminology shows that Aristotle has reconceived the taxonomy. Plato's top-level category is *narrative*: he identifies three ways in which a story can be told, two of which involve imitation (in the sense, taking on the role of a character). By contrast, the top-level category for Aristotle is *imitation*: Plato's 'simple narrative' and his 'narrative through imitation' are now both subsumed as modes of imitation.

In saying that all poetry is imitation, Aristotle departs from customary usage. In ancient Greek, as in modern English, 'poetry' could refer to any composition in verse. In this sense, one could say that the presocratic philosopher Empedocles wrote poetry, because he wrote in verse. Aristotle thinks that the use of verse is a superficial feature. Empedocles and Homer both compose in verse (indeed, they use the same verse form), but they are doing fundamentally different things. Empedocles uses verse to tell us about nature (1, 1447b13–20); Homer uses verse to imitate. Since Aristotle has substituted 'imitation' for Plato's 'narrative', we might suppose that to describe Homer's poetry as imitation is just to say that he, unlike Empedocles, uses verse to tell stories. But there must be more to it than that. Later in the *Poetics*, Aristotle says that Herodotus' history would not be poetry, even if it were in verse (9, 1451a39–b4). Historical narrative in verse would not be poetry; but poetry is imitation in verse. It follows that in substituting 'imitation' for 'narrative' Aristotle was not saying that all narrative is imitation: poetic imitation is a subset of narrative in verse. We might conjecture that Aristotle's motive for discarding 'narrative' as the top-level category in the taxonomy of modes was precisely to avoid classifying versified historiography as poetry. But what did he mean by choosing 'imitation' as the substitute? In what sense is simple narrative a kind of imitation?

Consider the diverse kinds of activity that can be described as 'imitation'. An apprentice and an actor may both imitate a master craftsman, on whose actions they model their own: but in doing so, the apprentice really engages in craft activity, while the actor only simulates it.[4] The same distinction applies when the imitation involves assimilating external

---

[4] The distinction is not absolute. Since children learn their first lessons through imitation (4, 1448b7–8: cf. Pl. *Laws* 643b–d), a child's imitation may move along a continuum from simulation to real engagement.

objects, rather than one's own actions, to a model. The apprentice who uses a couch as a model produces a real couch; the painter who uses a couch as a model produces something that resembles a couch but is not really a couch. In the light of this distinction, it is clear that the imitation that makes verse poetry is a subset, not only of narrative, but also of imitation.[5] An author who models his verse composition on Empedocles is imitating, and is doing so in verse, but is engaged in the same kind of activity as Empedocles, who is not a poet. This author is not imitating in the sense that is relevant to defining poetry.

Suppose, then, that poetry is the kind of imitation that produces a resemblance without the reality. If so, one obvious difference between poetic and historiographic narrative clamours for attention: the criterion of success.[6] A historian's task is to give a true account of what happened: if the account is false, the history is to that extent defective. Historiographical narrative is not unique in this respect. Telling the truth is important in most kinds of social interaction. But this norm does not apply to poetic narratives. Aristotle does not regard it as a defect in poetic narrative if it gives an account of things that did not happen. As the quotation at the head of the chapter shows, he licenses falsehood not only in the particular events in the narrative, but also in its underlying framework: stories about the gods that could not possibly be true are not at fault poetically. In paradigmatic cases, therefore, narrators produce an account that is subject to the norm of truthfulness; the accounts that poetic narrators produce are not subject to that norm. So one might say that poetic narrators imitate in the sense that what they produce is a resemblance of what other narrators produce without the reality. The story the poet tells is (so to speak) a *pretend* story.[7]

This explanation is speculative – inevitably, since Aristotle has not explained himself on this point. It is also incomplete, as two further

---

[5] Aristotle's use of 'imitation' can be very broad: the elements 'imitate' the eternal circular movement of the heavens (*Met.* 9.8, 1050b28–34; *GC* 2.10, 337a1–7).

[6] It should be stressed that Aristotle would have no reason to be troubled by ambiguous or borderline cases. Aristotle's analytical distinctions typically do not entail clear-cut dichotomies in the phenomena to which they apply. Even such basic oppositions as inanimate/living and plant/animal have gradations which make it hard to identify a borderline (*HA* 7.1, 588b4–6; *PA* 4.5, 681a10–15); defining characteristics may be possessed 'indeterminately' (*de An.* 3.11, 434a4–5); a single organism may combine characteristics of distinct kinds (e.g. *PA* 4.5, 681a36–b8). See Lloyd 1996, 67–82.

[7] That is not to say that the poet pretends to tell a story. Aristotle's concept of poetry as imitation is not a speech-act theory (e.g. Searle 1975). The object imitated in an epic battle narrative is a battle, not the narrating of a battle. Poets, like painters, imitate by virtue of what they produce, and poets are makers of stories or plots (*muthoi*: 9, 1451b27–9), and it is by virtue of its plot that a poem is an imitation (see §3.6).

observations about Aristotle's treatment of poetic imitation will show. More worryingly, these observations raise doubts about whether Aristotle's conception is coherent in itself. I shall argue that the apparent inconsistencies become more tractable when we take an Aristotelian approach to poetry's development (§3.2). Pursuing the implications of that insight through Aristotle's discussions of poetry's roots in human nature (§3.3), his theory of culture (§3.4), and his history of Greek poetry (§3.5), will eventually yield a more complete explanation of the sense in which poetry is imitation.

The first of the two observations is that when Aristotle denies that Herodotus in verse would be a poet he does not focus directly on truth, but on another, less immediately obvious, difference between historical and poetic narrative: history is concerned with particulars, poetry with universals (9, 1451b4–9). History records a series of particular events: this happened, then that happened, and then another thing. But the plot of an epic or tragedy should comprise a causally connected sequence of events: this happened, and as a consequence that happened, and another thing happened as a consequence of that. Good poetic plots are not just one thing *after* another, but one thing *because* of another (10, 1452a18–21). In a poetic plot, one thing should follow from another in accordance with necessity or probability (7, 1451a12–13; 8, 1451a27–8; 9, 1451a38, b8, b35; 10, 1452a19–21; 11, 1452a24; 15, 1454a33–6). Similarly, what a character does or says should be what such a person would necessarily or probably do or say (9, 1451b8–9).[8] Many epic poets, and some tragedians, have failed to grasp this; as a result, their plots and their poems are defective. So, while poetic narrative is not subject to the criterion of truthfulness that governs historical narrative, it is subject to a structural criterion of its own (see §3.6).

Secondly, Aristotle has high praise for one distinctive feature of Homer's narrative style (24, 1460a5–11):

Homer deserves praise for many reasons, but above all because he alone among poets is not ignorant of what he should do in his own person. The poet in person should say as little as possible; that is not what makes him an imitator. Other poets perform in person throughout, and imitate little and seldom; but after a brief preamble Homer introduces a man or woman or some other character – and none of them are characterless: they have character.

---

[8] This does not mean that poetic plots must conform to what would necessarily or probably happen *in the real world*: we have already seen that poetry may tell stories about the gods that could not possibly be true in the real world. Stories may conform to the way the gods of popular religious belief (or literary convention) would necessarily or probably speak and act.

Homer does not just tell us what happens: he lets his characters speak for themselves in a way that prefigures drama (cf. 4, 1448b34–9a2). Using Plato's terminology, we could say that Homer does not use simple narrative alone, but combines it with narrative through imitation. Indeed, Aristotle himself seems in the passage quoted to revert to Plato's terminology: when the poet speaks in his own person 'that is not what makes him an imitator'. But that is a puzzling claim. The apparent abandonment of the taxonomy of modes set out in Chapter 3 is, on the face of it, an inconsistency.

Another apparent inconsistency arises when the structural criterion is investigated further. The problem is not that Aristotle is sometimes willing to waive the requirement of necessary or probable connection. Consider his relaxed response to a 'problem' mentioned earlier – the Phaeacians leaving Odysseus asleep on the shore. Aristotle acknowledges the implausibility of this, but admires Homer's skill in concealing it (24, 1460a35–b2):

> The irrationalities in the *Odyssey* involved in Odysseus' being put ashore would be manifestly intolerable if a second-rate poet had composed them, but as it is the poet conceals the oddity with other good qualities, and makes it a source of pleasure.

This simply means that Aristotle is pragmatic and flexible in applying his principles: the relevant standard for judging poets is what they can make an audience accept as necessary or probable.[9] The apparent contradiction lies instead in Aristotle's recognition of a kind of poetry in which necessary or probable connection is not a requirement even in principle. Iambic poetry typically does not have a connected plot (5, 1449b7–9; 9, 1451b14–15). You can make fun of someone by saying: 'Bill did this stupid thing; and he did this other stupid thing, too.' The lack of causal connection is a standard feature of this genre, not a defect in the individual poem. By contrast, the habit of composing unconnected plots ('iambic form') was something that comic poets had to unlearn in the course of the genre's development (5, 1449b5–9): universality is a normative feature of comedy, and the absence of causally connected plots is a defect in individual plays.[10]

---

[9] Aristotle also approves impossibilities that are likely (24, 1460a26–7; cf. 25, 1461b11–12), not enacted in full view (24, 1460a11–17), kept outside the tragedy or narration (15, 1454b6–8; 24, 1460a27–32), or smoothed over by inducing the audience to make fallacious inference (16, 1455a12–16; 24, 1460a18–26). Coincidences can be effective if an apparently meaningful relationship between two events conceals the absence of a genuine causal connection (9, 1452a3–11).

[10] For this understanding of 'iambic form' see Rotstein 2009: 61–111; Heath 1989a: 348–52.

Aristotle's account of poetic imitation therefore seems to lead him into two self-contradictions. First, what makes a poet an imitator is making the characters speak for themselves; but according to the taxonomy of modes, poets are imitators even if they do not do this. Secondly, historical narrative, even in verse, is not poetry because it does not require a connected plot. So what makes a narrative poetry, i.e. imitation in verse, is the connected plot; but some kinds of poetry are not required to have a connected plot. Our next task is to unravel Aristotle's apparent confusions.

2 THINKING BIOLOGICALLY

Aristotle was a biologist: at a rough estimate, 20–25 per cent of his surviving works are devoted to detailed investigations of animals. This is important, not because it induced in him any tendency to confuse poems with living organisms, but because biology shaped his habits of thought, making salient certain concepts and analytical tools that, once grasped, prove to be fruitful when applied more widely.

One important fact about biology is that worthwhile work in the subject is impossible without the study of real organisms. First, you must observe the facts; only then can you try to explain them. Theoretical speculation is worthless if it is not anchored by careful observation. This is a basic methodological principle for Aristotle, not only in his biological works.[11] His political theorising was informed by a research project that produced studies of the constitutional histories of 158 different states. Similarly, when he discusses poetry, his ideas are based on scholarly research. The discussion of problems and solutions in *Poetics* 25, from which we started, is unusually dense and cryptic, even by Aristotle's standards, because it summarises the conclusions of the six books of Aristotle's *Homeric Problems*, of which only fragments survive. In the *Homeric Problems*, a corpus of poetry of acknowledged excellence provided the evidential basis for a theory of what it is or is not reasonable to expect in an excellent poem, what does or does not matter in poetry. Aristotle also conducted historical research, compiling production records for the Athenian dramatic festivals. We should not assume that this kind of fact-gathering is irrelevant to philosophy. When he compiled the lists of victors at the

---

[11] Priority of observation over theory: *GA* 3.10, 760b27–33. Theories developed on the basis of abstract assumptions and arguments are empty: *Cael.* 3.7, 306a5–17; *GC* 1.2, 316a5–14. He makes his point vividly in *GA* 2.8, 747b27–8a16, constructing a purely theoretical explanation of the infertility of hybrids, which he then shows to be inadequate: detailed empirical data is needed if an adequate explanation is to be achieved.

Olympic games, Aristotle observed a lack of correlation between junior and senior Olympic victories; in the *Politics*, his explanation of this phenomenon became the basis for a recommendation in educational theory (8.4, 1338b40–9a4).

A second important point about biologists is that they must think developmentally. A checklist of distinctive human characteristics might include fully upright posture, bipedal locomotion, rationality and language (*PA* 4.10, 686a27–8a11; *Pol.* 1.2, 1253a7–18). Human babies do not manifest these characteristics, but they possess them potentially. In favourable conditions, human babies grow up to manifest the distinctively human characteristics; kittens grow up to manifest a different set of characteristics. For Aristotle, what distinguishes something as *natural* is its possession of an inner principle of development towards at end-point characteristic of its kind, and a thing's *nature* is what it is when its development is complete (*Pol.* 1.2, 1252b32–3). A thing's nature, then, unfolds over time. The outcome is contingent, however: completion will not be achieved in unfavourable conditions. So Aristotle's formula has an important qualification: something that is natural will develop towards a particular end-point *provided there is no impediment* (*PA* 1.1, 641b23–6; *Ph.* 2.8, 199a8–12, 199b15–18, 25–6).

The relevance of this to poetry may not be immediately obvious. Poems do not write themselves: they are human artefacts, not natural organisms. However, Aristotle believes that there is a sense in which poetry exists by nature, and that the nature of poetry is what it is when its development is complete. His history of Greek tragedy concludes: 'tragedy was gradually enhanced as people developed each new aspect of it that came to light. After undergoing many transformations tragedy came to rest, because it had attained its nature' (4, 1449a13–15). That formulation combines two perspectives on tragedy: it develops towards a natural end-point, but its development is contingent on human skill finding ways to improve it. It might be thought that this involves Aristotle in a third contradiction. But he presumably saw no inconsistency between these two successive propositions. That poses two questions. First, can Aristotle say both of these things consistently? Secondly, if he can do so, does this help resolve the apparent inconsistencies noted earlier?

Take the second question first. Suppose that the development of a poetic tradition is a natural process. Then, according to Aristotle's conception of nature, it is the end-state that determines the nature of poetry. We can define poetry in terms of the characteristics that the most fully developed forms of poetry have – connected plots and dramatic form (or an approximation to it in the case of Homer). But poetry that has not yet reached that stage is still poetry. This is analogous to what we said about living organisms: we define human nature in terms of a mature adult human, but babies are still human. The analogy is imperfect, since Aristotle does not think of poetry on the model of a single developing organism. Nor can he think of it on the model of an evolving species: in his non-evolutionary biology species do not change.[12] Biology may foreground developmental issues, but does not provide any close analogy for the development of a cultural tradition. There is no reason why it should: the biological is a subset of the natural, and biological development is a special case of the wider phenomenon of natural change. Stones, for example, are by nature such as to fall, provided there is no impediment (e.g. *NE* 2.1, 1103a20–1).

Aristotle's biology does, nevertheless, have some help to offer, in the concept of a defective kind. For example, a healthy adult seal is not defective as a seal; but it is a member of a species which, because of the particular formation of its hind feet and auditory passages, Aristotle regards as impaired (*HA* 2.1, 498a31–b4; *PA* 2.12, 657a22–4). His point is not that the species-typical formation of these parts is dysfunctional: he is perfectly well aware that their distinctive morphology makes seals well adapted to their aquatic habitat and way of life (*GA* 5.2, 781b22–8). Aristotle's idea is a much stranger one: the morphology appropriate for seals is deviant relative to the quadrupedal norm. Normal quadrupeds in turn deviate from the norm set by the only animal in which 'the natural parts are disposed in accordance with nature' (*PA* 2.10, 656a3–13). The seal's morphology is appropriate to its characteristic way of life, but the form of life made possible by human morphology is objectively superior: different states of existence vary in value according to the level of cognition they involve (*GA* 1.23, 731a30–b4), and human intelligence depends on upright posture (*PA* 4.10, 686a27–b3). If we apply this hierarchical conception of kinds, it makes sense to think of iambus as a defective kind. An iambic poem that conforms to iambic norms is not defective, and the iambic norm is appropriate to what iambic poetry attempts to do; but iambus is defective relative to comedy, since the comic norm enables poets to achieve something superior to what iambus attempts. The natural development of a poetic tradition involves poets discovering how to produce progressively

---

[12] Modern evolutionary biology would also, though for different reasons, have no use for the teleological notion of a species developing towards a natural completion.

more complete realisations of each poetic kind, and progressively more complete kinds of poetry.

Aristotle can be acquitted of self-contradiction in his definition of poetry, therefore, if we remember that he thinks developmentally – provided that it makes sense to say that poetry exists by nature, and that its development has a natural end-point, even though poetry is a human artefact. Does it make sense to say that? There are three key points. First, poetry is a natural human behaviour (§3.3). Secondly, humans are good at finding better ways to do things. Thirdly, some kinds of poetry are objectively better than others. If those three premises are true, they yield three predictions. First, poetry will exist in every human community. Secondly, people in any given community will tend over time to improve the way they do poetry. Thirdly, they will eventually find the best way to do poetry (unless there is some impediment to their doing so). Poetry is natural, in the sense that humans do it by nature; and it is natural in the sense that its development will tend towards a particular end-point, if not impeded. That is entirely consistent with its development involving the exercise of human skill.

3 POETRY AS A NATURAL PHENOMENON

Aristotle's argument that poetry is a natural human behaviour comes at the beginning of chapter 4 of the *Poetics* (4, 1448b4–24):

In general, two causes seem likely to have given rise to the art of poetry, both of them natural. Imitation comes naturally to human beings from childhood (and in this they differ from other animals, i.e. in having a strong propensity to imitation and in learning their earliest lessons through imitation); also the fact that everyone takes pleasure in imitations.

Aristotle here draws attention both to the production of imitative behaviour (imitating) and to its consumption (taking pleasure in imitations). Since the roles of poets and of audiences are interdependent, both are needed to explain poetry as a natural human behaviour.

Aristotle offers various kinds of evidence that these behaviours are natural. First, imitating starts early: we do it from childhood. Natural traits do not necessarily manifest themselves early in life (for example, puberty is a natural stage in human development, but its onset is delayed). As a biologist, Aristotle was aware of that (*EE* 2.8, 1224b29–36). But if a behaviour does appear very early, that is evidence that it is natural: it is not a culturally transmitted behaviour that we have learned from caregivers.

Indeed, as Aristotle points out, imitation is itself the mechanism by which children first begin to acquire new patterns of behaviour.

Secondly, humans are more imitative than other animals. I stress *other* animals: another important point about Aristotle as a biologist is that he never forgets that humans are a kind of animal. If humans engage in imitative behaviour more than nonhuman animals, that is an indication that imitating is not only natural to humans, but also plays an important role in their characteristic way of life. No living organism is a random bundle of traits: its traits form an integrated functional system. There is a reason why birds that live in marshes have long legs: they need to be able to wade in a waterlogged habitat (*PA* 4.12, 694b11–17). There is a reason why raptors have sharp eyesight: they need to be able to detect prey at a distance (*PA* 2.13, 657b24–9; cf. 4.11, 691a20–7). So we may assume that there is a reason why humans are strongly imitative: the trait must be functionally important. Aristotle's reference to learning hints at one function: because human behaviour is far more varied and adaptable than that of any other species (*Pol.* 7.13, 1332a38–b11; cf. 1.2, 1253a29–39; *NE* 2.1, 1103a23–6, 1103b23–5), human children must be equipped by nature to absorb whatever ways of behaving are appropriate to the demands of the diverse physical, social and cultural environments in which they grow up.[13] But it does not follow that this is imitation's only function in human life. In particular, given the developmental cast of Aristotle's thought, we should not assume that its childhood function defines its function in adult human life (see §3.7).

A third indication that imitation is natural is that it is universal. All normal human beings imitate; they also enjoy being consumers of imitations. For example, we like looking at pictures – even pictures of things we do not like looking at in reality. Aristotle has a theory about the psychological basis of our enjoyment of pictures (4, 1448b9–19):

What happens in practice is evidence of this: we take delight in viewing the most accurate possible images of objects which in themselves cause distress when we see them (e.g. the shapes of the lowest species of animal, and corpses). The reason for this is that learning is extremely pleasant, not just for philosophers but for others too in the same way, despite their limited capacity for it. This is the reason why people take delight in seeing images; what happens is that as they view

---

[13] Modern research on imitation confirms that humans are imitative from a very early age, and that a strong propensity to imitation is distinctive to humans and of central importance in human life. For a wide-ranging overview see Hurley and Chater 2005. One should, however, be wary of assuming in any given case that Aristotle's use of 'imitation', itself expansive (n.5), equates directly to the phenomena, themselves diverse, addressed in modern research.

them they come to learn and infer what each thing is (e.g. 'This is so-and-so!'). If one happens not to have seen the thing before, it will not give pleasure as an imitation, but because of its execution or colour, or for some other such reason.

This argument is worth examining in detail. It begins with a proposition: (1) everyone enjoys imitations. The evidence for (1) is that (2) we enjoy very accurate pictures even of unpleasant objects. The explanation for (2) has two parts: (3a) everyone enjoys learning; and (3b) the source of our enjoyment of pictures is learning and inferring what each thing is. The evidence for (3b) is: (4) we do not enjoy the picture as an imitation unless we have seen the object before (i.e. unless we are equipped to make the connection between features of the picture and features of the object), although (5) we might take pleasure in other aspects, such as the execution or the colouring.

In (3b) Aristotle says that when we look at a picture, we learn 'what each thing is'. This seems to mean that we look at a picture and think 'that is so-and-so!' or 'that is a such-and-such!',[14] and derive enjoyment from this exercise of our cognitive powers. Many interpreters resist this interpretation, because it appears to trivialise art. That concern is misguided. In this context Aristotle is looking for a common element that is present in all appropriate responses to pictures. To affirm the existence of a minimal baseline element, lacking any sophistication, in all appropriate responses to pictures is not to deny that there are other, more complex and sophisticated, elements in many (perhaps most) responses to pictures: for example, appreciation of artistic technique (why the artist painted the dog in that way), or learning something about the object depicted. The point is simply that these more complex responses presuppose the minimal baseline element.[15]

This interpretation is supported by the important qualification in a parallel to (3a) in the *Rhetoric* (3.10, 1410b10–11): 'learning *easily* is naturally pleasant to all'. Aristotle is not talking about learning achieved through laborious study or research, but about the everyday experience of finding things out. The natural and universal desire to know which Aristotle attributes to humans (*Met.* 1.1, 980a21) is the seed of the greatest human achievements in science and philosophy, but is also manifested in

---

[14] Aristotle's expression at 1448b17 is individual, but his explanation must also apply to the examples he has already mentioned, such as 'the shapes of the lowest species of animal', which are generic.

[15] Compare the programme formulated by Fitch *et al.* 2009: 60: 'a future discipline of bioaesthetics should focus on the broadly shared capacity of any normal human to have *any* aesthetic experience'.

routine exercises of the senses (980a21–7). Sense-perception is not limited to humans (980a27–8), and Aristotle attributes learning to nonhuman animals (*HA* 9.1, 608a17–21, 27; 9.15, 616b11; *PA* 2.17, 660b1; *Met.* 1.1, 980b21–5), just as he does to human children (*Po.* 4, 1448b7–8). So there is no reason to deny that nonhuman animals have a share in the pleasure of learning: they are, after all, naturally inquisitive and like looking at things (or, depending on species, sniffing them).

But Aristotle does not say simply that we *learn* what each thing is: he says that we learn *and infer* what each thing is. That addition puts the kind of cognition he has in mind beyond the reach of nonhuman animals and human children, since inference depends on the developed capacity for reason. This addition is puzzling. On the face of it, perceptual recognition seems sufficient: when I look at a picture of a cow, I *see* that it is a cow, without any need for inference or reasoning.[16] Yet the addition of 'and infer' cannot be discounted as a casual oversight. In a related account of imitation in the *Rhetoric* (1.11, 1371a31–b10) Aristotle explains the pleasure we take in imitations (including visual arts and poetry) in terms of the pleasure of learning: 'there is an inference that this is that, so that something is learned'. The inferential component is therefore a settled part of Aristotle's theory.

To account for the element of inference, we might emphasise either the opacity of pictures or their transparency. These two options treat the picture as puzzle and as potential illusion respectively. Pictures are puzzles, in the sense that they are never visually identical to the objects they depict (for example, the picture is two-dimensional, the object three-dimensional). Perhaps, then, Aristotle's idea is that we have to work out what the picture is a picture of by identifying relevant similarities and discounting differences. A discussion of metaphor in the *Rhetoric* (3.10, 1410b9–27) might seem to support this conjecture. In Aristotle's example, when Odysseus invites Eumaeus to judge the corn from the stubble (*Od.* 14.213), Eumaeus has to search for the meaning: 'corn' is 'what I was like in my prime', 'stubble' is 'what I am like in my old age'. Metaphor thus prompts us to engage in a search for a connection; when we have found it we can say 'this is that'. However, while it is plausible that inference is needed to grasp the conceptual connections on which metaphor depends, visual art depends on perceptual similarities: and the problem we face is precisely why this should be thought to require inference. The passage on

---

[16] Aristotle's concept of incidental perception (*de An.* 2.6, 418a20–4) gives the senses extended reach without the need for inference.

metaphor does not solve the problem, therefore, so much as show more clearly where the problem lies. Furthermore, the incompleteness of the visual resemblance between a picture and the object is not what Aristotle emphasises in context: when he talks about 'the most accurate possible images', he is not thinking of images that are difficult to recognise, but of those which place the least demands on the viewer's capacity for perceptual recognition. This may turn our thoughts to pictures as potential illusions.

In *Rhetoric* I.II, as in *Poetics* 4, what Aristotle singles out for attention is our enjoyment of pictures of things that we do not enjoy looking at in themselves. That phenomenon is significant, because it reveals a feature of our consumption of visual images that might go unnoticed if we took account only of pictures of things we do enjoy looking at: we are able (to some extent) to dissociate our response to a visual image from our response to the thing of which it is an image, despite the visual similarity.[17] Consider an example:

(A) I see something that looks like a snake, think 'This is a snake', and move away.

If the thing that I have seen is a snake, my response is appropriate. If it is a stick or a painting, my response is inappropriate.

(B) I see something that looks like a snake, think 'This looks like a snake, but is not a snake', and ignore it.

If the thing that I have seen is a stick, my response is appropriate. If it is a painting, my response is incomplete.

(C) I see something that looks like a snake, think 'This looks like a snake, but is not a snake; it is a painting of a snake', and I look at it with pleasure.

If the thing that I have seen is a painting, my response is complete and appropriate. So the thought 'This is so-and-so/a such-and-such', if it is to be an appropriate response to a picture, involves a complex judgement: (i) this *looks like* so-and-so; (ii) this is *not really* so-and-so; (iii) it is an *artistically contrived* likeness of so-and-so. The third element requires causal understanding: that is, we understand the reason *why* this thing that is not an X looks like an X – i.e., because it is an artistically contrived

---

[17] Dissociation does not arise with images that are so like the object depicted that we take the same *pleasure* in their visual qualities as we do in those of the real thing (*Pol.* 8.5, 1340a23–8).

likeness of X. For Aristotle, there is a fundamental distinction between knowing 'the that' and understanding 'the why'. We can know *that* something is so just by sense-perception (for example, I can see that it is so), but understanding *why* it is so requires the developed capacity for reason; it is something that adult humans can do, but nonhuman animals and small children cannot (*EE* 2.10, 1226b21–5). The appropriate response to a painting therefore involves a complex judgement that includes causal understanding. The addition of 'and infer' may reflect the judgement's complexity, and its inclusion of a reason-dependent element. 'Complexity' is, of course, relative: this judgement is more complex than perceptual recognition, but is still very easy. As explained earlier, Aristotle is here concerned to establish the baseline component that is necessary to explain *any* appropriate response to a picture.

Pictures vary, so in principle it would be possible to combine these two options. Some pictures are not very like the object depicted, and pose a puzzle; others are so like the object depicted that they are potential illusions. The structure of an appropriate response varies across this range. But in every case there is some minimal complexity of judgement, and some element of causal understanding. In working out a puzzling picture, I have to ask 'what is this *meant* to be?', a question that does not arise with regard to the stick in the grass. But Aristotle's emphasis in the passage is on pictures as transparent likenesses. We might therefore recall an ancient anecdote, according to which the painter Zeuxis painted a bunch of grapes so realistically that birds flew down to feed on them (Pliny *NH* 35.65–6). A bird seeing Zeuxis' grapes will feel pleasure at the opportunity to feed; when it swoops down and encounters inedible two-dimensional colour patches, it will feel distress (frustration); then it will view the picture with indifference. Human observers, on discovering that the apparent grapes are a painting, may take greater pleasure in the picture than they would have taken in actual grapes, because of their recognition of the artistic contrivance.

Aristotle said that there were two causes of poetry. At first sight, it seems that they are the propensities to produce and consume imitations. But these would not, on their own, provide a complete explanation of poetry, which is not simply imitation, but imitation in language, enhanced by rhythm, with or without melody. It is possible, therefore, that the second cause is one that is mentioned very briefly at the end of the passage (4, 1448b20–24):

Given, then, that imitation is natural to us, and also melody and rhythm (it being obvious that verse-forms are segments of rhythm), from the beginning those who had the strongest natural inclination towards these things generated poetry out of improvised activities by a process of gradual innovation.

Why did Aristotle not feel the need to elaborate on the point about melody and rhythm in the way he does for imitation? Perhaps he thought it sufficiently obvious that music is universal, enjoyable, attracts us from childhood, and is characteristic of humans as against other animals. But Aristotle has interesting things to say about music in other works, which will later help us to answer a fundamental question which Aristotle does not address in his outline anthropology of poetry (§3.7).

Aristotle's outline does not cover every human trait that is relevant to explaining poetry. It identifies some of the natural characteristics that *motivate* poets and their audiences, while taking for granted other traits that *enable* poetry, such as the capacities for language and causal understanding. Aristotle singles out the instincts for imitating and consuming imitations, and for melody and rhythm, because the question he is addressing is what motivates us to use language *for poetry*. It is not puzzling that humans use language to exchange information with each other in everyday life. What needs to be explained is, first, why they use language to tell, and why they enjoy being told, stories of which truth is not required (§3.1), and, secondly, why they put such stories into rhythmical and melodic form. Since these peculiar stories, cast in a peculiar form, lack the obvious utility of other forms of linguistic interaction, the motivation of this behaviour needs to be explained. But an account of the traits which provide poetry's proximal motivations is not a complete explanation. Since an animal's characteristics are presumed to be functional, understanding poetry as a natural human behaviour also requires an account of its place in human life. What value does poetry have for human beings? We shall return to this fundamental question later (§3.7).

4 NATURE AND CULTURES

In modern understanding, *Homo sapiens* evolved, dispersed from a common point of origin to achieve its global distribution, and in the course of that dispersal developed many distinct (though often interacting) cultural traditions. Aristotle's worldview was profoundly different. His world had always, and would always exist; hence there is no need to explain the origin of species – the world has always been inhabited by the species now in existence. Therefore, no history, however complex and diverse, traces humans back to a common origin. Humanity is unified by a common nature, not a common descent.

If the past history of human civilisation has been infinitely long, how can we account for evidence of fairly recent progress from primitive conditions to civilisation? By contrast with the unchanging regularity of the heavens, what happens on earth is, within limits, unstable. Catastrophic natural events occur that intermittently devastate human societies and cultures (*Mete.* 1.14; F53 Rose = F74.1 Gigon; F13 Rose = F463 Gigon). The gradual ascent to civilisation has been repeated infinitely often, and is always followed eventually by its cataclysmic overthrow. This is what Aristotle means when he says that 'pretty well everything ... has been discovered many times in the long course of history, or rather an infinite number of times' (*Pol.* 7.10, 1329b25–7; cf. *Met.* 12.8, 1074b10–12; *Mete.* 1.3, 339b16–30; *Cael.* 1.3, 270b16–25).[18] Although Aristotle never makes the point explicitly, it must be assumed that the infinitely repeated process of social and cultural development includes the development of poetry from its most primitive to its most mature forms. Poetry, then, has both a natural history and infinitely many cultural histories. But naturalness implies that there is a certain end-point which each history would attain, in the absence of impediments. So there is a presumption that these histories follow, with whatever degree of variation, the same underlying pattern.

The history of Greek poetry which Aristotle presents in chapters 4–5 of the *Poetics* is therefore particular in its focus, but universal in its horizon. In accordance with Aristotle's scientific methodology, the history of Greek poetry is the starting-point ('the that') from which explanatory understanding ('the why') is sought. Given the premises that there are objectively best kinds of poetry, and that people tend over time to discover better ways of doing things, then it is reasonable to suppose that studying the trajectory of poetry's development will help us to understand what poetry, by nature, is. We may compare Aristotle's analysis of human societies, where he says that the origins and development of things provide the best view of them (*Pol.* 1.2, 1252a24–6). The point is not that we should look for a pristine original state, but that the primitive stage of any phenomenon reveals its minimal core, while the changes that ensued illuminate its fully developed state. In particular, it is only in its fully developed state that we see what human society really is: the city 'comes into existence for the sake of living, but continues in existence for the sake of living *well*' (1.2, 1252b27–30).

It is not possible to extract a universal account of poetry's development directly from particular data. First, the natural path of development may

---

[18] Catastrophe theory: Chroust 1973a; Palmer 2000.

be impeded. So it cannot be assumed that the actual outcome, or the path to it, in any given tradition is normative in every respect. Aristotle recognises detrimental developments even in the Greek tradition (*Po.* 9, 1451b34–52a1; 13, 1453a33–5). Secondly, where the data are incomplete, inferential reconstruction will be needed to fill in gaps. For example, Aristotle makes the reasonable inference that there was invective poetry before Homer, even though no pre-Homeric poetry of that kind was extant (4, 1448b28–30). Thirdly, and conversely, many contingent details in a particular tradition's history can be ignored because they have no universal significance. Aristotle mentions competing claims for the origination of tragedy, but they are not part of his history of poetry, and he does not feel it necessary to adjudicate between them (3, 1448a28–b2). On the other hand, some abnormal features of a particular tradition may reveal important things about the nature of poetry in general. One could not expect a poet of Homer's genius to appear in every tradition, but Aristotle finds it revealing to compare his poetry with that of lesser poets, and to analyse the reasons for its success. In a variety of ways, therefore, theory and data are reciprocally related. As in any scientific enquiry, theoretical analysis is recommended to the extent that it makes the observational data intelligible, while confidence in the reliability of our observations is reinforced to the extent that it yields to theoretical analysis. We must not expect Aristotle's history to provide historical evidence uncontaminated by theory (is there such a thing?); nor should we jump to the conclusion that the history is a purely theoretical construct, which treats the evidence in an arbitrary way.

A deeper problem is the fact that Aristotle had access only to a single tradition: this, surely, is an absurdly limited evidence base from which to extrapolate universals. Aristotle could legitimately reply that, without access to other traditions, there was no alternative. The problem will, in any case, seem less formidable on the assumption that poetry is natural than on a view which emphasises the contingency and diversity of cultural practices: for Aristotle, each tradition will have the same underlying pattern, however imperfectly manifested. It is, though, worth considering what options would have been available to him had he encountered comparative evidence that failed to match his analysis of the Greek tradition. He might have concluded that the analysis had reached the wrong conclusions, because it was based on too limited an evidence base. Alternatively, he might have tried to save the analysis by arguing that the anomalous non-Greek traditions had undergone an impeded development. Though the presence of detrimental developments shows that the Greek world was not free of impediments, Aristotle would have found it plausible that more serious impediments would exist elsewhere. His views on the effects of environment on character and intelligence (*Pol.* 7.7, 1327b18–31) suggest certain predictions: Northern European poetry would lack technical skill; Asiatic poetry would be skilful, but lacking in 'spirit' – perhaps sharing the preference for plots with happy endings which Aristotle blames on the 'weakness' of audiences when it manifested itself in the Greek world (*Po.* 13, 1453a33–4).

But Aristotle would have had a third option. He distinguishes between unqualified and relative goods. For example, the diet that is healthy for a person in good health is healthy without qualification, but may be unsuitable for an invalid; a diet suited to an invalid is a healthy diet in a qualified and relative sense. Unqualified goods are superior to qualified goods, but not always preferable. If I am in a less than optimal condition, I should choose the qualified goods which are appropriate to my condition in preference to the unqualified goods that would not be good *for me* – while also aiming to improve my condition, so that unqualified goods become good for me as well (*NE* 5.1, 1129b2–6; cf. 7.12, 1152b24–33; *EE* 7.2, 1235b30–6a7). This distinction between unqualified and relative goods carries over to ethics: what is fine for humans, without qualification, may differ from what is fine for a particular group of humans. Most strikingly, it is fine for Triballians to sacrifice their fathers (*Top.* 2.11, 115b22–6). In saying this, Aristotle is not simply making an ethnographic report about what Triballians *regard* as fine behaviour. The passage says that sacrificing their fathers *is* fine for Triballians, in just the same way that a particular diet may be genuinely beneficial in unhealthy conditions (b18–21), or taking medicine may be beneficial when one is ill (b26–9), although neither is beneficial in an unqualified sense.[19] This principle can be generalised to all arts and sciences (*Pol.* 4.1, 1288b10–21). So Aristotle could maintain that other poetic traditions were significantly impeded, while still granting them qualified approval.

5 A CULTURAL HISTORY OF POETRY

Imagine the survivors of a catastrophic natural disaster that has wiped out their civilisation, sending them back to the struggle for bare survival. They

---

[19] Ethnographic accounts of ritual killing of elderly parents in other ancient sources understand it as an honorific act, which pleases the parent (Timaeus *FGrH* 566F46; Demon *FGrH* 327F18). If so, then the virtuous Triballian who sacrifices his father is respecting the two most fundamental ethical principles – honouring one's parents and the gods (*Top.* 1.11, 105a3–9).

are human, and have not lost the power of speech: they have language; they talk to each other; they tell each other things they need to know. But, being human, they are also naturally given to imitative behaviour. They engage in it from childhood: imitating what people around them do is one important way in which their children learn how to do things, and the right way to behave. Being human, they also enjoy it when others engage in imitation. So even in their most primitive state, when their energies are absorbed in bare survival, these people spontaneously take to story-telling that goes beyond the communication of things they need to know: they make up stories that are not judged by whether they are true or false, and enjoy listening to such stories. Furthermore, being human, they enjoy rhythm and melody: so they spontaneously start to tell these stories rhythmically, and even to sing them.

Because these people are starting from scratch, they do not have any established traditions that tell them how best to do this. So they improvise: people tell stories in whatever way seems best to them. Over time, they notice which ways of telling a story get the best response from audiences. Feedback from audiences gradually shapes the ways in which the most skilled story-tellers tell their stories. Skilled story-tellers compete with each other for the approval of audiences, experimenting with new ways of doing things, abandoning experiments that do not succeed, and building popular innovations into their repertoires. So we would expect to find a gradual progression from improvised performances to distinct forms of poetry, shaped by the experience and ingenuity of performers interacting with their audiences' responses.

Is that the story Aristotle wants to tell? As always, we are dealing with a text that leaves much of the detail implicit or undeveloped. But the scenario just presented is a plausible way of unpacking the characteristically compressed introduction to Aristotle's history of (Greek) poetry (4, 1448b20–4):

Given, then, that imitation is natural to us, and also melody and rhythm (it being obvious that verse-forms are segments of rhythm), from the beginning those who had the strongest natural inclination towards these things generated poetry out of improvised activities by a process of gradual innovation.

The story continues like this (4, 1448b24–7):

Poetry bifurcated in accordance with the corresponding kinds of character: more serious-minded people imitated fine actions, i.e. those of fine persons; more trivial people imitated those of inferior persons. The latter at first composed invectives, while the others composed hymns and encomia.

Aristotle established in the preliminary chapters that what poets imitate (the *object* of imitation) is people doing things. People and the things they do vary in their ethical character: the agents 'must be either admirable or inferior', since 'character almost always corresponds to just these two categories, since everyone is differentiated in character by defect or excellence' (2, 1448a1–4). That is an oversimplification: people cannot be sorted into two clearly distinguished groups, since ethical character varies along a continuum from the very good to the very bad. There are people in the middle, as Aristotle recognises: 'alternatively they must be better people than we are, or worse, or of the same sort' (2, 1448a4–5). That alternative will be important in the analysis of tragic plots (13, 1453a7–12: §3.6), but for the purposes of the historical sketch the over-simplified binary opposition is useful to the extent that the poetic tradition is observed to have sorted itself into two distinct streams – one leading from hymns and encomia through epic to tragedy, the other leading from invectives through iambus and narrative burlesque to comedy.

The bifurcation of poetry into two streams does not depend on the affinity of poets of inferior character to bad actions (that would make them *praise* bad actions), but on their tendency to malicious denigration (cf. *Rh.* 2.6, 1384b9–11). Homer's abusive trouble-maker Thersites (*Il.* 2.211–75) might serve as an example, but also reminds us that epic is not devoid of inferior individuals. The two streams are differentiated by their *dominant* tendency towards celebration or denigration. It is in this sense that it is possible to see epic poetry as a sophisticated descendant of primitive encomia. But Aristotle's next move is surprising (4, 1448b27–30):

We are not in a position to identify a poem of that kind by any of the poets who preceded Homer, although they are likely to have been numerous; but beginning with Homer we can do so – e.g. his *Margites* and similar poems.

We might assume that 'a poem of that kind' refers to the hymns and encomia just mentioned. That would agree with our image of Homer as a serious-minded epic poet, imitating fine actions. But the reference to *Margites* proves that this is not what Aristotle meant. The few surviving fragments of *Margites* show that it was not a serious epic poem: it was about an idiotic anti-hero, who got into ridiculous situations because 'he knew many things, but knew them all badly' (F3).[20] This was an imitation of an inferior person.

---

[20] *Margites*: West 2003: 225–8 (introduction), 240–53 (fragments).

Modern scholars do not agree with Aristotle in associating *Margites* with the *Iliad* or *Odyssey*; they would date it much later. The attribution was not accepted by everyone in the ancient world, either. Aristotle may have felt that it was supported by the poem's distinctive technical affinities with the two epics. If so, his respect for what he took to be the evidence deserves credit, since it would have been theoretically tidier if *Margites* were not by Homer. There are two points. First, the fact that Homer's *Margites* was the earliest surviving example of the stream of poetry that imitates inferior persons is chronologically awkward. On Aristotle's theory of poetry's natural course of development, invective (which is relatively primitive) should come before burlesque narrative (which is relatively sophisticated), just as hymns and encomia come before heroic epic. Yet *Margites* was a burlesque narrative, not a simple invective, and the earliest surviving invectives were those of Archilochus, who was later than Homer. This is not a major difficulty, since Aristotle's inference that this is no more than an accident of survival is reasonable. Elsewhere he observes that little is known about the early development of comedy because it was not taken seriously (5, 1449a37–b4): the same would plausibly apply to invective. Secondly, and more significantly, Homer's authorship of burlesque narrative as well as serious epic makes him a paradoxical figure. Aristotle has said that the two streams of poetry divided 'in accordance with the corresponding kinds of character'. But if Homer, an epic poet who imitated fine actions, also composed a narrative poem that imitated an inferior person, what kind of character did he have? Was he a serious-minded person, or a trivial person? Apparently, he was both: he was so exceptionally versatile that he excelled in both kinds of poetry.

Aristotle concludes this part of the history by saying that 'some of the ancients became composers of heroic poetry, others of lampoons [*iamboi*]' (4, 1448b32–4).[21] He does not say that some became composers of heroic poetry, others of comic narratives like *Margites*. The evidence would not allow that, not only because Homer composed both heroic and comic narratives, but also because *Margites* was an isolated case. Narrative form took root in the stream of poetry that imitates fine actions, but not in the stream of poetry that imitates inferior persons. Even after Homer, the

---

[21] At some point poets in the stream that imitates inferior persons discovered that iambic metre was most appropriate to their kind of poetry; hence the metre acquired its name because people used it to lampoon (*iambizein*) each other (4, 1448b30–32). For the characteristics of iambic metre that made it appropriate for *iamboi* see 4, 1449a22–7; 22, 1459a10–14. Aristotle assumes that the appropriate metre for heroic poetry was also discovered empirically (24, 1459b31–7).

greatest poets in this stream (such as Archilochus) typically composed iambic poetry rather than comic narratives.

We have seen two respects in which Homer was exceptional. First, he excelled in both streams of poetry. Secondly, he saw how to apply narrative techniques that had taken root in the imitation of fine actions to the imitation of an inferior person, and did so at an early date; other poets failed to follow his lead. There are two further respects in which Homer was exceptional, and in which other poets failed to follow his lead. One is the excellence of his plot-construction. That is not discussed in the history of poetry, but in two later passages Aristotle singles it out as an area in which Homer saw what was best, while other epic poets did not, even though Homer had shown them the way (8, 1451a16–30; 23, 1459a17–b2). We shall return to this in the next section. The history of poetry does emphasise a further exceptional excellence: both in his serious epics and in *Margites* Homer developed a narrative technique that was quasi-dramatic. This is an idea we met earlier, as formulated in a later chapter (24, 1460a5–11: see §3.1). In the history of poetry, Aristotle interweaves Homer's unique anticipation of dramatic form with his ability to compose in both streams of poetry (4, 1448b34–9a2):

But just as Homer was the outstanding poet of the serious kind, since he did not just compose well but also made his imitations dramatic, so too he was the first to adumbrate the form of comedy; what he composed was not an invective, but a dramatisation of the laughable. His *Margites* stands in the same relation to comedy as the *Iliad* and *Odyssey* do to tragedy.

So Homer was an exceptional figure in many respects. Since a genius of this kind cannot be taken for granted, his presence in the Greek poetic tradition must make the history of Greek poetry atypical. Aristotle thinks that cultural traditions generally develop by the gradual accumulation of small changes (*SE* 34, 183b17–36, 184b1–8; *NE* 1.7, 1098a22–6). Hence, in the Greek tradition, 'tragedy was *gradually* enhanced as people developed each new aspect of it that came to light' (*Po.* 4, 1449a13–14). But sometimes an especially gifted individual can make a big advance (Aristotle thinks of his own contribution to logic in that light). That does not mean that other traditions will not reach the same natural end-point; but they will arrive there by a different route.

Although Homer showed the way for both tragedy and comedy, this was only an anticipation: drama proper developed at a later date (4, 1449a2–6):

When tragedy and comedy made their appearance, those who inclined towards either kind of poetry became, in accordance with their nature, poets of comedy (instead of lampoons) or of tragedy (instead of epic), because these forms were greater and more highly esteemed than the others.

The importance of audience feedback in poetry's development, already implicit in the interdependent production and consumption of imitations, is here made explicit. Tragedy and comedy supersede epic and invective because they are 'more highly esteemed'. Poets now preferred to compose in dramatic forms because audiences preferred to consume them. The fact that audiences recognise from experience that dramatic form makes for more effective poetry is, for Aristotle, evidence that drama is poetry at its best.[22] Drama is therefore the natural end-point of poetry's development.

Since other epic poets did not follow Homer either in his approach to plot-construction or in his quasi-dramatic narrative technique it would be implausible to suppose that drama arose as a modified form of epic. Nor would it have been plausible to trace a direct line of descent from epic, with its single performer, to drama, which requires multiple performers. Choral song, in which the body of the chorus was distinct from the chorus-leader and the leader might take on the role of one or more characters in the story being sung, provides a more convincing developmental resource. From the interaction between chorus and chorus-leader it is a relatively small step to the creation of the first actor, and thus the simplest kind of drama. This is the line of development which Aristotle suggests (4, 1449a7–13):

Originally it [i.e. tragedy] developed from improvisations. This is true of tragedy, and also of comedy: the former arose from the leaders of the dithyramb, the latter from the leaders of the phallic songs which are still customary even now in many cities.

Scholars have seized on this passage for the evidence it does (or does not) provide about the early history of Greek tragedy and comedy. We do not know how far Aristotle's derivation of drama from dithyramb and phallic songs was based on the kind of argument from probability with which I

---

[22] Aristotle believes that what people think has evidential value. The empirical data (*phainomena*) include observational data, but also people's opinions, especially opinions that have some claim to good standing (*endoxa*): e.g. those held universally, or very widely, or by those most qualified to judge: *Top.* 1.1, 100a29–b23; cf. 1.10, 104a8–11; note especially *EE* 1.6, 1216b30–1 ('every individual has some contribution to make to the truth'), *Met.* 2.1, 993a30–b7. *Endoxa* are likely to conflict, but a theory will be most in harmony with the empirical data if it shows that conflicting opinions all (or at least the 'the greater number and the most authoritative': *EE* 7.2, 1235b13–18; *NE* 7.1, 1145b2–7) have some element of truth. Some *endoxa* are false (*Top.* 8.12, 162b27); it is then important to explain how the error has come about.

introduced it, and how far it was supported by evidence. But that is not our present concern. Our aim here is to understand the rationale of the pattern of development he suggests.

In the classical period, elaborate and well-rehearsed dithyrambs were performed at major festivals like the Dionysia, but the reference to tragedy's development from an improvisatory origin (4, 1449a9–10) shows that Aristotle had something more primitive in mind. So he must be tacitly assuming that the impromptu performances mentioned at the beginning of the history (1448b23–4) persisted alongside more formal kinds of poetry. These were informal activities, not elaborate and not taken very seriously either by performers or by audiences. Perhaps they included elements of dramatic mimicry. That would explain the otherwise puzzlingly late appearance of drama in Aristotle's account. He starts his explanation of poetry's existence with the observation that imitation comes naturally to human beings, and that we do it from childhood. But in pretence games, children do not only tell stories: they act things out. So why was dramatic mimicry not present in the poetic tradition from the start? Perhaps it was. Aristotle's idea may be that, though drama was formalised relatively late, dramatic mimicry was present all along in these marginal forms of informal poetry. They lacked the prestige of more formal kinds of poetry, but provided a reservoir of potential which would eventually enrich the formal poetic tradition.

That would fit with the comment that 'tragedy acquired dignity at a late stage', having begun with trivial plots and laughable diction, like satyr plays (4, 1449a19–21). These plays were mythological burlesques with a chorus of satyrs (followers of Dionysus, part-human and part-animal, idle, drunken and lustful). In the classical period, tragedians competing at the Dionysia in Athens normally staged three tragedies and a satyr-play. Aristotle sees satyr plays as preserving characteristics of tragedy's informal, pre-dramatic choral antecedents. Improvised songs with an element of dramatic mimicry gave rise to the earliest drama; when poets saw how popular this format was, they gradually learned how to exploit the new medium for themes as serious as those of epic narrative. And so 'after undergoing many transformations tragedy came to rest, because it had attained its natural state' (4, 1449a14–15).

Although dithyrambs and phallic songs are not mentioned in the history of poetry until they become relevant to tragedy and comedy, they must have been present in the background all along; so may other kinds of poetry. Aristotle's account of poetry's history does not aim to be comprehensive: it picks out the crucial steps in the tradition's development (the split into two streams, the transition to narrative structure, the transition to dramatic form). If the history is to give a clear picture of these key elements, it must not get bogged down in tracing every complicated thread. Particular kinds are therefore mentioned only when, and if, they become relevant to the main line of development.[23] In the same way, when Aristotle embarks on his technical analysis of poetic forms he concentrates on the most mature forms, tragedy and comedy – and also epic. One reason why the attention given to epic, a poetic form which in Aristotle's view is not fully mature, does not strike us as anomalous is that Homer's exceptional excellence makes his work so revealing about what poetry is at its best.[24]

Plato's Socrates allowed hymns to the gods and encomia of good men to remain in the ideal city (*Rep.* 10, 607a). At first sight, this seems to be another radical difference between Plato and Aristotle: the only kinds of poetry that Plato allows are precisely the kinds that Aristotle sees as primitive forms that poetry must progress beyond to begin developing towards its natural end-point. But that is not quite right. Plato uses 'encomium' in an extended sense, in which an epic narrative might count as an encomium of the heroes (*Rep.* 10, 599b). So limiting the permissible kinds of poetry to hymns and encomia does not rule out epic narratives; even epic narratives making limited use of narrative through imitation would be consistent with Socrates' prescription (§2.7). Plato, then, could allow poetry to proceed some of the way along the developmental pathway which Aristotle maps out. But he could not allow it to go the whole way: Homer and drama go beyond an acceptably limited use of narrative through imitation. That, in Aristotle's view, is what poetry is like when it reaches its natural fulfilment.[25]

We can now return to the speculative and incomplete explanation of Aristotle's concept of poetry as imitation suggested earlier (§3.1). Plato's taxonomy of poetic modes was a static map of the possibility space; Aristotle's reconfiguration fits his developmental approach. The nature of poetry, as of any natural phenomenon, is shown in its fully developed form; the initial stages should contain this end-point potentially, though manifesting it incompletely (§3.2). Poetry's developmental trajectory is

---

[23] Dithyrambs and nomes (another kind of lyric poetry) were mentioned in the opening chapters: 1, 1447a14, b26; 2, 1448a14–15.

[24] Iambus might therefore not have received comparably extended treatment alongside comedy.

[25] Not everyone agreed: Aristotle confronts the advocates of epic in chapter 26. That there was still debate about whether epic or tragedy was superior is another reason for the attention given to epic.

from (in Plato's terms) simple narrative to narrative through imitation. But this terminology fails to capture the difference between simple poetic narrative and historiography. One advantage of substituting imitation as the top-level category is that it marks this difference by means of a feature that is common to all poetry – the fact that it is not bound, like narrative proper, by the criterion of truth. It also characterises the fully developed nature of poetry more adequately, reflecting poetry's tendency to develop towards dramatic form. Imitation therefore spans the whole of poetry's developmental trajectory, applying in a restricted sense to its early stages and in an enriched sense to its most fully developed stage.[26]

6 PLOT: THE 'SOUL' OF POETRY

In the opening chapters of the *Poetics* Aristotle distinguishes the medium, object and mode of poetic imitation. The linguistic medium is the vehicle for a story or plot (*muthos*). Plot is the imitation of the action (6, 1450a3–4; 8, 1451a31–2). Strictly speaking, therefore, a poem is an imitation by virtue of its plot. Aristotle speaks of plot as being 'as it were the soul of tragedy' (6, 1450a38–9). With a proviso to cover incomplete poetic kinds, such as iambus (§3.2), this principle can be extended to poetry in general.

What plot imitates is people doing things (2, 1448a1). More precisely, plot as the imitation of action imitates the things people do – 'things' in the plural, since one event does not constitute a story. A plot is an imitation of an action (*praxis*), and is a structure of acts (*pragmata*, 6, 1454a4–5, 15–17, 22, 32–3, 36–7; 7, 1450b22; 8, 1451a32–3; 14, 1453b2–3, 1454a13–14; 15, 1454a33–4). Clearly, if plot is poetry's soul, and plot is a structure, it is crucially important that poems and plays should have the right kind of plot-structure. We shall begin by looking at Aristotle's views on the proper structure of poetic plots, with closer analysis of Homer's exceptional insight into the requirements of plot-construction. But Aristotle is concerned with the content of poetic plots, as well as their structure. The actions that comprise a good tragic (or, by implication, epic) plot will evoke a certain kind of emotional response from the audience. The fact that Aristotle defines a good plot in terms of the emotional response it evokes will bring us back to the differences between his views on poetry and Plato's.

---

[26] Plato and Aristotle are, in a sense, agreed on this trajectory. But Aristotle sees the progressive disclosure of poetry's normative nature (in the absence of impediments) where Plato saw a tendency to degenerate towards indiscriminate imitation (in the absence of philosophical regulation).

The question of plot-structure is the question of what makes a plurality of acts or events a single action: it is, in other words, a question of unity. Plato anticipated this concept in the *Phaedrus*: though he does not use the term 'unity', he does speak of a 'whole' and introduces the now familiar organic analogy (264c):

Every text [*logos*] should be constructed like a living organism, with its own body; it should not lack head or feet, but should have its middle parts and extremities, composed so as to fit appropriately with each other and with the whole.

There are two differences between Plato's and Aristotle's use of this concept. First, Plato is concerned with a principle of appropriate structure at the level of the *text*; Aristotle, however, is concerned with the appropriate structure of the action imitated by the *plot*. The action is not co-extensive with the text, since some of the actions may occur before the beginning of the text or after its end (14, 1453b31–2; 15, 1454b3–8; 18, 1455b24–5; 24, 1460a27–32). Secondly, Plato does not translate his abstract principle into concrete criteria that a text must satisfy if it is to be an appropriately ordered whole;[27] by contrast, Aristotle specifies concrete criteria of unity for poetic plots with some care.

Aristotle thinks that an epic or tragedy should have a plot that is single and complete. That is to say: a poetic narrative should tell a story that consists of a single, complete series of events. Aristotle identifies two misconceptions that have resulted in the failure of many epic poets to satisfy this requirement. One is to suppose that a plot is unified if it is constructed round a single focal figure, such as Heracles or Theseus (8, 1451a16–22); the other is to suppose that a plot is unified if it deals with events that occurred within a single period of time (23, 1459a21–30). The latter structure is historiographic, and we have already seen that Aristotle distinguishes poetic narrative from historiography by the requirement of necessary or probable connection (9, 1451a36–5: §3.1). In poetic plots, events should be causally connected: one thing because of another, and not just one thing after another (10, 1452a18–21). The fact that events happened in one person's life, or within one period of time, does not ensure that they are causally connected, and is therefore not enough to give the plurality of actions narrated the requisite unity.

Aristotle has one way of formulating his criteria in which the requirement of causal connection is not immediately apparent (23, 1459a17–20):

---

[27] That creates a trap for unwary interpreters, who may unthinkingly import their own criteria into Plato's formula. Heath 1989b gives a (regrettably imperfect) survey of unity in ancient poetics.

As for the art of imitation in narrative verse, it is clear that the plots ought (as in tragedy) to be constructed dramatically: that is, they should be concerned with a unified action, whole and complete, possessing a beginning, middle parts and an end.

This may seem a trivial point: self-evidently, a story must begin somewhere and end somewhere, and there must be something in the middle to keep the beginning and end apart. But Aristotle has something more specific in mind (7, 1450b27–31):

A *beginning* is that which itself does not follow necessarily from anything else, but some second thing naturally exists or occurs after it. Conversely, an *end* is that which does itself naturally follow from something else, either necessarily or in general, but there is nothing else after it. A *middle* is that which itself comes after something else, and some other thing comes after it.

Even here, Aristotle is not quite explicit: he leaves it to the reader to understand that the qualifiers applied to beginnings and ends ('necessarily', 'naturally', 'in general') must also be supplied in the definition of middles: a middle should be something that would necessarily, naturally or in general, be a consequence of that beginning.

The beginning happens *after* other things, but it must not be a necessary or probable *consequence* of anything else. How is that possible? One possible explanation lies in the fact that adult humans are capable of acting from deliberated choice (*prohairesis*). This is one crucial respect in which they differ, not only from inanimate objects, but also from children and nonhuman animals, whose behaviour is driven by pleasure and distress (*NE* 3.2, 1111b6–10; *EE* 2.10, 1226b21–5; *Ph.* 2.6, 197b6–8). Such choices are starting-points: as decision-making agents, human beings are originators of actions (*EE* 2.6, 1222b18–3a20). But if that were sufficient to constitute a beginning in the sense required for a plot, suitable middles would be hard to come by. Though choices that are necessary or probable responses to prior events (the kind of choice a person of this kind would make in such a situation) count as starting-points in ethics, in poetics they are just what is needed for a properly connected middle. This approach does not seem satisfactory, therefore. An alternative approach is suggested by Aristotle's discussion of chance events in the *Physics*. Consider this scenario, based on Aristotle's examples (*Ph.* 2.4, 196a3–5; 5, 196b33–7a5). I go to the market to do some shopping; when I am there, I meet someone who owes me money. If I had known that he would be in the market at that time I might have gone there to ask for my money back; and he might have avoided the market then if he had known that

I would be there. Since neither of us knew that the other would be there, it was just luck (good for me, bad for him) that we happened to be in the market at the same time. There is an explanation of my being there at that time; there is an explanation of his being there at that time; but there is no explanation of our both being there at that time. It is true that the meeting could have been predicted by anyone who knew about my and his respective market-going intentions, but this would be knowledge of two separate and unrelated facts. There is no *single* situation from which this meeting follows as a necessary or probable consequence.[28]

It is easy to see how this meeting could be the starting-point for a chain of subsequent events, unfolding in accordance with necessity or probability. Having, by chance, met my impecunious debtor, it is probable that I ask for my money back; that he asks for an extension to the loan; that I, being generous, agree. The agreement is an ending. *Something* must happen after that (we will not stand frozen in the market for ever); but there is nothing that will necessarily or probably follow what has just happened. The sequence of events initiated by the chance encounter has run its course, and what happens next depends on decisions that are not determined, necessarily or probably, by the consequences of the encounter. Consider the situation at the end of Sophocles' *Oedipus*. Something must be done about Oedipus, but what will be done depends on Creon's decision, which is not determined in advance (in this case, the decision depends on an oracle's response). Or consider the *Iliad*. An unpredictable constellation of events (it was not necessary or probable that Agamemnon's allocated booty should include the daughter of a priest of Apollo) precipitates a quarrel between Agamemnon and Achilles; given the respective characters of the two men and the tensions between them, the quarrel is necessary or probable in these circumstances, and it leads, by a circuitous but probable chain of further choices and actions, to the deaths of Patroclus and Hector, to the ransoming of Hector's corpse, and to his funeral. What then? We know that the war will continue; we know that Troy will be taken; but we cannot identify specific, causally significant events leading to that outcome which must necessarily or probably happen next. Beyond this point, we would have to fall back on one thing happening after another.[29]

Homer, then, met the basic requirement of plot-construction (8, 1451a22–30):

---

[28] There is no 'connected explanation': Sorabji 1980: 3–25.

[29] An ancient attempt to connect the end of the *Iliad* to the start of the next epic in the Trojan cycle (the *Aethiopis*) illustrates the point: 'Such was the burial they gave to Hector. And an Amazon came …'.

Just as Homer excels in other respects, he seems to have seen this point clearly as well, whether through art or natural talent. When he composed the *Odyssey* he did not include everything which happened to Odysseus ... instead, he constructed the *Odyssey* about a single action of the kind we are discussing. The same is true of the *Iliad*.

Note the phrase 'whether through art or natural talent': Aristotle does not assume that Homer understood the technical requirements for a good plot-structure, so that he could have explained them in the way that Aristotle has done. He may just have been gifted with the ability to recognise a well-structured plot. But that is not the full extent of Homer's insight: he went beyond the basic requirement (23, 1459a30–4):

So (as we have already said) Homer's brilliance is evident in this respect as well, in comparison with other poets. He did not even try to treat the war as a whole, although it does have a beginning and an end. Had he done so, the plot would have been excessively large and difficult to take in at one view – or, if it had been moderate in magnitude, it would have been over-complicated in its variety.

One could, in principle, compose an epic about the whole Trojan War which would have a single, complete plot. The beginning would be whatever it was that made the war inevitable (perhaps Paris running off with Helen), and the end would be the fall of Troy. But the middle connecting the one with the other would be overwhelming, either in length or in density of detail. That would be less effective than what Homer has done (23, 1459a35–b2):

Instead, he has taken one part and used many others as episodes (e.g. the catalogue of ships, and other episodes which he uses to diversify his composition). The other poets write about a single person, a single period of time, or a single action of many parts.

The *Iliad* and *Odyssey* are alike in this respect (8, 1451a28–30). The *Odyssey* does not narrate the whole of Odysseus' life, or even the whole of his journey from Troy. In Aristotle's analysis, the plot begins near the end of Odysseus' absence, and comprises only the final stages of his return (17, 1455b15–23):

A man has been away from home for many years ... Despite being shipwrecked he reaches home, reveals his identity to a number of people and attacks. He survives and destroys his enemies.

Aristotle comments: 'that much is integral; the rest is episodes.' The rest includes Odysseus' account of his past wanderings. Aristotle was not forced to exclude the past wanderings from the *Odyssey*'s plot since, as noted earlier, he recognises that elements of a plot may lie outside the chronological boundaries of the narrating text. But counting the past wanderings as part of the plot would produce an inferior 'single action of many parts'; in treating them as episodes, Aristotle does more justice to the poem's structural excellence.

Though the *Iliad* and *Odyssey* both have properly constructed plots, the plots differ in ways that make it possible to see the poems as different *kinds* of epic (24, 1459b7–15):

Epic must also have the same kinds as tragedy; it is either simple or complex, or based on character or on suffering ... Homer was the first to use all of these elements in a completely satisfactory way. Each of his two poems has a different structure; the *Iliad* is simple and based on suffering, the *Odyssey* is complex (recognition pervades it) and based on character.

This looks back to an earlier classification of kinds of tragedy (18, 1455b32–6a2):

There are four kinds of tragedy (since that was also the number of component parts mentioned): complex tragedy, depending entirely on reversal and recognition; tragedy of suffering (e.g. plays about Ajax or Ixion); tragedy of character (e.g. *Women of Phthia* and *Peleus*); and, fourth <??> (e.g. *Daughters of Phorcys*, *Prometheus* and plays set in the underworld).

The description of the fourth kind has been garbled in the manuscript tradition. If epic has the same kinds as tragedy, tragedy must have the same kinds as epic; so it would be logical to supply 'simple', bringing the two classifications into alignment. The fact that many scholars have preferred other solutions is perhaps less indefensible in a passage which starts with a reference to four 'component parts' of tragedy that has never been satisfactorily explained. This is a problematic passage, and the fact that most of the tragedies mentioned to illustrate the kinds have not survived compounds the uncertainties.

But there is some firm ground. Aristotle has explained in chapters 10–11 that tragic plots are complex if they involve recognition and/or reversal, and are otherwise simple. Recognition is self-explanatory: it is a change from ignorance to knowledge. Oedipus discovers that the man he killed was his father, and the woman he is married to (and who bore his children) is his mother. In this case the recognition comes after the event, but it is equally possible for recognition to precede and pre-empt disaster. In Euripides' *Iphigeneia in Tauris* Iphigeneia discovers that the stranger she is going to sacrifice is her brother Orestes in time to avoid that catastrophe. The second complicating plot-component, reversal, is not self-explanatory, and is not clearly explained: 'a change to the opposite in the actions being performed' (11, 1452a22–3). One thing that is perfectly clear (though frequently overlooked) is that a reversal is *not* simply a change of fortune: reversal (*peripeteia*) makes a plot complex, but a change of fortune, from good to bad or from bad to good, will occur in any tragedy, whether complex or simple (7, 1451a11–15; 10, 1452a14–18). The idea seems to be that actions which are intended to bring about one result, or seem to be leading to one result, paradoxically lead to the opposite outcome. In *Oedipus*, the messenger's attempts to put Oedipus' worries to rest actually result in the discovery of the terrible truth – a combination of recognition with reversal that Aristotle admires (11, 1452a24–6, 32–3). A third plot-component mentioned alongside reversal and recognition is suffering, defined as 'an action that involves destruction or pain (e.g. deaths in full view, extreme agony, woundings and so on)' (11, 1152b9–13). Sophocles' *Ajax* is an example of a tragedy of suffering (18, 1455b34–6a1).

In the case of epic, the *Iliad* is simple, because it has no recognition or reversal; it is based on suffering, because the changes of fortune depend on the deaths of Patroclus and Hector (24, 1459b14). The *Odyssey* is complex, because there are recognitions all the way through (there is a whole succession of scenes in which Odysseus' identity is revealed, deliberately or inadvertently: to the Phaeacians, to Telemachus, to the dog, to the Nurse, to Eumaeus, to the suitors, to Penelope, to Laertes); it is also based on character (24, 1459b14–15). The point is not that the plot exists to depict character: Aristotle's argument for the primacy of plot means that such a subordination of plot to character would be an aberration (6, 1450a2–22). Rather, the whole plot, and the eventual change of fortune, is driven by Odysseus' deliberate choices and (therefore) by his underlying character.[30]

Aristotle thinks that the best tragic plot would be complex rather than simple (13, 1450b30–2). Part of his argument for the primacy of plot is that 'the most important devices by which tragedy sways emotion are parts of the plot, i.e. reversals and recognitions' (6, 1450a33–5). This does not mean that a tragedy with a complex plot is necessarily better than a tragedy with a simple plot, but that a tragedy with a complex plot would be better than a tragedy with a simple plot *other things being equal*. Since the quality of a play depends on many factors, we cannot take it for granted that other things are equal. A tragedy in which a recognition made it possible for a very bad man to commit a terrible crime that enables him to escape from misfortune and enter into the enjoyment of great good fortune

---

[30] The correlation of simplicity with suffering and complexity with character is not fixed. Taking the recognitions out of the *Odyssey* would produce a simple character-based epic; putting a reversal into the *Iliad* would produce a complex suffering-based epic.

would satisfy the definition of a complex plot, but Aristotle would regard it as untragic, because it has none of the effects that tragedies aim for (13, 1452b36–53a1). In particular, it does not evoke pity or fear, which Aristotle regards as a defining characteristics of tragedy (6, 1449b27; 9, 1452a1–3; 11, 1452a38–b1; 13, 1452b32–3a7); hence the 'characteristic pleasure' of tragedy is 'the pleasure which comes from pity and fear' (14, 1453b10–13). Aristotle does not say explicitly that the same applies to epic, but the fact that the kinds of epic are the same as the kinds of tragedy suggests that this is a legitimate conclusion to draw.

As well as distinguishing between simple and complex plots, Aristotle recognises a distinction between single and double plots.[31] This distinction is invoked in the context of a problem that arises from the change of fortune in tragedy. Suppose there is a change from good to bad fortune: if someone good falls into misfortune, that is repugnant; if someone bad falls into misfortune, that is morally satisfying. Suppose, on the other hand, there is a change from bad to good fortune: if someone good ends up in good fortune, there is nothing to pity; if someone bad ends up in good fortune, that is morally outrageous. So there is no combination of character with change of fortune that produces a satisfactory tragic plot (13, 1452b14–53a7). Some of Aristotle's contemporaries escaped from that impasse by recommending a 'double' plot, in which the good ended happily and the bad unhappily (13, 1453a12–13, 31–3). The idea is, presumably, that this kind of plot can evoke pity and fear by exposing the good characters to danger and distress, while ensuring that the ending is morally satisfying by assigning to every character their just deserts. Aristotle rejects this view (13, 1453a30–9):

Second-best is the structure which some say comes first – that which has a double structure like the *Odyssey*, and which ends with the opposite outcome for better and worse people. It is thought to come first because of the weakness of audiences; the poets follow the audiences' lead and compose whatever is to their taste. But this is not the pleasure which comes from tragedy; it is more characteristic of comedy. In comedy even people who are the bitterest enemies in the story, like Orestes and Aegisthus, go off reconciled in the end, and no one gets killed by anybody.

This passage is surprising. In the history of poetry (4, 1448b38–a2) and the discussion of kinds of epic (24, 1459b13–15) Aristotle associates both the *Iliad* and the *Odyssey* with tragedy; here, however, the *Odyssey*'s

---

[31] This is even more confusing in Greek, since Aristotle uses the same word for 'simple' and 'single'.

plot-structure is described as characteristic of comedy. And yet the comic ending described here is exactly what we do *not* find in the *Odyssey*: Odysseus is not reconciled to the suitors, the suitors do get killed. It seems that Aristotle is having a joke at the expense of his opponents by pretending that their theory turns tragedy into comedy. But that self-indulgence is pardonable: he has already explained the real reason why their argument fails.

In a famous passage in *Poetics* 13, Aristotle points out that a single plot can avoid falling foul of the problem about tragic changes of fortune if it is concerned with someone who occupies the ethical middle ground (13, 1453a7–10):

> We are left, therefore, with the person intermediate between these. This is the sort of person who is not outstanding in moral excellence or justice; on the other hand, the change to bad fortune which he is undergoing is not due to any moral defect or depravity, but to an error [*hamartia*] of some kind.

The point is reinforced a few lines later: the change to bad fortune 'must be due not to depravity but to a great error on the part of someone of the kind specified, or better than that, rather than worse' (1453a15–17). This specification of the optimal tragic subject as someone at or above the mid-point reveals the importance of the ethical continuum which Aristotle acknowledged but elided in the preliminary chapters (2, 1448a1–5; 4, 1448b24–6: §3.5). But what of the great 'error' (*hamartia*) which is the cause of the tragic subject's misfortune? Aristotle's use of this word is extremely flexible. The kind of ignorance that makes people unjust or bad can be described as *hamartia* (*NE* 3.1, 1110b28–30); so can adultery (*Pol.* 7.16, 1335b38–6a2). In *Poetics* 13, however, such cases are excluded by the logic of the context: the tragic subject's misfortune must not be due to moral depravity. But contextual logic does not require us to exclude any cause other than moral depravity. In particular, it does not require us to restrict the tragic subject's error to non-culpable ignorance of particular facts, even though tragic plots involving recognition are hospitable to errors of that kind. It is true that according to Aristotle's discussion of voluntary action in the ethical writings, only acts performed in non-culpable ignorance of particular facts are pitiable (*NE* 3.1, 1110b31–1a2), but that is the answer to a different question. The pity with which *Poetics* 13 is concerned is not a response to the act itself, but to the act's consequences for the agent. The tragic subject, whose moral character is not at the very top of the ethical continuum, must be capable of culpable action. There is no reason in principle why culpable actions of a kind consistent with an

intermediate or better moral character should not be the causally implicated in the tragic subject's misfortune, since culpable actions of that kind
ex hypothesi do not entail depravity or preclude pity.[32]

The change to bad fortune may seem the least surprising aspect of
Aristotle's attempt to specify the best kind of tragic plot: in fact, it brings
us to one of the most perplexing problems in the *Poetics*. Chapter 13 seems
to say that in the best kind of plot someone of this intermediate character
undergoes a change to bad fortune; Chapter 14 clearly says that it is best
if the bad fortune is averted by a recognition (as in *Iphigeneia in Tauris*).
In view of cross-references between the two chapters, there can be no
solution to this problem which does not read the two chapters as a single,
consistent whole. That means recognising that the passage just quoted,
despite its fame, is not Aristotle's final conclusion, but an interim stage in
a more complex argument. The change of perspective which that requires
is not easy, since the passage is so firmly fixed at the centre of our conception of Aristotelian tragedy. But it is worth noting that when he speaks of
the change of fortune in chapter 13, Aristotle uses Greek verb forms which
indicate a process without specifying completion (hence the translation:
'the change ... which he is undergoing'). The focus is on the trajectory
of the change, rather than its outcome. In chapter 13 Aristotle maintains
that the best kind of tragic plot includes plots in which the change to
bad fortune is completed. This argument is directed against the advocates of the double plot, and also against those who criticise Euripides for
ending plays in misfortune (13, 1445a23–6). Endorsing plots in which
a change to bad fortune is completed does not entail rejecting plots in
which the change is not completed, unless one supplies the additional
premise that the best kind of tragic plot must be defined so narrowly that
it admits of no variants. Aristotle does not supply that premise, and the
argument in chapter 14 for the superiority of plots in which the change is
pre-empted by recognition shows that he would not have accepted it. My
own hypothesis, therefore, is that Aristotle's conception of the best kind
of tragic plot is an inclusive one: the subtype discussed in chapter 13 is an
admissible variant of the best kind of plot, and Aristotle's opponents are
wrong to condemn it, but chapter 14 argues that a different subtype is the
best of the best.[33]

---

[32] *Hamartia*: Stinton 1975; Sorabji 1980: 295–8; Schütrumpf 1989; Sherman 1992; Freeland 1996.
On the moral errors of good people: Curzer 2005.
[33] See Heath (in preparation).

Whatever view we take of this problem, Aristotle clearly believes that emotional impact is a criterion of a good epic or tragic plot, and consequently of a good epic or tragedy. This does not mean that poets should seek any kind of emotional impact by any means, as is clear from Aristotle's debate with the advocates of 'double' plots. Plots which have a happy ending for the good characters and an unhappy ending for the bad characters do have emotional impact, and many people enjoy them; but Aristotle regards this as a 'weak' preference. That is why the double plot is not a subtype of the best kind of tragic plot – though it is *second* best, which means (despite the jocular caricature) that it is not untragic (13, 1453a30–9). Aristotle is more critical of dramatists who depend on visual effects to achieve emotional impact, and especially of those who use visual effects to achieve the wrong kind of emotional impact, 'the monstrous' (14, 1453b1–14): we might think of horror films that rely on special effects. So Aristotle is not indiscriminate in his demand for emotional effect. But he does believe that the right kind of emotional impact is a criterion of a good epic or tragedy. Here he is at odds with Plato. Socrates acknowledges in *Republic* 10 that epic and tragedy excite emotions, and that people think that the poets who are most successful in doing that are best, but he describes the psychological damage which imitative poetry causes by stimulating the audience's emotions as the 'most serious' allegation against it (*Rep.* 10, 605c–d). This does not seem to worry Aristotle. Why not?

Aristotle has a much less suspicious view of emotions than Plato. As a biologist, with a particular interest in zoology, he recognises the importance of affect in animal behaviour: that is, of perceptions that (being associated with pleasure or distress) incorporate evaluations of changing environmental conditions and prime appropriate responses. Mice that were not afraid of cats, and were not primed by fear to take evasive action on detecting a cat, would not live long. Human emotions, though cognitively and behaviourally more complex, are also important in guiding action. Emotions are therefore fundamental to ethics. Someone whose emotional responses are inappropriate will tend to act inappropriately, and virtues are (in part) properly calibrated dispositions to feel emotions (*NE* 2.5–6). If I am in danger I ought to feel fear: if I do not, I will behave recklessly. If I am insulted I ought to feel anger: if I do not, I will not display proper regard to my status and rights.

It is also possible to feel too much fear (cowardice) or too much anger (bad temper). So it is important to ensure that emotional dispositions are properly formed in a young person's upbringing. Malformed emotional dispositions are hard to change in adulthood. It might, however, be possible to mitigate their effects. That possibility underlies one interpretation of Aristotle's concept of *katharsis*. Here we touch on an extremely controversial topic. There is only one brief mention of *katharsis* in the *Poetics*: tragedy 'effects through pity and fear the *katharsis* of such emotions' (6, 1449b27–8). Aristotle says a little more about musical *katharsis* in the *Politics* (8.7, 1341b32–2a15), but refers us to the *Poetics* for a fuller account. Faced with the consequent wilderness of inconclusive philology and undisciplined fantasy, it may be most prudent to accept that we have no clear idea what Aristotle meant by it and move on. But there is at least a case for saying that in *Politics* Aristotle sees *katharsis* as regulating excessive tendencies towards the expression of an emotion.[34]

It is easy to see how such an interpretation of *katharsis*, or any other interpretation that takes seriously the description of it as being 'as it were' healing and relief (*Pol.* 8.7, 1342a10–11, 14), might be understood as an argument against Plato: tragedy and epic do not damage our emotional stability, but restore it. But the uncertainty about the nature of *katharsis* may not matter very much, since Aristotle's disagreement with Plato regarding the emotional effect of poetry and drama is not critically dependent on the concept of *katharsis*. In the *Republic*, Socrates regards comedy as damaging because it undermines our self-control with regard to laughter (10, 606c). The assumption is that even the best adult character might be destabilised by comedy. But Aristotle is confident that adult character is sufficiently stable to be immune to harm. In the *Politics*, although he recommends a general ban on abusive and obscene language, and on indecent images and stories, an exception is made for the abuse and obscenity that were customary in some religious cults, including those which were the context for performances of iambus and comedy. He thinks it sufficient to exclude impressionable young people from these performances: adults, whose character has already been formed, will not be harmed by them (*Pol.* 7.17, 1336b12–23). As was said at the beginning of the chapter, Plato and Aristotle disagree about poetry for reasons that lie beyond the competence of poetics. Whether comedy should be allowed, and under what restrictions, is a decision for the architectonic discipline of politics. Plato and Aristotle reach different conclusions in

[34] Halliwell 1986: 350–6 provides a useful survey of interpretations of *katharsis*. Recent discussions include Heath 2001; Destrée 2003; Halliwell 2003; Ford 2004. The theory is placed in a larger context in Sorabji 2000, esp. 288–300.

politics, because their judgement is informed by different views of adult psychology.[35]

The immunity of adult character to harm from comedy suggests that adults would not be likely to be changed for the better by exposure to poetry, either. That leads us, finally, to the question of poetry's positive value.

7 POETRY'S VALUE

When Socrates issued an invitation to lovers of imitative poetry to speak out on its behalf, he asked to be shown 'that it is not only enjoyable but also beneficial for societies and for human life' (*Rep.* 10, 607d). Aristotle thinks that epic and tragedy are enjoyable because of their emotional effect: the characteristic pleasure of tragedy is the pleasure that comes from pity and fear (14, 1453b10–13). He also thinks that this emotional stimulus is not psychologically damaging. But does he meet Socrates' demand? That is, does he show that epic and tragedy are beneficial as well as enjoyable? Many interpreters have assumed that Aristotle must have tried to meet this challenge on its own terms. I shall argue that Aristotle would reject Socrates' demand as misconceived. That does not mean that he is committed to denying that poetry has any possible benefits; but he does not regard such benefits as fundamental to poetry's value. As I said at the outset, allowing Plato to set the agenda will lead to misunderstanding if Aristotle's agenda is different.

We have seen how Aristotle explains poetry as the product of the natural human traits that motivate it – the inclination towards imitation and towards rhythm and melody. But that is only half of a biologist's approach to explanation. Why do birds build nests? Saying that birds have a natural inclination to collect twigs and weave them together is uninformative, since it does not tell us why birds have this natural inclination. To understand why nature has equipped birds with the instincts that motivate nest-building we must specify the function of nesting in avian life. Analogously, to complete Aristotle's explanation of poetry we need to understand, not just what natural inclinations motivate human beings to

---

[35] Plato's Socrates never gives any evidence to support his claims about the damaging effects of imitative poetry's emotional stimulus on audiences; nor does he show that the portrayals of gods and heroes of which he disapproves have the specific effects he attributes to them. Nor, however, does Aristotle provide evidence in support of adult immunity. Modern research suggests that his emphasis on human imitativeness should have made him more cautious: see Hurley 2004, drawing in part on work synthesised in Hurley and Chater 2005.

produce and consume poetry, but also what place this behaviour has in a characteristically human way of life.

The analogy may seem to return us to Socrates' demand that we show how poetry is beneficial. We explain why birds build nests by showing what benefit birds get from nest-building in terms of the fundamental biological imperatives of survival and reproduction. But in Aristotle's eyes, it would be a vulgar error to impose the same constraints on the explanation of human behaviour. For humans, uniquely, the goal is not mere living, but living *well* (*Pol.* 1.2, 1252b29–30; 1.4, 1253b24–5; 1.9, 1257b40–8a1; 3.9, 1280a31–2; *PA* 2.10, 656a5–6). Humans, accordingly, have access to an extended range of values. Birds use their calls to communicate (*PA* 2.17, 660a29–b2); but, like other nonhuman animals, their communication is restricted to objects of pleasure and distress (*Pol.* 1.2, 1253a10–14). Human language is distinctive in that it is also used to communicate about what is beneficial and harmful, just and unjust, good and bad (1253a14–18). Awareness of this extended range of values means that adult humans need not submit to being steered by pleasure and distress, as nonhuman animals and small children are (*NE* 10.1, 1172a20–1). It opens up the possibility of deliberate choice (*prohairesis*), in which desire is combined with deliberative reasoning.

When we make a deliberated choice, we do something for a reason. Sometimes the reason lies beyond the immediate object of choice: one thing is chosen because of something else. I make a phone call to book a taxi to get to the station to travel to … and so on. But any chain of deliberative reasoning must have a limit (*NE* 1.2, 1094a18–22; cf. *Met.* 2.2, 994b9–16):

> If, then, there is some end of the things we do, which we want for its own sake, and everything else for the sake of this, and if we do not choose everything for the sake of something else (for in that case the process would go on indefinitely, so that our desire would be empty and futile), clearly this would be the good and the best good.

It is not possible to choose one thing because of another, and that in turn for something else, *ad infinitum*; at least one thing must be chosen for itself. Furthermore, at least one thing must be *worth* choosing for its own sake, or there would be no ultimate reason for choosing anything. We may express this as a distinction between the *intrinsic* value of an object of choice, and the *derived* value that it has by virtue of its relation to some separate object of choice. Instrumental value is one obvious kind of derived value, though not the only kind.

The insufficiency of derived value is urged with vigour in a fragment of Aristotle's *Protrepticus*,[36] in which he is trying to persuade practically-minded people that philosophy, which they regard as unproductive and pointless, is in fact the most worthwhile activity that any human being can engage in. He explains why it is ridiculous to imagine that everything needs to be justified in terms of its producing some benefit beyond itself (F42 Düring = Iamb. *Protr.* 52.23–8):

It is not the case that this is chosen because of that, and that because of something else, and this goes on and on, proceeding to infinity: it comes to a stop somewhere. So it is utterly ludicrous to seek from everything another benefit separate from the thing itself and to ask 'So what's the benefit to us?' and 'What use is it?'

A thought-experiment illustrates the point: in the Isles of the Blessed, where all needs have been met, nothing would have the kind of value that Aristotle's opponents demand (F43 Düring = Iamb. *Protr.* 53.2–10). It follows that there is nothing odd in principle in claiming that philosophy, even if it is not useful, is still worthwhile (F44 Düring = Iamb. *Protr.* 53.15–18):

So there is nothing untoward in it [i.e. philosophy] not being seen as useful or advantageous; the claim is not that it is advantageous, but that it is *good*, and one should choose it not because of something else but because of itself …

The next step reminds readers that they already accept the principle (F44 Düring = Iamb. *Protr.* 53.19–25):

… We go to Olympia for the sake of the sight itself, even if nothing further is going to come of it; being a spectator [*theōria*] in itself is beyond monetary value. And we are spectators at the Dionysia, not because we are going to get something from the actors – in fact, we have to pay. And there are many other sights that we would choose in preference to a large sum of money …

Aristotle can be confident that his upper-class Greek readers would accept that athletics and drama are worth watching in themselves. He must now induce them to see even greater value in philosophy (F44 Düring = Iamb. *Protr.* 53.25–54.5):

… In the same way, contemplation [*theōria*] of the universe is to be valued more highly than all the things that appear to be useful. After all, there is no sense in going to see human beings imitating women and slaves, or fighting and running,

---

[36] On the fragments of the *Protrepticus* see Hutchinson and Johnson 2005.

with great seriousness, just for the sake of the sight of them, while thinking that there is no reason to contemplate the nature of reality and the truth – for free!

When Aristotle uses the word *theōria* ('watching', 'looking at') to describe the activity of the philosopher, the reference is not to scientific research or the effort to solve a philosophical problem; these evidently are chosen for the sake of something else, the attainment of understanding. *Theōria* is the insightful appreciation that becomes possible when the goal of understanding has been achieved. Such understanding is a source of greater joy than enquiry: 'it is to be expected that those who know will pass their time more pleasantly than those who inquire' (*NE* 10.7, 1177a26–7). Philosophical understanding is a source of greater joy, to the extent that the universe is a better thing to be a spectator of than, for example, athletes and actors (*NE* 10.7, 1177a19–21).

Plato, too, recognises a distinction between things that are worthwhile in themselves and things that are worthwhile because of their consequences. The challenge which Glaucon and Adeimantus pose to Socrates in *Republic* is to show that justice is worthwhile in itself, and not only for its consequences (2, 357a–367a). Plato would also agree that philosophy is more worthwhile than drama or athletics. But it is not clear that Plato would accept that drama or athletics are worthwhile in themselves. The demand that Socrates makes of imitative poetry's defenders assumes that poetry and drama are only worthwhile if they have some beneficial consequence. If so, this is another point of disagreement between Plato and Aristotle.

Does Aristotle really regard drama and athletics as worthwhile in themselves? These examples are selected because they are both forms of *theōria*, and so in some way analogous to philosophical *theōria*. But when Aristotle singles out actors 'imitating women and slaves', he exploits an assumption he shares with his upper-class Greek male readers: women and slaves are less worth taking seriously than heroic male characters (e.g. *Po.* 15, 1454a17–22). This turn of phrase is designed to emphasise the greater value of philosophy over drama and athletics. So it is possible that Aristotle is arguing *ad hominem*, using his addressees' existing commitments to establish the principle of intrinsic value, without sharing those commitments himself. The value they attach to athletics and drama is the ladder up which Aristotle invites his readers to climb; but perhaps he expects them to discard the ladder when they have seen that philosophy is what they should really value. Since Aristotle nowhere explicitly asserts or denies that drama, or poetry more generally, is worthwhile in itself, we must approach this question indirectly. His views on the value of music provide a promising point of departure, since listening to music is also *theōria* (*EE* 7.12, 1245a18–22).

Aristotle undoubtedly thinks that listening to music is valuable in part because of its useful consequences (*Pol.* 8.5–7). People who have been working hard or are stressed need to rest and relax; listening to music is a good form of relaxation because it is enjoyable. Music is also useful in moral education: young people's character can be shaped by listening to music. (Plato, too, thinks that musical education shapes character: *Rep.* 3, 398b–402c, 410a–12a.) Furthermore, Aristotle thinks that some music is useful for *katharsis*. This is an obscure and controversial issue (§3.6), but what little Aristotle says about musical *katharsis* in the *Politics* is consistent with a model in which music of a certain kind is capable of provoking an ecstatic frenzy in people who are prone to over-excitement, leaving them in a calmer frame of mind; and he is willing to extend this model to music that stimulates other emotions (8.7, 1341b32–2a15; cf. 8.5, 1340a9–12, b4). If this is right, *katharsis* would be a way of regulating the expression of people's emotional dispositions.

All of these uses give music a derived value: that is, the music is valued as a means of achieving something beyond itself. But this leaves open the question whether music has intrinsic value, since things may have both derived and intrinsic value. Of these it can be said that, because of their intrinsic value, 'we would choose each of them even if nothing came of them' (*NE* 1.7, 1097a22–b6). For example, it is useful to have friends, but friendship is also something that one would wish to have for its own sake; if you value your friends only for their usefulness, you have misunderstood what is most important about friendship.[37]

Aristotle refers to musical *theōria* as an illustration of how the pleasure of good things is enhanced when they are shared with friends. The other examples he mentions are bodily pleasure and philosophy (*EE* 7.12, 1245a18–22). Obviously, he thinks philosophy is more of a good thing than bodily pleasure; listening to music is somewhere in between.

When Aristotle talks about bodily pleasure, he is generally thinking of the pleasures of eating and drinking, and of sex. These pleasures, which are pleasures of touch and taste, are common to human and nonhuman

---

[37] Note, therefore, that if a certain kind of music is defined as kathartic, in the sense that the capacity to effect *katharsis* is what differentiates this from other kinds of music, it does not follow that *katharsis* is 'the' purpose of such music: that is, there is no implication that *katharsis* is the only, or the primary, value of such music. For the same reason, the *katharsis* clause in the definition of tragedy (*Po.* 6, 1449b27–8) does not entail that *katharsis* is the only, or primary, purpose or value of tragedy.

animals. They are the pleasures directly involved in the most basic biological functions of animals, reproduction and feeding (*de An.* 2.4, 415a24–26; *HA* 8.1, 589a2–9). They are also the pleasures with regard to which it is possible to show self-indulgence or moderation (*EE* 3.2, 1230b25–31a4; cf. *NE* 3.10, 1118a1–26). Aristotle observes that people are not called self-indulgent because they take pleasure in looking at a beautiful picture or statue, a fine horse or a beautiful human body, or in listening to beautiful singing. These pleasures are distinctively human. It is not that nonhuman animals get no pleasure at all from hearing sounds, but they do not take pleasure in a sound in its own right: the pleasure comes from something that is incidentally associated with the sound, such as the prospect of feeding or sex. A lion that hears an ox lowing is delighted, not because of the intrinsic qualities of the sound itself, but because the sound signals his next meal (*NE* 3.10, 1118a20–23). When Aristotle talks about pleasure from looking at a beautiful human body he is explicitly not thinking of sexual arousal (*EE* 3.2, 1230b26–7): that would be the same kind of incidental pleasure by association. Spectators at Olympia, watching athletes with delighted admiration, provide a better idea of what he has in mind.

Aristotle does not assert that no animal ever takes pleasure in listening to harmonious sounds as such, but only that the effect is negligible except in abnormal cases (*EE* 3.2, 1231a2–4). The possibility of nonhuman animals being responsive to music is confirmed in the discussion of music in education in the *Politics*. Aristotle says that there will come a point at which young people (if they are properly educated) will be able 'to take delight in melodies and rhythms that are fine [*kalon*], and not merely in the common element of music, as even some nonhuman animals do, and also the mass of servile people and children' (*Pol.* 8.6, 1341a14–17). Music, then, can be appreciated on two levels. On the one hand, there is what Aristotle had described a few pages earlier as a 'common' and 'natural' pleasure, available to everyone who has perception (8.5, 1340a2–5). Humans, who have a natural inclination to rhythm and melody (*Po.* 4, 1448b20–1), will be especially sensitive to this; but if it is accessed through sense-perception, there is no reason in principle why some animals should not have some sensitivity to it. On the other hand, properly educated adult humans are capable of appreciating 'fine' melodies and rhythms, which offer more than just the common or natural pleasure of music.

To understand this distinction, we must consider an important difference which Aristotle sees between adult humans and all other animals. The behaviour of nonhuman animals is driven by pleasure and distress.

Pleasure and distress are built into their perceptions of the world around them. They are naturally disposed to find things that are good for them (for example, food) pleasurable, and things that are bad for them (for example, predators) distressing, and they seek out things that evoke pleasurable perceptions and avoid those that produce distressing perceptions. Pleasure and distress are the limits of the values that nonhuman animals are capable of grasping. By contrast humans have access to a range of values that extends beyond the reach of sense-perception: only rational animals can communicate about things as beneficial and harmful, just and unjust, good and bad (*Pol.* 1.2, 1253a7–18). This is why it makes sense to talk about ethics and morality in the case of humans, but not of other animals.

In Aristotle's ethical theory, virtuous action involves more than doing the right thing: the criteria include the action being chosen *because* it is the right thing (*NE* 2.4, 1105a27–b4). Aristotle can express this by saying that the action should be chosen for its own sake; he can also say that the action should be chosen because of (or for the sake of) 'the fine' (*to kalon*). This is the same word that Aristotle uses to describe beautiful pictures, statues, horses and human bodies, and to distinguish the 'fine' melodies and rhythms that go beyond the common or natural pleasure of music. Aristotle himself recognises this parallel between the 'fine' in ethics and in music: 'a good man ... delights in virtuous actions and is displeased by ones arising from vice, just as a musical man takes pleasure in fine tunes but is pained at bad ones' (*NE* 9.9, 1170a8–11).

In the *Rhetoric* Aristotle defines 'the fine' as 'whatever, being worth choosing in itself, is praiseworthy; or whatever, being good, is pleasant because it is good' (1.9, 1366a33–4). The second part of this formulation illuminates the two levels of musical appreciation. Most people are responsive to the common and natural pleasure of music. The value they attach to the music is derived value, being conditional on the pleasure it gives; if it ceases to give pleasure, the music loses its value for them. By contrast, fine music has intrinsic value. When I listen appreciatively to music of this kind, my pleasure depends in part on my recognising that intrinsic value. This value is objective, and has a normative claim on me: if music of this kind ceases to give me pleasure, that would reveal a deficiency, not in the music, but in me.

In making this distinction, Aristotle is not condemning music that is valued only for the pleasure it gives. Such music may help us to relax and recover from hard work or stress; in that respect it would be beneficial as well as enjoyable. Relaxation is such an important benefit that Aristotle is willing to allow genuinely bad music into his hypothetical city. The souls of the lower classes are so distorted from their natural state that they only enjoy a debased and unnatural style of music; but because they need relaxation, this kind of music should be performed for their benefit (*Pol.* 8.7, 1342a18–28). People whose souls are not unnaturally distorted will get the benefit of relaxation from the natural pleasure of music, even if it is not fine (though they will find music that is debased and unnatural unpleasant). There is therefore nothing wrong in principle with music that is valued because it gives pleasure. But even when this kind of music is *naturally* pleasurable, its value is derived: it is valued for the pleasurable relaxation it affords. By contrast, music that is 'fine' affords a pleasure that results from our recognising that the music is good *in itself.*

That distinction is important to Aristotle, because it matters how people use their leisure (*Pol.* 8.3, 8.5). Leisure is not the same as rest and relaxation. Relaxation is a kind of remedy (8.3, 1337b41–2; 8.5, 1339b16–17); if a trivial amusement is effective in aiding our recovery from the exertions of work and preparing us to return to work, it achieves its goal. But Aristotle's readers, drawn from a wealthy social elite, are people with significant amounts of time that is entirely at their disposal. This leisure time is not needed for relaxation and recovery; its use is unconstrained by necessity, and is associated with the goal of living well (*Pol.* 8.3, 1338a1–4; *NE* 10.7, 1177b4–5). Leisure time should therefore not be spent on trivial amusements, but should be devoted to things that are intrinsically worthwhile. Education should prepare for leisure as well as for work (8.3, 1338a9–13), and music, unlike the other components of education, is not taught because of its practical uses, but with a view to leisure (1338a13–24). It is not studied because it is useful or necessary, but because it is 'free and fine' – that is, appropriate to a life of cultivated leisure because of its intrinsic value (1338a30–2).

If something is good in itself, then it seems reasonable to say that it is worth our giving attention to it for its own sake. That is why, in Aristotle's view, philosophy is an activity that is worth choosing for its own sake, and why it is ridiculous to insist that it must lead to some beneficial consequence beyond itself if it is to have any value. The universe is the best possible object of our attention. So the best human life is one that is structured round philosophical *theōria*, contemplating the universe with appreciative understanding (*NE* 10.7–8). However, human beings cannot spend all their time doing that. Even philosophers will have leisure time to spend on other things; so will those who, because they do not have the inclination or aptitude for philosophy, make the exercise of ethical and political virtues the structural core of what is (secondarily, but still genu-inely) an intrinsically valuable human life (*NE* 10.8, 1178a9–14). Since fine music is good in itself, and gives pleasure because it is good, such music is worth listening to for its own sake. Fine paintings or statues, fine bodies (including fine bodies in action in athletic competition), and fine poetry or drama are also intrinsically worthwhile objects of attention. They, too, afford a pleasure that results from our recognising that they are good in themselves – not good only as a means to some further goal (such as relaxation), but good *in themselves*. Listening to fine music, or watching drama or athletics, are activities less worthwhile than philosophy, but still worth choosing for their own sake. So it is ridiculous to insist that they must lead to some beneficial consequences beyond themselves if they are to have any value. Socrates' insistence that a defence of Homer or tragedy must show that they are useful is therefore inadmissible: 'to be asking all the time what use something is, is most inappropriate for great-souled and free people' (*Pol.* 8.3, 1338b2–4).

CHAPTER FOUR

Ways to find truth in falsehood

Later Platonists came to hold a view of poetry – or, more precisely, of Homer and some other ancient poets – radically different from the one which Plato's *Republic* seems to offer us. The new consensus is exemplified by Porphyry (in the third century AD), who regards Homer as a profound philosopher (§4.7). This chapter investigates the background to the transformation of Platonist poetics by exploring various ways in which the relationship between poetry and truth was conceived. A preliminary outline may be helpful, since the path will be circuitous and wide-ranging. We begin with Plutarch (around the end of the first century AD), whose approach to poetry in education is motivated by a sense of the dangers of poetry inherited from the *Republic* (§4.1). We then consider three other approaches which Plutarch mentions and rejects: the alleged Epicurean repudiation of poetry (§4.2); the long-standing tradition of allegorical interpretation (§4.3); and the Stoic approach to myth (§4.4). The Stoics made a distinction between myth in poetry and religious myth; in interpreting the latter they emphasised symbolic representation, and showed respect for non-Greek religious traditions. This constellation of ideas was widely shared: we can trace its influence in Plutarch's treatise *On Isis and Osiris* (§4.5), and in Greek debates about images of the gods (§4.6). Against this background, it is easy to define the nature of the transition that occurred between Plutarch and Porphyry: Homer crossed the boundary line between poetic and religious myth, and thus became eligible for a different kind of interpretation.

I PLUTARCH: POETRY IN EDUCATION

Plato's *Republic* presents a society which, though unlikely to be realised, may serve as a paradigm for the ordering of our souls in the corrupt societies which we inhabit (9, 592a–b). These societies expose us to potentially harmful poetry, against which Socrates' arguments may protect us

(10, 608a). But people in such societies will already have been exposed to these corrupting influences at the most impressionable age (2, 377a–c), when they are too young to understand the need for prophylaxis. Bad education will pre-empt Socratic argument, leaving only a few who can be won over to philosophy in adulthood (6, 496a–e). There is, then, a serious educational problem in the real world. How do the few respond to that challenge? There is no prospect of their reforming the educational system at the public level: Socrates has advised them not to enter politics (9, 591e–2b). But they cannot ignore the challenge in their private lives. They must at least be concerned to protect their own children from harmful influences, to whatever extent it is possible to protect impressionable young people from things that are all around them. Plutarch considers this problem in his essay *How to Read Poetry*, addressed to a friend whose son is the same age as Plutarch's own.[1] Naturally, they share a concern about their sons' education.

When the very young encounter 'philosophy' in the form of fables, stories from the poets and philosophical myths, it does not seem philosophical, or even serious, and they enjoy it (1, 14e). But this creates a risk that they will read self-indulgently, attaching more value to the enjoyable sauce than the nourishing substance (14f). That danger is increased when they start reading poetry, which is very enjoyable indeed. It can be nourishing, but is liable to cause indigestion (15b–c). Plutarch recommends approaching this problem in the same way that we deal with excessive drinking: the solution is not to impose prohibition (or, as Plutarch puts it, not to cut down the vines) but to encourage moderation (15e–f).[2] Since Greeks and Romans routinely diluted their wine, moderation in the ancient world meant mixing in the right amount of water, so that the pleasurable effects of mild inebriation and increased sociability are achieved without drunkenness. In the same way, Plutarch suggests, the pleasurable effect of poetry can be gained safely by mixing in philosophy.

Plutarch says at the outset that denying young people access to poetry altogether (a strategy he associates with Epicurus: 15e; see §4.2) is not only impossible, but also not beneficial (15a). If he sees potential benefits in young people's encounter with poetry, Plutarch must believe that Socrates' challenge to poetry's defenders (*Rep.* 10, 607d) can be met. But

---

[1] Commentary: Hunter and Russell 2011. See also Schenkeveld 1982; Zadorojnyi 2002; and, for a broader perspective on Plutarch and poetry, van der Stockt 1992.

[2] The comparison recalls Plato's argument that drinking wine can be beneficial, despite its bad effects (*Laws* 1, 636e–650b; cf. 2, 671a–2d). Proclus also makes this connection in his discussion of poetry (*in Remp.* 1.75.28–76.17).

he does not reject Socrates' critique entirely. He has reasons for thinking that poetry is dangerous that are recognisably related to those put forward in the *Republic*; and we cannot infer any opinion on Plato's restrictions on poetry in an ideal community from an essay concerned with children's education in the world as it is. Plutarch's point is that, in an environment in which children will inevitably be exposed to poetry, they will benefit from a properly managed exposure. Young people must be shown a way to engage with poetry that will turn its dangers to educational advantage by making it a preparation for philosophy (15f). That does not mean that poetry itself is philosophical. Plutarch's imagery presents philosophy as something that must be introduced into the poetry, like water poured into wine. To read poetry philosophically, therefore, is not to look for truths hidden within the poetry. Rather, young people must be trained to supply truths for themselves when they are reading poetry.

Plutarch is not saying that there is nothing true in poetry at all: there is a mixture of good and bad. Plato would not disagree: his Socrates praises Diomedes' disciplined response to Agamemnon, as well as criticising Achilles' indiscipline (*Rep.* 3, 389e–390a; cf. 2, 383a). But philosophy has to be imported into the poem in the sense that the distinction between good and bad is something that readers must ultimately judge for themselves. At first, young people can only make the necessary discriminations under the guidance of a teacher, but in guiding the pupil's judgement the teacher should also aim to develop it. Young people should be brought ever closer to the point at which they can read poetry independently, relying on their own capacity to discriminate good from bad. The techniques of reading that Plutarch wants young people to be taught are designed to steer them towards increasingly autonomous exercises of critical judgement. That may sound like a modern and progressive approach to education, but Plutarch's programme fosters autonomy only within a highly directive framework. The relevant techniques of reading and standards of judgement are acquired under the close supervision of an adult instructor. The teacher's guidance is essential in bringing students to the point where they can be trusted to exercise their own judgement; it is the adoption of the values and methods acquired from the teacher that makes their judgement trustworthy.[3]

Plutarch starts his exposition with two basic principles. First (chapter 2), poetry distorts the truth (2, 16a). Poets sometimes do that deliberately:

---

[3] Konstan 2004: 8 therefore exaggerates when he says that 'Plutarch places his confidence in the astuteness of the audience or reader, indeed the young reader.'

there are pure inventions, designed to make the stories more entertaining (16b–f). But they sometimes go astray because they share the widespread ignorance of the truth about, for example, the gods or the afterlife (16f–17f). The direct connection to Socrates' complaints in *Republic* 2 is obvious. Pure inventions are easier to detect, because of their fantastic nature: no one is likely to imagine that Zeus really set up a pair of scales to decide the combat between Hector and Achilles (*Il.* 22.210–13). Errors that arise from ignorance are more insidious, because they reflect widely held beliefs. So the young person needs a firm grasp of the principle that poets are not to be trusted.

Secondly (chapter 3), poetry is imitation. It portrays both good and bad behaviour, and there is a risk that young people will model their own behaviour on bad behaviour in a poem if they confuse a good imitation with an imitation of something good (3, 17f–18f). They must not be so seduced by the quality of the imitation that they forget that poetry imitates bad people acting badly, as well as good people acting well. To alert them to this, when a character in tragedy or Homer says something disgraceful, the teacher should point out that the poet has put these disgraceful sentiments into the mouth of a disgraceful character: this will put the student on guard against everything else that character does or says.

Are there clues which the student can use to see what a poet is doing? Plutarch goes on (chapter 4) to describe some techniques for distinguishing good from bad. Sometimes poets give a clue by commenting explicitly on a character's words or actions. When Athene prompts Pandarus to break the truce, Homer calls him 'foolish' (*Il.* 4.104), making it easy to see that he is misbehaving. Even in the absence of explicit comment, an evaluation may be implicit in the narrative's outcome: it should serve as a warning if someone who behaves badly comes to a nasty end. Hera's seduction of Zeus ends badly for her; so, even in the absence of explicit comment, the narrative exhibits the self-defeating nature of manipulative sexual relationships. The same is true of the adultery of Ares and Aphrodite. Plutarch does not draw attention to the bad theology of these stories, perhaps thinking that they are among the obviously fantastic inventions. He is, at any rate, certain that allegorical interpretation of such passages is an unnecessary distraction, since the narrative carries a clear moral message on its surface (4, 19e–20b: see §4.3).

When the poet has not given explicit or implicit guidance towards the right assessment of what someone says or does, we can exploit poetry's

contradictory voices (20d–21d).[4] If one character praises wealth, and
another disparages it, the contradiction invites us to make our own assessment: which is right? Sometimes a corrective contradiction is found in the
immediate context; sometimes it must be sought more remotely. When
the gods fight each other or are wounded, other passages from Homer can
be quoted which give a more elevated picture of the gods living in eternal
bliss without pain or sorrow (20e–f). Plutarch does not make the point
that this applies to stories like the seduction of Zeus or the adultery of
Ares and Aphrodite: his readers are presumably trusted to make the connection themselves.

When the poet makes an explicit evaluation, implies one through the
outcome of the action, or shows contrasting opinions in a single passage,
the student should be capable of seeing that for himself. But when remote
contexts supply the corrective, the passage itself gives no indication that
anything is amiss. How, then, is the student to know that he should look
for something better elsewhere? At this stage, Plutarch must rely on adult
guidance: when they come across a questionable passage, the teacher can
produce correctives from other contexts. The young person is still dependent on a teacher whose task it is to cite contradictory passages as antidotes
to poetry's toxic content. That is even clearer in the next suggestion, in
which correctives are cited from other authors (21d–22a).

Additional resources which are likely to need the teacher's guidance,
at least initially, are introduced in chapters 5 and 6. These involve paying
attention to details of expression, in order to find different ways of interpreting the words. For example, 'such is the fate the gods give wretched
men, to live in sorrow' (*Il.* 24.525–6) might be read as saying that humans
in general are wretched, and that the gods inflict on them the fate of living in sorrow. But that is a shocking way of thinking about the gods (as
Plato said, the gods are the source only of good: *Rep.* 2, 379b–c). Plutarch
suggests a better way to read it: 'Homer did not say that the gods doom
all men indiscriminately to a life of sorrow, but foolish and thoughtless
men, whom he is accustomed to call "wretched" and "miserable" because
their immorality makes them wretched and pitiable' (5, 22c).

Though this kind of subtlety is something one might look to a teacher
to provide, some subsequent chapters place progressively greater demands
on the young person's judgement. Chapter 7 revisits the idea that poetry is
imitation, and draws two further implications from it. First, poetry must

---

[4] Compare Pl. *Laws* 4, 719c, where it is stressed that poets do not know on which side of a contradiction the truth lies.

portray a world that is not made up of people who are straightforwardly either good or bad if it is to be at all realistic. To make their narratives plausible, poets sometimes show good people acting misguidedly (7, 25b–c). Secondly, poetry is not *just* realistic: it must entertain us, astonish us, move us. So events are sensationalised; characters undergo sudden changes of fortune, are intensely emotional, and make mistakes (25d). Here we take a step beyond the simple idea in chapter 3, that the poet puts disgraceful sentiments into the mouth of disgraceful characters. If characters who are basically good do not always behave well, the student must make more sophisticated judgements to decide whether to approve or disapprove of what is in the poem. Actions should not be judged simply on the basis of who is doing them (chapter 8). Even the heroes in poetry ought not to be taken uncritically as role-models (8, 25d). For example, the young person should not imagine that, since Achilles is a great hero, whatever he does is admirable. Agamemnon behaves badly in the assembly in *Iliad* 1; but when he sends Chryseis back to her father he shows more restraint and dignity than Achilles, who weeps when Briseis is taken away from him (26b–f). So we should always judge the particular action, and not place indiscriminate trust in the person.

The quality of a character's words or actions is not always apparent: it depends on their motives, which are not necessarily made explicit in the poem. When Nausicaa tells her companions that she would like to marry someone like Odysseus (*Od.* 6.244–5), was she sexually aroused or did she admire Odysseus' intelligence and virtue (27a–b)? Here the reader must first discern the different ways in which the character's behaviour might be understood, and then make an appropriate judgement of each. Difficult though that complex of interpretation and assessment is when the poem leaves the character's motives implicit, it is even harder when a character's motives are actively disguised by plausible-looking pretexts. But the judgement is then especially important: young people need to learn how to look beneath the surface of what is said, and draw their own conclusions about agents' real motives. In fact (chapter 9), the student should always be encouraged to ask 'why?' That does not apply only to poetry. Young people should be obedient, but not mindless: they should always try to understand the reason why they are being told to do this or not to do that. Otherwise, they will end up obeying stupid or immoral orders. But in the case of poetry, which we know contains falsehoods, it is essential that they do not swallow uncritically every bit of purported 'wisdom'. They must acquire the habit of examining and assessing it for themselves.

Plutarch's overriding educational interest in poetry is its moral content. The essential thing is that students should pay attention to what will
help them develop their moral understanding and character (chapter 11).
So they should observe the differences between good and bad characters,
and give close attention to comments on, or speeches that are expressive
of, the virtues. Plutarch's objection to Stoic interpretation is that its focus
on physical processes is likely to distract the student from the proper
ethical focus (11, 31e: see §4.4). But even morally dubious passages can
provide the source for useful reflection (chapter 12). Plutarch is unhappy
with Thetis' suggestion that Achilles cheer himself up with some sex (*Il.*
24.128–31); but the passage is instructive, since it draws attention to the
self-control which Achilles displays when he does not follow the advice. In
the absence of such resources for reflection, the teacher can at least make
a critical response: when the poet or a character says something bad, the
teacher counters it with a correction. This much, Plutarch concedes, the
Stoics got right (12, 33c–d).

The reader should also try to generalise, moving from the individual instance in the poem to a more general truth (chapter 13). This goes
beyond finding the moral implications of, for example, the seduction of
Zeus. In that case the generalisation is from the instance to similar cases;
here the generalisation is to analogous cases. For example, both Paris and
Hector are described (by hostile speakers) as 'good for nothing but looks'
(*Il.* 3.39, 17.142): the implication is that beauty is a superficial quality, of
no use (indeed, potentially harmful) if not accompanied by more solid
virtues (13, 34e–35a). That principle can be generalised to such qualities
as wealth and social status. Attacks on the superficiality of beauty alone
should prompt readers to ask themselves what is genuinely worthwhile,
and to reflect that whatever has no value in itself is not a matter for pride
unless underpinned by something that has real value. Plutarch remarks
that this example shows the importance of paying careful attention to
what is praised or criticised in poetry. So he does not deny that poets
sometimes tell the truth; when there is wisdom there, we should take note
of it and reflect on its general implications. Interestingly, he says that it is
especially worth noting what is praised or criticised by Homer (35a). The
privileged place accorded to Homer recalls the Athenian Stranger's claim
that men of mature judgement will rightly prefer Homer and Hesiod
(*Laws* 2, 658d), and foreshadows the later Platonists' attitude to Homer.

By this stage the young person reading poetry has begun to engage
in active questioning. Plutarch's programme started with relatively simple devices by which the teacher can protect the pupil from being misled

by poetry; but it has moved on, making progressively greater demands on the young person's critical judgement and initiative in posing questions to the text and drawing general lessons from the answers. Reading poetry has become an introduction to philosophy, and a basic training in how to think philosophically. Finally (chapter 14), the teacher should show the student that the good things that poets say are in agreement with what philosophers say. Here the student starts to encounter properly philosophical texts – is, in fact, ready to make the transition to the study of philosophy.

At the end of the essay (14, 36d–38a), Plutarch describes the difficulties young people will have if they come to philosophy unprepared. From the nursery upward, they have been fed a diet of stories and myths by people who have a profoundly misguided moral outlook. So when they encounter philosophy, they are bewildered. Philosophers say weird things, which seem to make no sense. Since exposure to myths and poetry cannot be prevented, the question is, first, how to protect young people from the harm that poetry can do, but also how to turn their exposure to poetry to positive advantage by making it a preparation for their encounter with philosophy. If they are taught to read poetry in the way that Plutarch recommends, they will acquire the habit of evaluating poetry's content. They will pass judgement on what happens in stories, rather than absorbing them uncritically. They will discover that there are questions to be asked about what is right and wrong. The falsehoods and contradictions they find in poetry will provide a positive stimulus to critical reflection. So in reading poetry they will have begun to learn to think philosophically even before their first encounter with philosophy in the raw.

Plutarch says that when young people are bewildered by their first encounter with philosophy, it is as if they have been living in the dark all their lives, and are dazzled when they go out into the sun for the first time. The echo of Plato's image of the Cave (§2.5) is obvious. If you are going to take people out of darkness into bright sunlight, it is a good idea to give them some preparatory exposure to subdued artificial light. That is what Plutarch's programme for reading poetry is like.

2 EPICURUS: POETRY FOR PLEASURE

The fleeting reference to Epicurus in the introduction to Plutarch's essay implies that the Epicureans thought that poetry should be avoided altogether: young people are advised to stop their ears, like Odysseus' crew protecting themselves from the Sirens (*Od.* 12.37–101), and sail past, full speed ahead (1, 15e). That is undoubtedly a tendentious oversimplification of the Epicurean position, but the truth is hard to retrieve from fragmentary evidence derived in part from authors unsympathetic to Epicureanism (as Plutarch was), and in part from Epicurean writings preserved on papyri buried when Vesuvius erupted in AD 79. The main author represented in the Herculaneum papyri is Philodemus, an Epicurean of the first century BC. His style would not have made for easy reading even if his works had been transmitted in pristine condition; when they have been reconstructed from tatters of carbonised papyrus, the challenge they present is correspondingly greater. A brief discussion cannot hope to provide more than a few pointers.[5]

Plutarch's nautical image alludes to Epicurus' letter to Pythocles: 'flee all education ... raising your sail' (F163 Usener = F89 Arrighetti = D. L. 10.6.7). Several other Epicurean fragments express the same disparaging view of the standard liberal education, of which the study of poetry was one important component. Epicurus congratulated Apelles because he was untainted by any education when he started out on philosophy (F117 Usener = F43 Arrighetti = Ath. 13, 588a; cf. Plut. *Non posse* 12, 1094d). Epicurus' associate Metrodorus, in his *On Poems*, advises us not to worry if we have to admit to ignorance even of the most elementary facts about the *Iliad* (Plut. *Non posse* 12, 1095a = F24 Körte).

Plutarch finds Epicurus' position puzzlingly inconsistent (*Non posse* 1095b–d = F20 Usener = 12.2 Arrighetti). On the one hand, he makes no allowance for 'musical problems and questions of literary scholarship' even at drinking parties; on the other, he says that 'the wise man is a lover of sights and more than anyone enjoys hearing and seeing Dionysiac performances'. We may find it strange that Plutarch treats scholarly discussion as particularly suitable to drinking parties, but posing problems on literary topics and suggesting solutions to them had become a leisure activity of the cultured elite, and in symposiastic contexts the seriousness of the discussion was not necessarily sustained.[6] Contrasting examples of the literary genre which this practice inspired can be found in Plutarch's own *Table-talk* (*Quaestiones convivales*) and Athenaeus' *Learned Banqueters* (*Deipnosophistae*). Plutarch therefore finds it incomprehensible that anyone should be eager to spend the day listening to music, but unwilling to engage in intellectual discourse on the subject (13, 1095e). For Epicurus, however, the difference of context is crucial. The arts are a

---

[5] For fuller discussion see Asmis 1991; 1993; 1995; Obbink 1995a; Halliwell 2011: 304–26. On Epicureanism: O'Keefe 2010; Warren 2009.

[6] Heath 2009a: 253; Slater 1982.

source of pleasure, on a par with gustatory and sexual pleasures; without them, the notion of a good life has no intelligible content (F67 = Ath. 12, 546e; Cic. *Tusc.* 3.41). But devoting time and effort to serious study of music, poetry and other components of a liberal education adds nothing to our pleasure in the arts, and contributes nothing to – indeed, is a distraction from – one's progress in philosophy and the living of a good life (Cic. *Fin.* 1.71–2).[7]

Aristotle agrees that the wise man is a lover of *theōria* of music and poetry (§3.7), but would reject the way that Epicurus understands the value of such *theōria*. Epicurean ethics is able to discriminate between pleasures, but cannot sustain Aristotle's distinction between what is good because it is pleasurable and what is pleasurable because of its intrinsic value: in Epicureanism, virtue and 'the fine' have only instrumental value (F69 Usener = 22.2 Arrighetti = Cic. *Tusc.* 3.42; F70 Usener = 22.4 Arrighetti = Ath. 12, 546f–7a). It would not surprise Plato to find such ethical opinions expressed by a materialist who describes the wise man as 'a lover of sights' (*philotheōros*), and thus effectively confesses to being a 'sightseer' (*philotheamōn*, *Rep.* 4, 475c–d: §2.5). Epicurus' exclusive emphasis on poetry as a source of pleasure would certainly be unacceptable to Plato. Conversely, Plato's demand that poetry should be beneficial to the city, as well as enjoyable (*Rep.* 10, 607d), is unacceptable to the Epicurean Philodemus (*On Poems* 5, col. 4.10–13 and 29.9–23 Mangoni). In Philodemus' view, imposing this demand must lead to a wholesale expulsion of poetry – the word he uses (*ekrapizei*, 'beat out') concisely echoes Heraclitus' pronouncement that 'Homer deserves to be thrown out [*ekballesthai*] of the contests and given a beating [*rapizesthai*]' (B42: §2.4). The majority of poems are not beneficial; some, indeed, are harmful; and even poetry that is beneficial does not benefit by virtue of being poetry – it is the thought that is beneficial, and that could be expressed more effectively in prose.

One way in which Philodemus believes that poetry can cause harm is in promoting false beliefs about the gods. Epicureans held that there is a universal, empirically evoked pre-conception (*prolēpsis*) of the divine (Cic. *ND* 1.43–5). A correct theology could be derived from this by anyone whose reasoning is not corrupted or distorted, but in practice people have been led stray by superstition and falsehood – a process to which poets have contributed. The Epicurean speaker in Cicero's *On the Nature of the Gods* observes that the harm done by the poets' absurd theology is exacerbated

---

[7] Blank 2009.

by the pleasantness of their poetry (1.42). The brief selection of examples given there is abbreviated from a much more extensive catalogue, which Philodemus presented more expansively in his *On Piety*.[8] A similar catalogue in Sextus Empiricus *Against the Grammarians* (1.279–98),[9] in a passage explicitly based on an Epicurean source (299), maintains that poetic theology is no better than that of lay people (287), and in many cases worse (288–91). Moreover (279–80), poetry's claims are mere assertions, without proofs; so they cannot produce rational conviction. Proof is the task of philosophy. In addition, poetry makes inconsistent claims, in ethics as well as theology. Inevitably, some of the inconsistent things that can be found in poetry are wrong, and therefore harmful, since people tend in the absence of rational proof to choose the worse option. But, again, it is philosophy that can adjudicate the conflicting claims. So if studying poetry is worthwhile because of the usefulness of what the poets say, what is needed is not literary scholarship, but philosophy – and why (Philodemus asks) would a philosopher, who has a proof, pay attention to a poet, who does not (*Rhet.* 1.262 Sudhaus = *PHerc.* 1669, col. 27.10–14)?[10]

One can see, then, why Epicureans dismissed conventional education as a useless distraction, and also the sense in which Epicurus could say that only the wise man would discourse correctly on music and poetry (F569 Usener = D. L. 10.121). But one should not overlook the fact that Plutarch has more in common with Epicurus than his dismissive reference implies. Both hold that poetry is attractive, full of inconsistencies, and potentially harmful; and both regard philosophical judgements imported from outside as the only antidote to that harm.[11]

3 ALLEGORY: HIDDEN TRUTH

A second approach that Plutarch rejects in *How to Read Poetry* (4, 19e–f) reads passages about the gods as allegories of physical processes. For

---

[8] There is no up-to-date edition of this part of *On Piety*: for the transitional passage see *On Piety* 2479–96 Obbink. Discussion: Obbink 1995a.

[9] Translation and commentary: Blank 1998.

[10] What if the poet does give proofs, as in Lucretius' experiment in Epicurean didactic poetry? One might then argue that, just as poetry's harm is amplified by the poetry's pleasantness, so is the benefit: thus Lucr. 1.933–50. But the proofs could have been given in prose; and the pleasure, though it may make the proofs more palatable and persuasive, does not make them any more rationally compelling. Poetry is not a route to philosophical wisdom.

[11] For this comparison see Asmis 1991: 20–2. The suspicion that Plutarch has adapted material from Epicurean sources is reinforced by his persistent description of poetry as 'disturbing' (*taraktikon*, 1, 15c; cf. 2, 16e, 17d; 6, 25a; 7, 25d; 9, 28c); significantly, philosophy's power to relieve the disturbance caused by poetry is illustrated by Epicurean examples (14, 37a).

example, Hera's seduction of Zeus is outrageous if it is really about the gods: but it gives no grounds for outrage if Hera (*Hēra*) is a coded reference to the atmosphere (*aēr*) and the story is describing what happens when air comes into proximity with fire. There is evidence that such allegories were already being proposed in the sixth century BC. According to Porphyry, Theagenes of Rhegium, 'who was the first to write on Homer', defended apparently objectionable stories about the gods by physical allegorisation (A2 = Porphyry on *Il.* 20.67–75). But the work of Theagenes and other early allegorists has not survived, and it is unclear how much the later sources who mention them actually knew: sparse information may have been filled out from knowledge of later allegorists.[12] So there is little that can be said with confidence about their interpretations or their motives: for example, were they really mounting a defensive response to critics such as Xenophanes (§1.2), or were they annexing Homer's prestige in support of their own cosmological theories?

One remarkable source, however, does allow us to glimpse a relatively early allegorical interpreter at work. A papyrus excavated at Derveni (northern Greece) in 1962 preserves fragments of a book, probably written in the late fifth or early fourth century BC, by an unknown author. This copy was placed on a funeral pyre, but not completely burnt. The surviving fragments, scrappy and difficult to read, are mainly taken up with an allegorical interpretation of a poem attributed to the mythical poet Orpheus.[13] Like Hesiod's *Theogony*, the poem was about the origins and history of the universe. It contained a version of the Succession Myth related to Hesiod's, but with some differences. As in Hesiod, Zeus overthrew his father Cronos, who had himself deposed and castrated his father Uranus; but this version has an additional twist – Zeus swallowed the detached genitals and had intercourse with his mother Rhea. The commentator maintains that Orpheus deliberately used this myth to communicate a cosmology in 'riddling' form. The commentator's cosmology is clearly derived from presocratic philosophy, and this is not the only evidence for presocratics claiming that Homer expressed their own theories about the universe. Diogenes of Apollonia, for example, 'praises Homer for having spoken about the divine not mythologically, but truly: he says that he regarded Zeus as *aēr*, since he says that Zeus knows everything'

---

[12] Kingsley 1995: 26. Allegory and presocratic philosophy: Naddaf 2009. General accounts of allegory in antiquity: Brisson 2004; Struck 2004.

[13] Derveni papyrus: Betegh 2004. See also: Laks and Most 1997; Bernabé 2007; Frede 2007; Rangos 2007.

(A8 = Philodemus *On Piety* 6b Gomperz).[14] The Derveni commentator, too, associates Zeus (not Hera) with *aēr* (col. 17.1–6, 19.2–4, 23.1–4).

Plato's Socrates would disapprove of this Orphic myth (*Rep.* 2, 377e–8a; *Laws* 10, 886b–e), and would not agree that reading it allegorically renders it unobjectionable. He mentions this defence, but argues that young people, or people lacking in discernment, will be unable to see past the surface narrative to the deeper truths (*Rep.* 2, 378d–e). Socrates does not deny that some poems are deliberately allegorical. The examples of Parmenides and Empedocles, who expressed philosophical ideas non-literally in mythological verse, would have made denial difficult. Socrates has no reason, either, to object to allegorical poetry in principle. He is content with stories that are literal falsehoods but convey truths, and could agree that allegorical composition is acceptable provided that the surface meaning is not potentially harmful. Then it would not matter if some people read the text only at a superficial level: though they will not discover the deeper truths, they at least will not be infected with false theology or bad morality. Socrates is, indeed, willing to mention allegorical readings of Homer, and even to cite one as the 'crown' of an argument – with irony, perhaps, but without protest (*Tht.* 153c–d, on *Il.* 8.17–27; cf. 152e, 180c–d).

When Plutarch rejects allegorical interpretation (4, 19e–f), he does not reproduce Socrates' objection that young people cannot discern the deeper meaning. His essay assumes that the student is reading Homer with a tutor, who would be able to explain the allegory. In the context of his argument, it is more important that the allegories would be a distraction from poetry's moral content, which is what Plutarch wants young readers to focus on. In the examples of allegorical interpretation he criticises, he maintains that there is a moral lesson to be learned from the Homeric passages; reading them as allegories of physical processes would miss the moral point.

Plutarch also says that these passages are violently distorted by allegorical readers (4, 19f), which suggests that he regards allegorical interpretations, not simply as unsuitable for the education of young people, but as perverse and absurd. That would be a typical modern reaction, too: modern readers are unlikely to be persuaded that Homer's account of the seduction of Zeus was intended as the vehicle for an account of the interaction of physical elements. Yet if allegory is taken in the broad sense of text that is talking about one thing on the surface level, but at

---

[14] Diogenes: Laks 2008.

a deeper level is talking about something else, allegory is undeniably a widespread feature of poetry. A text of the first or second century AD, the *Homeric Problems* by Heraclitus (not to be confused with the presocratic Heraclitus), begins by saying that Homer would be on a par with mythical blasphemers if his stories were spoken 'without any philosophical insight, with no allegorical figure lurking within them, following a poetic tradition' (1.3). The main part of the work demonstrates that Homer is not blasphemous by working through the poems and explaining apparently objectionable passages allegorically. The author is aware that such interpretations will meet with resistance, and prepares his ground by illustrating their continuity with universally acknowledged forms of non-literal expression. Alcaeus describes a storm at sea, but is really talking about political upheavals. Anacreon describes a frisky foal, but is really talking about an unco-operative lover. Homer speaks of the time when 'the bronze drops straw in plenty on the ground, but there is little harvest' (*Il.* 19.222–3): he describes farming, but is really talking about battle.[15] The point is that objections to allegorical interpretation need a sounder basis than instinctive incredulity. Doubters must show that such allegories are objectionable in a way that these uncontroversial examples are not.

What would be the point of the riddling strategy that allegorical interpretation attributes to poets? If Homer meant to convey a cosmology, why did he compose mythological stories that appear to be about gods seducing each other and fighting? One possible motive is control of access to privileged truths. Only those with special insight will be able to understand fully a meaning that is hidden beneath the surface. This idea would not have seemed strange in the ancient world, where mystery cults had secrets that were not to be disclosed to the uninitiated. The Derveni commentator attributes this motive to Orpheus (7.4–11):[16]

His [i.e. Orpheus'] poetry is something strange and riddling for humans. But Orpheus did not intend to speak [? captious] riddles to them, but great things in riddles. In fact, he is speaking a sacred discourse from his first all the way to his last word, as he also makes clear in the [? well-chosen] line: for in ordering them to shut the doors on their ears, he is saying that he is [? not legislating] for the many ... [? but teaching only] those pure in hearing.

[15] In this case, Homer makes the application explicit in context. Heraclitus needs an explicit example to establish that Homer does make use of non-literal expression; once this has been established, the burden of proof lies on those who deny that Homer ever does it implicitly.

[16] Cf. 25.12–3: the poet did not *want* everyone to understand. For 'riddling' see also 9.10–11, 10.10–11, 13.5–6; for misunderstandings see 9.2–4, 12.3–6, 26.8, 23.7. Note in particular 18.10–15, against the popular misconception that Zeus was born (compare Xenophanes B11). On the Derveni commentator's hermeneutics: Betegh 2004: 364–70.

Plato's Socrates would like the Succession Myth to be kept secret, even if it were true (*Rep.* 2, 377e–8a). For him, access controls are needed to ensure that people are not exposed to a surface meaning that they will be unable to handle. For the Derveni commentator, by contrast, the surface meaning is itself the access control, designed to ensure that unqualified people are excluded from the deeper truth.

A second possible motive is self-protection. In late fifth-century Athens, people who did not believe in the gods that everyone else believed in, and substituted purely physical explanations of the world, attracted suspicion and hostility. This could have serious consequences. The charge on which Socrates was put to death included not believing in the gods worshipped by the city; according to Plato, his prosecutors alleged that he thought that the sun was a stone and the moon made of earth (*Ap.* 26c–d). It would be possible to imagine that the poets had expressed their philosophical insights in mythological form in order to avoid that suspicion. Plato's Protagoras speaks of the hostility to sophists, claiming that sophists used to disguise themselves: some (Homer, Hesiod, Simonides) used poetry as their cover, others (Orpheus, Musaeus) used religious rites and prophecy (*Prt.* 316d–e). Plato's Protagoras himself uses myth as an expository device (320c–3a). So, of course, did Plato.[17]

4 ANCIENT WISDOM: TRUTH OBSCURED

Allegorical interpretation credits poets with wisdom of their own. That wisdom is not expressed in the surface meaning of their poetry, which may be false or otherwise discreditable, but must be uncovered by the interpreter. But is it right to regard ancient poets as a source of wisdom? Xenophanes had one reason for doubting that: 'the gods did not disclose all things to mortals from the beginning, but mortals in time by searching find out better' (B18: §1.2). Yet the idea that people in the past were better than we are today was deeply embedded in ancient ways of thinking. So a more pressing question, perhaps, is whether the 'ancient' poets are ancient enough. Homer and Hesiod already looked back to a better past. Homer contrasts the heroes with 'mortals as they are now',[18] but even the heroes were not living in an age of innocence and unclouded insight. When Hesiod recounts how the idyllic Golden race was replaced by races

---

[17] See Kingsley 1995: 79–132, 159–71 on the background to the eschatological myth in the *Phaedo*.
[18] *Il.* 5.302–4: Diomedes can throw a stone that two men now could not lift; cf. 12.381–3, 447–9; 20.285–7.

of Silver, Bronze and Iron (with the heroes inserted between Bronze and Iron) he is telling a story of deterioration (*WD* 106–201).

Plato's Socrates echoes this kind of thinking when he says that 'the men of old, who were superior to us and lived nearer the gods, handed on this saying … ' (*Phlb.* 16c). In another dialogue one speaker (not Socrates) says: 'as to the other gods, to say or know their origin is beyond us, and we must accept those who have spoken before us, who were offspring of the gods (as they say) and presumably had clear knowledge of their ancestors' (*Tim.* 40d–41a). Plato does not always look back to the very origins of mankind: he also makes use of the idea that human life is repeatedly disrupted by natural catastrophes. The stories of Deucalion's flood and of Phaethon, who borrowed the chariot of the sun and drove it too near the earth, causing destruction by fire, preserve memories of such catastrophes in mythical form (*Tim.* 22a–d).[19] In the *Critias*, an incomplete dialogue which tells the story of Atlantis, the flood which destroyed both Atlantis and the ancient Athenians who had successfully resisted their aggression wiped out knowledge of the great deeds of ancient Athens: the survivors preserved only the names of some ancient Athenians (109d–110c). In the *Laws* the 'Athenian Stranger' (the main speaker) mentions ancient accounts of such catastrophes, and imagines how society would develop in the aftermath of one of them (3, 677a–682e). The survivors would have been sent back to absolute basics, without even the memory of civilised life. However, for precisely that reason they had no difficulty in meeting their simple needs, and there was nothing to cause violence or injustice among them. There follows an account of the decline from this primitive simplicity as a more complex and less virtuous form of society develops.

In *Timaeus* and *Critias* this view of human history is wrapped up in a multi-layered fiction: Plato invented the story about Atlantis; he invented a story in which Solon learned about it in Egypt, which enjoyed a long cultural tradition unbroken by natural catastrophes; and he invented the conversation in which Critias reports all this to Socrates and others. The history of civilisations in the *Laws* may be simply a thought-experiment that is helpful in thinking about the origin and function of laws in society, just as the City of Pigs (of which the unspoiled post-catastrophic community is reminiscent) and the feverish city in *Republic* (§2.2) are imaginary aids to thinking about justice. So Plato provides evidence that this theory

---

[19] Xenophanes is reported to have cited marine fossils on dry land as evidence of floods that wiped out mankind (A33).

of human history was current in his day, but we cannot be sure that he is committed to it as a literal truth.

Aristotle was committed to this theory. His world had no beginning, and without the recurrent devastation of human societies and cultures by natural calamities it would have been impossible to account for evidence of fairly recent progress from primitive conditions to civilisation (§3.4). Unlike Plato, Aristotle does not think of the post-catastrophic communities as ideally virtuous and wise: the survivors, struggling to stay alive, would be like ordinary, stupid people today (*Pol.* 2.8, 1269a4–6). Understanding the universe requires a sophisticated society, able to support a leisured class that can sustain the pursuit of knowledge for its own sake, independently of its derived value (*Met.* 1.1, 981b13–25). It does not follow that Aristotle must discount the possibility of ancient wisdom, but the wisdom would not be that of primitive innocence, but of pre-catastrophic sophistication, some fragments of which might have been passed on through the collapse of civilisation (*Met.* 12.8, 1074a38–b14):[20]

> Remnants from the remotest antiquity have been transmitted to posterity in the form of a myth that these [i.e. heavenly bodies] are gods, and that the divine encloses the whole of nature. The rest has been added with a view to persuading the masses and to legislative and practical utility: it is said that these gods have human form, or are like certain other animals, and other things consequent on and very similar to those I have mentioned. But if one separates out the first point, and takes it on its own, that they thought the primary substances are gods, one would regard it as an inspired statement, and that in all likelihood while every art and philosophy has been developed as far as possible, and then been destroyed again, these beliefs have been preserved like relics to the present day. The ancestral belief, held by the earliest people, is visible to us to that extent, and no further.

The knowledge and understanding attained by the pre-catastrophic civilisation survived in fragmentary form, but made no sense to the survivors.[21] Because the inherited material no longer made sense, poets and others felt free to manipulate and distort it for various purposes. It may be possible to peel off the mythological elaboration and see the original insights – although Aristotle is generally cautious about the value of alleged ancient wisdom (*Met.* 1.3, 983b27–4a2; 3.4, 1000a9–18; *Cael.* 2.1, 284a18–23).

---

[20] See Palmer 2000; Johansen 1999.

[21] Aristotle is reported to have described proverbs as remnants of ancient wisdom lost in cataclysms, preserved because of their conciseness and cleverness (F13 Rose = F463 Gigon). The point may be that, since proverbs are self-contained, their intelligibility was not impaired by the fragmentation of pre-catastrophic wisdom.

If myths transmit ancient wisdom in a distorted form, the best way to gain access to the insights of early or pre-catastrophic people may be to study, not myths, but words. If names were bestowed correctly, they would have had a meaning that embodied the name-givers' wisdom. Aristotle is willing to make use of etymology as a tool for recovering the knowledge originally encoded in ancient words. For example, in two passages he suggests that the word for the element of which the heavens are made, *aithēr*, can be etymologised as 'always [*aei*] runs [*thei*]', expressing the eternal motions of the heavens (*Mete.* 1.3, 339b16–30, *Cael.* 1.3, 270b16–25). In these passages, Aristotle speaks of ideas being rediscovered infinitely often (cf. *Pol.* 7.10, 1329b26–7). What etymology tells us, therefore, is that the latest science is a rediscovery of what people had understood before the last catastrophe. Of course, we can only recognise something as a truth understood by the ancients because we have ourselves understood its truth. Etymology is not a method for discovering truths we have not already rediscovered for ourselves.

Etymology appears in Plato, too, especially in the *Cratylus*. For example, Socrates gives much the same explanation of *aithēr* as Aristotle: '*aithēr* I should interpret as *aeitheēer* ... because this element always runs in a flux about the air [*aei thei peri ton aera reōn*]' (410b). He also relates 'god' (*theos*) to 'run' (*thei*), expressing the eternal motion of the heavenly bodies (397c–d):

> Something like this is my own suspicion: it seems to me that the first human inhabitants of Greece only believed in those gods that many non-Greeks do nowadays – sun, moon, earth, stars, and sky. Seeing that they were always moving at speed and running, because it was their nature to run [*thein*] they called them gods [*theoi*]. Later, when they became aware of all the other gods, they called them by the same name.

The changes and ignorant distortions that words have undergone over time make it hard to trace them back to their original form with confidence (414c–e). Moreover, Socrates goes on to argue that etymological analysis reveals that the primeval language already embodied philosophical errors (436b–440d). So Plato attests to the currency of etymologising,[22] but again we cannot be sure that he is committed to the etymologies proposed in the dialogue. The point for him is a negative one: etymology cannot provide a route to the truth, because it may lead us to reconstructing false beliefs. Only philosophy can tell us what is true.

---

[22] Baxter 1992: 107–63 surveys the evidence. On *Cratylus*: Barney 2001; Sedley 2003.

Etymology was a characteristic feature of allegorical interpretation, too. The allegory of the seduction of Zeus that Plutarch rejects (4, 19e–f) identifies Hera (*Hēra*) with the atmosphere (*aēr*),[23] and the interpretation of divine names is one of the techniques used by the Derveni commentator. Cronos is a combination of 'strike together' (*krouein*) and 'mind' (*nous*), showing that divine intelligence lies behind cosmogonically important collisions between pieces of matter. This overlap in method makes it easy to confuse those who used etymology as a tool for recovering fragments of ancient wisdom appropriated and distorted by poets with allegorical interpreters who sought to recover the wisdom which the poets themselves had expressed in riddling form. This confusion could prove polemically useful to those who viewed allegorical interpretation of poetry with scepticism. According to a passage in Cicero's *On the Nature of the Gods*, the Stoic Chrysippus 'aims at reconciling the myths of Orpheus, Musaeus, Hesiod and Homer with what he himself said … about the immortal gods, so that the most ancient poets (who had no inkling of these things) appear to have been Stoics!' (1.41). Though this view of Stoic exegesis has often been accepted at face value, it is a tendentious attack by a hostile witness: the speaker is an Epicurean. In a later part of the dialogue, where a Stoic is speaking, ancient insights into the physical world are sharply distinguished from the impious myths which poets have made out of them (2.63–4). The Stoic rejects the portrayal of the gods in poetry out of hand as totally false, misleading and absurd; but when those myths have been abandoned, there remain gods 'whose identities and natures can be understood from the name which custom has assigned to each of them': 'it is not only philosophers who distinguish superstition from religion – our ancestors did so, too' (2.70–1).[24]

Whereas allegorists used etymology as a clue to the riddling intentions of wise poets, therefore, the Stoics used etymology as a way of getting *behind* the fanciful intentions of misguided poets. Though the stories that the poets tell are the product of poetic elaboration and invention, the divine names which the poets inherited originally expressed true insights into nature. Those insights were, of course, in agreement with Stoic doctrine: that is how the Stoics recognised that they were true. But

---

[23] This echo is exploited in the Homeric text itself (*Il.* 5.775–6, 21.6), though not necessarily with allegorical intent.

[24] Stoics and allegory: Long 1992; Boys-Stones 2003; Goulet 2005. Nussbaum 1993 discusses aspects of Stoic views of poetry related to the concerns of Plato and Plutarch; it is clear that Plutarch adapted material from Stoic as well as Epicurean sources. On Stoicism: Sellars 2006; Inwood 2003.

why should Stoics have expected to find truth in very ancient thoughts about nature? Stoics, like Epicureans (§4.2), held that cognition depends on empirically evoked pre-conceptions or 'natural notions' (*phusikai ennoiai*).[25] Such pre-conceptions are a latent potential for knowledge, but may not be accurately expressed in an individual's actual beliefs. An Epicurean and a Stoic would agree, not only that there was a universal pre-conception of gods, but also that widely held beliefs about the gods are inconsistent with that natural pre-conception. (Each would maintain that the other is mistaken in his beliefs about gods, and in his beliefs about the pre-conception of gods: for example, the pre-conception postulated by the Epicurean excludes providence, while that postulated by the Stoic entails it.) Since social influences are a factor in preventing a pre-conception's accurate expression in actual belief, error is likely to be self-perpetuating and cumulative. But the earliest humans, as yet uncorrupted, were able to form beliefs from these pre-conceptions without the distortions which subsequently led people's thinking astray; they had a natural virtue and wisdom.[26] Their unclouded insights into the nature of the universe were encoded in the words of their language: their words expressed the real nature of things. Languages change over time, and the words we use now have taken on new forms, but determining the original form of the words may enable us to recover primordial insights.[27] Or perhaps not. Opponents could deride the arbitrariness of Stoic etymologies: 'there won't be any name the derivation of which you can't explain on the basis of a single letter'; the Stoic project of finding sense behind fictive myths by explaining why things have the names they do is a pointless waste of effort (Cic. *Ac.* 3.62–3). Stoic exegesis could meet with scepticism even when it was not conflated with allegorical interpretation of poetry.

The ancestors who, according to Cicero's Stoic, distinguished superstition from religion were scrupulous in their religious observances (Cic. *ND* 2.72). Cornutus, a Stoic of the first century AD,[28] concludes his *Compendium of Greek Theology* with the claim that the key to leading young people away from superstition to true piety and a proper practice of religion is to treat apparently mythical traditions in the manner he has demonstrated, in the confidence that 'the ancients were no ordinary people, but capable of understanding the nature of the universe and adept

---

[25] 'Pre-conceptions': Dyson 2009; Todd 1973; Obbink 1992.
[26] There are complications in the reconstruction of different stages of Stoic thinking about early humans: discussion and references in Boys-Stones 2001: 18–59; see also Algra 2009.
[27] Stoic theories of language: Allen 2005; Long 2005.
[28] Cornutus: Most 1980.

at philosophising about it by means of symbols and riddles' (35, 75.18–76.5). Cornutus is interested primarily in divine names and epithets, the iconography of the gods, and the myths told in connection with religious rituals. When he cites poets, he does so with an awareness that their evidence is potentially compromised. Hesiod derived some things from more ancient sources, but others were his own excessively 'mythical' additions (17, 31.12–17). Cornutus warns against relying on fictitious supplements added by people who did not understand the riddles, and who treated them as mere fictions (17, 27.19–28.2). Homer has 'distorted' a fragment of ancient myth, 'according to which Zeus was said to have suspended Hera from the upper air (*aithēr*) by gold chains (because the stars have a golden glitter in their appearance) and hung two anvils from her feet – obviously, the land and the sea, by which the air (*aēr*) is stretched out downwards, and cannot be torn away from either side'. Homer has thus transformed an innocuous cosmological image into a punitive act and incorporated it into an exciting, but utterly false, story of conflict among the gods (17, 26.6–28.2, on *Il.* 15.18–21). It is worth noting, however, that in Cornutus' account the ancients themselves already expressed their wisdom in symbolic and riddling form.[29] For example, Zeus's sceptre is a symbol (*sumbolon*) of his power, or (if you make a connection with someone using a staff for support) of the secure stability of his rule (9, 10.10–13); the myth of Dionysus' dismemberment and reassembly is a riddle (*ainigma*) of the harvesting of grapes and their reconstitution as wine (30, 62.101–6). Just as allegorical interpretation of the wisdom *in* poetry makes use of etymology, so the search for ancient wisdom *behind* poetry may need to make use of allegorical interpretation to make sense of what it finds there. The distinction between these two approaches will not be easily maintained.

The distinction between poetic and religious myth is a more stable element of the Stoic approach, as is the emphasis on the symbolic interpretation of the latter. Cornutus' interest in non-Greek thought is also significant. In the course of his discussion of Greek theology he refers to the religious traditions of Persians, Phrygians, Egyptians, Celts, Libyans (17, 26.9–11), Phoenicians (15, 18.10; 28, 54.18), Syrians (2, 6.11–12) and Egyptians (28, 54.15–17, on Isis and Osiris). The Greeks had a long-standing interest in the customs and beliefs of other nations: Herodotus' history includes many ethnographic excursuses, and Aristotle wrote a work (unfortunately lost) on non-Greek customs.[30] Greek philosophers, in

---

[29] Cf. Strabo 10.3.23.

[30] The assimilation of foreign cults also had a long history in the Greek world. At the start of the *Republic* Socrates has gone to the Piraeus to observe the first celebration in Athens of the festival of the Thracian goddess Bendis (1, 327a, 354a).

particular, had long been interested in the relation between the beliefs of non-Greek peoples and philosophy. In the introduction to his philosophical biographies, Diogenes Laertius mentions (but rejects) the view that philosophy originated among non-Greeks – he mentions Persians, Babylonians and Assyrians, Indians, Celts, Phoenicians, Thracians, Libyans and Egyptians. He cites sources stretching back to the fourth century BC, including Aristotle's lost *On Philosophy*.[31] In the second century AD, Numenius (a Pythagorean who had an important influence on subsequent developments in Platonism) adduced the rites, doctrines and cult-objects of the Indians, Jews, Persians and Egyptians as a source for theology in agreement with Plato and Pythagoras (F1a des Places).[32]

The Greeks were aware of how varied and (from their point of view) how strange the customs and beliefs of foreign nations could be, but philosophers interested in comparative religion searched for common elements underlying that diversity. The belief in ancient wisdom makes sense of that search. Where common elements can be identified in the beliefs of different nations, it is a reasonable inference that those elements descend from the primordial insights that were the common possession of the earliest humans. That origin is testimony to their truth.[33]

5 PLUTARCH REVISITED: *ON ISIS AND OSIRIS*

We have seen that in *How to Read Poetry* Plutarch rejects approaches to poetry based on allegorical interpretation or the recovery of inherited wisdom (§4.1). It may seem puzzling, then, to find Plutarch himself exploiting these approaches in other works. A striking case is the treatise in which he interprets the Egyptian myths and religious rituals relating to the gods Isis and Osiris.[34] The myth is clearly inconsistent with the criteria laid down in the *Republic*: for example, the god Osiris dies and his body is torn apart. Plutarch introduces his summary of the myth by warning that the myth is not a true record of events (11, 355b), and declares at the end of the summary that these things cannot truthfully be said of gods (20, 358e–f). Just before his introduction to the myth, he compares

---

[31] Chroust 1973b: 2.206–15, 421–30; White 2001.

[32] Numenius: Dillon 1977, 361–79; Frede 1987.

[33] The Epicureans, however, remained unmoved by comparative evidence: the monstrosities (*portenta*) of the Magi and Egyptian madness simply confirm the universality of the corruption of religious belief, and are dismissed with as much contempt as the poets (Cic. *ND* 1.43).

[34] Commentary: Griffiths 1970.

figuratively expressed Pythagorean aphorisms to Egyptian hieroglyphic writing, which he understands (wrongly) as ideogrammatic (10, 354e–5a). This comparison invites us to read the myth in a 'holy and philosophical' way (355c). When he reviews interpretative options later in the treatise, he is immediately dismissive of attempts to demythologise the stories and interpret them as confused accounts of things that happened to people from human history (22, 359d–24, 360d). A better solution, in his view, would be to interpret the myths as recording the experiences of super-natural beings below the divine level (25, 360d–31, 363d: the Greek word, *daimōn*, does not have the malevolent associations of the Christian derivative 'demon'). Others give a 'more philosophical' explanation. The reference is to Egyptians who interpret the myths allegorically, as accounts of the physical world (32, 363d–44, 368f). Plutarch compares this to allegorical interpretation of Greek mythology (363d), noting the Stoic parallel (41, 367c). However, he regards these purely physical interpretations as superficial, because they do not penetrate to the deepest theological truths (45, 369a; cf. 64, 376f–67, 378a). For Plutarch, the deep theological truth about the world is a form of dualism: that is, there is a divine source of all that is good, but also a resistant source of disorder.[35] This, he thinks, is what is expressed in the mythical opposition between Osiris and Typhon (45, 369a–49, 371a).

In Plutarch's view, therefore, the myth of Isis and Osiris and its associated religious rituals are symbolic expressions of the deepest truths of religion, which are also the most advanced truths of philosophy. It is clear why this dimension of Plutarch's thinking is not in evidence in *How to Read Poetry*: these deep truths are not appropriate for young people who have not yet begun their philosophical studies. But, like the Stoics, Plutarch makes a distinction in principle between the 'outrageous myths and empty fictions' of poets and religious myths and rituals (especially mystery cults) that express deep truths in a symbolic or riddling way. Poets elaborate their myths without any basis in reality, like spiders spinning webs out of material produced from within themselves (20, 358e–f). Plutarch's diagnosis of the falsehoods in Homer and other poets, stemming from deliberate inventions and from ignorance, makes it clear that Homer lies on the wrong side of this distinction. Reading Homer allegorically with young people would be inappropriate, not only to their educational attainments and need, but also to his poetry's real nature.

---

[35] The dualist interpretation of the myth is further developed in 54, 373a–c. Plutarch cites *Tim.* 35a and *Laws* 10, 896d–e to provide Platonic warrant for his dualism (48, 370f).

Plutarch's willingness to apply allegorical and etymological (49–64) techniques to the myths and rituals associated with the Egyptian cult of Isis and Osiris shows that he shares the belief in ancient wisdom with the Stoic Cornutus. He, too, believes that, while myths in poetry had been elaborated and fictionalised by the poets, religious ritual and myth preserve deep truths. He grants that myths associated with religious ritual may not have been perfectly preserved: the interpreter needs to be selective – some elements of the myth are useless and can be set aside (12, 355d; cf. 58, 374e for the principle of selectivity). Nor have worshippers necessarily understood the religious tradition correctly (70–1, 379b–e). But such myths are still a valuable source, provided that one does not fall into the reductive materialism (as Platonists would see it) of the Stoics.[36] Plutarch's respectful interest in Egyptian myth and cult,[37] and in other non-Greek traditions – the Zoroastrian religion of Persia provides him with an example of dualism (46–7, 369d–370c), and there are also references to the Chaldaeans (that is, Assyrians and Babylonians), Phrygians and Paphlagonians (47, 370c–d; 69, 378e) – is another point of resemblance to Cornutus.

6 IMAGING THE GODS

Egyptian religion confronts Plutarch with one severe challenge. The Greeks generally represented gods in human form; the Egyptians had gods who were represented in animal form. Since Greeks tended to think it degrading to represent gods as animals, Plutarch has to explain and defend theriomorphic images of gods.

The Egyptians regarded certain animals as sacred. Plutarch admits that the majority of Egyptians misunderstand this practice, and worship the animals themselves, but points out that ignorant Greeks fall into a similar confusion when they speak of statues of gods as if they were gods (71, 379c–e). Properly understood, sacred animals are revered either for their usefulness or for their symbolic properties (74, 380e–1e). Consider, for example, Anubis (the god of the dead, who Plutarch equates with Hermes in his role as escort of dead souls to the underworld): why is he

---

[36] Plut. F157 Sandbach, which interprets mythology, mysteries and religious rituals in terms of physics, is anomalous. It is possible that this view was expressed by one speaker in a dialogue, but later superseded: see Hardie 1992: 4466–72 for discussion. F200–201 ascribe 'riddling' expression of philosophical doctrine to Homer, but the attribution is debated. Smith includes it among Porphyry's fragments (F382): see Smith 1987: 726 n.48; Helmig 2008 argues for Plutarch.

[37] Plutarch addresses the treatise to his wife, a worshipper of Isis (2, 351e) and an initiate in the rites of Osiris (35, 364e), as well as a leader in the worship of Dionysus at Delphi.

represented with a canine head? Plutarch recalls a passage in the *Republic* where Socrates speaks of the philosophical qualities of dogs: guard dogs are vigilant, and discriminate between familiar friend and unfamiliar foe, so they display a philosophical love of knowledge (11, 355b; cf. *Rep.* 2, 375e–6b). This explanation comes just after Plutarch has compared the Egyptian use of symbols and riddles to their hieroglyphic writing (10, 354e–5a). It might still be objected that animal forms are degrading, and Plutarch concedes that it brings religion into contempt and leads to superstition or atheism when people mistake the animals for gods (71, 379d). On the other hand, he suggests that living animals are, as such, better images of divinity than inert bronze or stone statues (76, 382b–c).

Symbolism offers an alternative to imitation as way of thinking about poetry and visual art, since it works by conceptual mediation rather than likeness. Someone who reads an image of Anubis correctly does not conclude that the god looks like a man with a dog's head, but is led to an understanding of the god's nature by following the train of conceptual associations that leads from a dog's head to wisdom by way of a characteristic canine disposition. Consider a modern example: no one thinks that justice looks like a woman blindfolded and/or holding a pair of scales. Even if we believed in a divine being who regulates justice, we would not imagine that the conventional iconography supplied us with a visual likeness of that being. We recognise that the meaning of the image resides in the conceptual associations of the conventional attributes. There are therefore two prerequisites for successful symbolic communication: we must not mistake the symbols for likenesses, and we must identify the right middle terms. If we use the wrong mediating concepts to read an image of justice, we might infer from the blindfold that the legal system is easily deceived, and from the scales that the legal system, like a shopkeeper weighing out goods, will only give you what you pay for.

The anthropomorphic form of Greek representations of the gods was itself not exempt from criticism. Any thoughtful Greek would realise that gods are not really beings with a human-like physical appearance: the arguments are at least as old as Xenophanes (B14). So the Greek practice also needed to be explained and justified. An example that occurs repeatedly as a test-case in discussion of the problem of divine images is Pheidias' much admired statue of Zeus at Olympia. According to an anecdote, Pheidias claimed that he got the idea for his statue from the passage in *Iliad* 1 where Zeus nods his head in solemn assent to Thetis' supplication, and great Olympus is shaken (*Il.* 1.528–30: cf. Str. 8.3.30 (354a); D. Chr. 12.25–6). The connection thus made between Pheidias' statue and

Homer reflects the fact that the question of how divinity should be represented arises for visual arts and poetry alike.

The analogy between poetry and visual arts is familiar from Plato. The comparison between poetry and painting is introduced in *Republic* 2: a poet who makes a bad image of what gods and heroes are like is comparable to a painter whose painting does not resemble the thing he wants to make a likeness of (2, 377e). The censorship applied to poetry is extended to visual arts: gods fighting against giants must not be described in stories, nor embroidered (378c) – an allusion to the embroidered robe presented to Athene at the Panathenaea (§2.8). Socrates exploits the parallel between poetic and visual media when he examines the nature of imitation in *Republic* 10 (§2.6). Aristotle also makes extensive use of the analogy between poetry and painting (*Po.* 2, 1448a5–6; 6, 1450a26–9, 39–b3; 15, 1454b9–10; 25, 1460b8–11, 31–2), and in *How to Read Poetry* Plutarch calls it a cliché (3, 17f–18a). So it is not surprising that discussions of visual and verbal representations of gods became entwined. In the rest of this section, three authors, ranging in date from the late first through to the early third century AD, will illustrate both the common threads and the scope for diversity of opinion in discussion of these issues.

Dio Chrysostom, a contemporary of Plutarch whose philosophical outlook was Stoic and Cynic, uses Pheidias' statue of Zeus as a device to set up a comparison of visual and poetic representations of gods in a speech written for delivery at the Olympic games (*Or.* 12).[38] The comparison is preceded by an overview of the different sources from which humans derive their conceptions of the divine. First, and fundamentally, there is a natural and universal conception of god that must arise in rational beings simply as a result of their experience of an ordered universe that sustains their life (27–39). This is the familiar Stoic pre-conception (*prolēpsis*) of the divine (§4.4). Though it is natural, this conception of god can be obscured if our reason is corrupted (36–7); it was more readily available to the earliest men, since they were closer to nature than we are. Other sources of our conception of god arose later: poetry encourages us to revere the gods; custom and law compel us to do so (39–43). There are also the visual arts (44–5). Finally, there is philosophy, which through reasoning provides the truest and most perfect interpretation of the divine (47).

The natural conception is the indispensable basis for belief in god, philosophy is the perfect fulfilment of it, and we do not hold law to

---

[38] Commentary: Russell 1992. For the Stoic background to Dio's discussion see Algra 2009: 238–47.

account – quite the reverse (48)! Dio thus deftly clears the field for a comparative evaluation of poetry and visual art as sources of valid conceptions of divinity. Dio imagines Pheidias being challenged by auditors with regard to his statue of Zeus. This scenario alludes to stories that Pheidias had been prosecuted for embezzlement both in Athens and at Elis (the city which ran the Olympic games); but now he is called to account, not for the expenses incurred in making the statue (49), but for representing Zeus in material form and human shape (52). The question whether this was proper is important precisely because of the outstanding qualities of Pheidias' statue: other images of gods have little effect on us, but Pheidias' statue is so powerful as to make it impossible for us to think of Zeus in any other way (53).

In his defence, Pheidias carefully reformulates the point at issue: is his likeness of Zeus the best that is *humanly* possible (56)? He takes for granted the common philosophical conviction that mankind's conception of divinity is evoked primarily by the heavens, whose perfectly regular movements manifest the providential ordering of the universe.[39] But though the heavenly bodies themselves evoke amazement and a sense of purposeful agency, visual representations of them fail to have that effect (58). On the other hand, we cannot do without visual representations altogether, because the heavenly bodies themselves do not satisfy our need for something accessible as the focus of devotion (60–1). No direct visual portrayal of the divine intelligence which the heavens manifest is possible, since mind and intelligence are invisible. But the human body is a vehicle of mind and intelligence with which we are directly familiar. So the human body is the best visible symbol (*sumbolon*) of mind and intelligence – certainly better than the theriomorphic images used by non-Greeks (59).

Pheidias points out that Homer's poetry provides a precedent for anthropomorphic representations of god. If anthropomorphism is a fault, Homer should be called to account first. If, on the other hand, anthropomorphism is acceptable, Pheidias has done it better. Though Homer wrote the passage which inspired Pheidias (62, cf. 25–6), he extended his anthropomorphism too far, attributing to the gods things unworthy of them: 'meetings and deliberations and speeches ... and journeys from Ida to heaven and Olympus, and sleep and parties and sexual intercourse,

---

[39] E.g. Pl. *Crat.* 397c–d; *Laws* 10, 885e–6a, 889b; 12, 966e; [Pl.] *Epin.* 983d–4c; Arist. F10 Rose = 947 Gigon (S.E. *M.* 9.20–2); F12 Rose = F838 Gigon (Cic. *ND* 2.95); Zeno *SVF* 1.165 (Cic. *ND* 1.26); Cleanthes *SVF* 2.528 (Cic. *ND* 2.15).

adorning all this in a very lofty way in his verse, but still adhering to a likeness to mortals'. In fact, Homer even compares Agamemnon, a mortal, to Zeus (*Il.* 2.478), whereas Pheidias' statue is beyond comparison with any actual mortal (62). Pheidias' representation also shows more restraint. There are few limitations on what poetry can represent, since anything can be put into words, and Homer fully exploits that freedom of invention (63–9); but what can be represented in visual art is subject to practical limits (69–72). Homer has shown many fine images of Zeus, but he also portrays Zeus in ways that inspire fear. By contrast, Pheidias' Zeus is peaceful, mild, gentle, majestic, the source of everything good (73–4). According to the basic premises of Socrates' theology, gods are sources only of good, not of harm (*Rep.* 2, 379b–c). Whereas Homer frequently misrepresents the divine, therefore, Pheidias' visual representation is appropriate to a proper understanding of the divine nature. Furthermore, the titles by which Zeus is known (such as king and father), all of them indicating his goodness, are expressed by the statue as well as is possible without the use of words (75–8). What Pheidias could not do in a statue was to show Zeus using lightning and storms as signs of war (cf. *Il.* 10.5–8, 17.547–9, 4.75–7), or actually sending strife (*Il.* 11.3–4) – all things that Homer does. But even if he could have done this, Pheidias would have refrained (78–9). Homer chose to portray Zeus in a way that is inconsistent with a true theology; Pheidias' statue is a worthier image of the god, because he has not done this.

In the early third century AD, Philostratus took up the issue of Egyptian theriomorphic gods in his fictionalised account of Apollonius of Tyana, an itinerant wise man of the first century. In one episode (6.19), Philostratus shows Apollonius in conversation with Egyptian intellectuals, challenging their absurd representations of the gods. He maintains that Greek anthropomorphic images (including Pheidias' Zeus) represent gods more appropriately. The Egyptians, holding on to the concept of painting as imitation, ask satirically whether Greek artists went up to heaven to copy the appearance of the gods. But Apollonius maintains that visual art is not limited to reproducing what the artist has seen: the formation of mental images (*phantasia*) makes it possible for us to conceive and portray unseen reality. Apollonius also maintains that animal forms are inherently incapable of expressing an adequate conception of the gods. The Egyptians dismiss this criticism as superficial. They are not so bold as to represent the divine appearance: rather, they use symbols and hidden meanings, which is more reverent. Philostratus retorts that the use of animal forms makes the divine into an object of contempt. It would be better to worship without any images at all than to use theriomorphic images. The mind can form an image superior to anything that an artist can produce; but if, like the Egyptians, you give people unworthy images, you encourage them to form unworthy mental conceptions of the god.[40]

Maximus of Tyre was a Platonist of the late second century AD. We shall consider his treatment of poetry in the next chapter (§5.2): here we focus on his short discussion of images of the gods (*Or.* 2). He begins by saying that gods are 'helpers to mankind' (1): they are sources of good, and universal in their care for the whole human race. But he immediately notes the diversity of ways in which gods are worshipped by different peoples. He associates nature-worship (for example, taking mountain-peaks as images of Zeus) with the earliest humans, and briefly mentions artistic images, before raising the question whether worship is possible that uses only speech, without any visual image. To answer this question he compares the relation between spoken worship and images to the relation between speech and writing (2). Speech can exist without writing, but the possibility of recording speech in written symbols is useful – for example, as an aid to memory. Images of the gods are also useful symbols: 'the nature of the divine is such that there is no need of statues and dedications; but humanity, being utterly feeble and as far removed from the divine as heaven is from earth, contrived these signs in which to preserve the gods' names and what is said of them.' Some people, with a strong memory, can spontaneously reach out to the heavens with their minds and encounter god; but they are few, and there is no community in which everyone has remembrance of the divine. Just as teachers help children learn to write by providing models to help them remember the letter-shapes, so images of the gods are signs that help us remember.

So we need images. But what form should they take? The Greeks reasonably represent god in human form: it makes sense to represent God as clothed in a body similar to that which clothes the human soul, since 'the human soul is something very close to God and like him' (3).[41] But

---

[40] On *phantasia* see Watson 1994; Platt 2009. In another conversation (2.22) Apollonius suggests that, as well as imitation by hand and mind (as in painting), the existence of chance likenesses (e.g. in cloud formations), where the likeness is recognised but not designed or constructed, shows that imitation may be in the mind alone. A natural imitative faculty is implicated in the recognition, as well as in the production, of visual images (whether artefactual or coincidental), since observers must form an image of the object in their minds.

[41] But even the best anthropomorphic image (e.g. *Il.* 1.528–30, with an implicit reference to Pheidias) falls laughably short of the reality; so what our *phantasia* (n.40) raises us to is not high enough (11.3, from an essay on Plato's theology).

Maximus is critical of some non-Greek representations of god: Persian fire-worship (5), Egyptian animal-gods (5), and Indian worship of snakes (6). Other examples (Celtic, Paeonian, Arab, Cypriot, Lycian, Phrygian, Cappadocian) are listed without comment, except on their diversity (7–9). That allows Maximus to make the point that, underlying this diversity, there is one universally shared feature: all nations have some kind of symbolic representation of god.[42] This supports the conclusion that it is right to use images in worship: humans need them. But there is still an open question about the first two options mentioned: natural images, and images produced by human art. Maximus suggests that, if we were legislating from a blank slate, for people who had just sprung from the earth, it might be appropriate to leave them to their natural images. But since we start with diverse peoples, each with their established practices, it is better to leave the diverse symbols and names of the gods as they are (9). After all, God cannot be named, or spoken of or seen: the divine essence transcends our grasp. We are forced to rely on these proxies, like lovers taking pleasure in things that call their absent partners to mind. So it is pointless to debate the merits of different kinds of image: 'let men know the race of gods – let them only know it! If Greeks are aroused to the memory of God by Pheidias' art, and Egyptians by the honour paid to animals, and a river or fire arouses others, I have no objection to that diversity. Let them only know God, let them only love him, let them remember him!' (10).

The authors reviewed in this section all know that gods do not really look like humans, and acknowledge that anthropomorphic images do not represent gods as they are: they are symbols, rather than likenesses. But symbols may be better or worse. They may be more or less effective in communicating a proper conception of god, and they may be more or less likely to evoke an inappropriate conception. This is where the disagreements lie. For Dio, the human form is an appropriate symbol because it evokes a sense of purposeful agency and intelligence; he and Philostratus are not impressed by symbolic representations in animal form. Even Plutarch admits that Greeks do better when they associate animals *with* gods (like the owl and Athena) rather than representing gods *as* animals (71, 379d). But he is willing to defend the use of animal images, and points out that anthropomorphic representations are also open to misunderstanding. In Plutarch's view, then, animal symbols are better than none. By contrast, Philostratus thinks that such bad symbols are worse

---

[42] Cf. 11.4 for the universal consensus that the gods exist.

than none. Dio, on the other hand, argues that humans cannot do without symbolic images as an aid to worship. Maximus agrees, and thinks that the variation between symbols is too small to make much difference when compared with the absolute gulf between the divine essence and what humans can grasp. No image will be truly adequate to god: what works best for a given set of people depends less on how good the image is in principle, and more on their cultural background.

What about images of the gods in poetry? Plutarch thinks that religious traditions such as those he examines in *Isis and Osiris* are better sources than poetic fictions. Dio provides support for that view by showing that Homer's representations combine things that are symbolically appropriate with things that emphatically are not. What he objects to are the things that Socrates objects to in the *Republic*. It seems clear that Homer needs these elements for narrative effect: an *Iliad* in which gods never caused bad things to happen would lack the variety and excitement which, as Plutarch argues in *How to Read Poetry*, poetry needs. This is why, as Plutarch and the Stoics both believed, poetic representations of the gods have been elaborated in ways that distort the supposedly uncorrupted insights of early humans. Even so, Dio does not close the door on poetry. He accepts that poetic representations of the gods are older than those in visual art, and that poetry is in principle capable of representing the gods in a symbolically appropriate way.

7 FROM PLUTARCH TO PORPHYRY

Porphyry, one of the most important philosophers of the third century AD, studied with Longinus (§5.4) before becoming a student and associate of Plotinus (§5.3). In his *On Images* he endorsed the symbolic interpretation of statues of the gods: they are the product of a theological wisdom that used images (*eikōn*) accessible to sense-perception to declare god and the power of god, 'representing what is invisible in visible forms' (F351 Smith = F1 Bidez). For Porphyry, as for Dio, the human form is an appropriate 'indication' (*deikēlon*) of Zeus as creative intelligence (F354 Smith = 3 Bidez):

He is seated, as a riddling expression of the stability of his power. His upper body is bare, because he is manifested in the intellective and heavenly parts of the cosmos. His feet are shod because he is invisible in the things hidden below. He holds his sceptre in his left hand, the side on which ... the most authoritative and intelligent organ, the heart, resides; for the creative intellect is the king of the cosmos. He holds out in his right hand either an eagle, because he rules over the gods that traverse the air, or victory, because he is himself victorious over everything.

But these statues speak only to those who have learned to read them: to the ignorant, they are as unintelligible as books are to the illiterate (F351). The treatise begins by quoting a line from an Orphic poem (F245 Kern: cf. Pl. *Smp.* 218b): 'I shall speak to those to whom it is lawful: close the doors, profane ones.' This line, or its variant 'I sing to those with understanding ...', seems to have appeared at the beginning of the Derveni theogony (col. 7.9: cf. §4.3). For Porphyry, as for the Derveni commentator, riddles and symbols control access to truths that not everyone can understand.

Like Longinus, Porphyry was a wide-ranging polymath. His works included a collection of *Homeric Problems*, gathering and reassessing material from the whole tradition of problem-and-solution literature. But this contribution to mainstream literary scholarship introduces itself as a preparatory exercise to 'larger' enquiries into Homer (1.22–8 Sodano). The reference must be to interpretations such as that in Porphyry's essay *On the Cave of the Nymphs*, which provides an elaborate symbolic interpretation of the cave on Ithaca described in *Odyssey* 13.102–12.[43] Setting out three ancient uses of cave imagery – as symbol of the material world, or of cosmic powers, or of the intelligible world – Porphyry argues that the darkness, solidity and moistness of Homer's cave is consistent only with the first; and from that premise he goes on to explain the detailed attributes of Homer's cave symbolically. The interpretation owes an acknowledged debt to the second-century Pythagorean Numenius (§4.4) and his pupil Cronius.[44] Having found evidence in the geographer Artemidorus that the cave was real, Porphyry rejects Cronius' assumption that the cave is a Homeric fiction. Since the consecration of caves was an act of religious devotion older than the building of temples, and caves were chosen because of their multi-layered symbolic meaning, Porphyry thinks it perfectly likely that Homer was accurately describing a real cave, and that the symbolic meanings are those of the people who originally consecrated the cave to the nymphs. Yet he is also willing to entertain the possibility that Homer added details of his own to the description, without any sense that this would diminish the significance of the symbolic interpretation. Cronius and Poprhyry would agree, therefore, that if Homer did contribute any inventions or additions, these were not designed for merely poetic effect: if the description of the cave is fictitious, in whole or part, Homer

---

[43] Porphyry and Homer: Lamberton 1986: 108–29; 1992; Pépin 1965.
[44] Numenius: Lamberton 1986: 54–77; cf. n.32 above.

himself intended the fiction to serve as a symbolic vehicle for theological truths. The extent to which the symbols are owed to Homer, or to a religious dedication more ancient than Homer, is therefore secondary. The point of primary importance to Porphyry is that the cave as Homer describes it is a symbolic expression of truth.

In his conclusion Porphyry rejects the charge that this kind of interpretation is 'forced': 'when one considers ancient wisdom and the extent of Homer's intelligence and his perfection in every virtue, one should not discount the possibility that in the form of mythical fiction he gave riddling images of matters divine' (36). 'Forced' is the very word which Plutarch applied to allegorical interpretation of Homer (4, 19f). For Plutarch, Homer is on the poetic side of the distinction between religious tradition and poetic myth; for Porphyry, he is on the religious side. A fragment of his work on the river Styx makes it even clearer that Porphyry saw Homer as communicating theological truths (F372 Smith):

The poet's thought is not, as one might suppose, easy to grasp. All the ancients communicated matters concerning the gods and *daimones* by means of riddles, but Homer concealed these matters even more by not making them the principal subject of his discourse, while appropriating what he says to the presentation of other things.

Hesiod's *Theogony*, the poems attributed to Orpheus, and the works of philosophical poets like Parmenides are openly cosmological and theological. Their discourse may need careful decoding, but it is at least clear that it is a discourse about gods. In Homer's case, that is not obvious: he communicates theology through discourse that is, on the surface, concerned with other things. There are therefore two layers of concealment: it is necessary to recognise the latently theological nature of Homer's poetry before one can begin to extract the latent meaning of its riddles.[45]

Homer is now viewed, not as an inventor of entertaining, though shocking, fictions about the gods, but as a theological poet – in fact, the most profound theological poet of them all. Since the deepest truths of philosophy are theological truths (a point on which Porphyry and Plutarch agree), it follows that Homer is also a profound philosopher. Porphyry's lost history of philosophy included Homer and Hesiod (F201–2, F204), and he wrote a treatise *On the Philosophy of Homer* (T371). In this he

---

[45] Porphyry goes on to underline the difficulty of grasping Homer's thought by criticising Cronius: though he is the most successful interpreter of Homer's hidden meanings, he has often imported his own opinions into the Homeric text. Porphyry himself composed a poem on the Sacred Marriage which conveyed theological meaning in veiled form – impenetrably so to at least one of those who heard it (Porph. *VP* 15.1–6): cf. §5.3 n.38.

was not alone. His teacher Longinus wrote a work *Whether Homer is a Philosopher* (*Suda* Λ645); since it has not survived, its conclusions are a matter for conjecture – though there are grounds for conjecturing that he would answer in the affirmative (§5.4). There is no doubt about the position on Homer's philosophy and related topics defended in extant works by Maximus of Tyre: as we shall see (§5.2), he regards Homer and Plato as differing in antiquity and in literary form, rather than in their substantive philosophical outlook. Similarly, a sixth-century introduction to Platonic philosophy, listing philosophical schools before Plato, begins with the 'poetic' school, of which the leaders were Orpheus, Homer, Musaeus and Hesiod (*Anon. prol.* 7.2–6 Westerink). That seems to be a long way from Plato's Homer. But Porphyry and the many other later Platonists who took this view thought that they were in agreement with Plato on this point. Moving Homer across the barrier between poetic and religious myth might be a small step: but it ought, surely, to be a hard step for Platonists to take. How could it be reconciled with a professed allegiance to Plato? That question will concern us in the next chapter.

CHAPTER FIVE

The marriage of Homer and Plato

It is tempting to speak of a later Platonist reconciliation of Homer and Plato. But from their point of view, this description would miss the point. According to them, Homer and Plato have no need of reconciliation, since they were never seriously estranged. Perhaps, then, marriage provides a more appropriate symbolic image of their relationship. As Homer says, 'there is nothing better or finer than this, when husband and wife keep house, the two of one mind in their thinking' (*Od.* 6.182–4). The question which this chapter addresses is not whether the later Platonists were right to believe that Homer and Plato were of one mind, nor whether the interpretative approach to Plato that sustained this conclusion was correct. The aim is to understand how the later Platonist consensus, paradoxical though it may seem, was a reasonable one, relative to its own premises. There is not space to follow in detail the development of the tradition from Porphyry (§4.7) to Syrianus and his pupils Hermias and Proclus in the fifth century AD.[1] I have therefore chosen to focus on three case studies from the late second and third centuries, illustrating different ways in which these ideas could be applied at the transition between what modern scholarship terms Middle Platonism and Neoplatonism.[2] But first, I survey some of the resources available to later Platonists when they attempted to demonstrate that Homer and Plato were of one mind.

I PLATONIC RESOURCES

Plato himself provided an opening by saying apparently positive and respectful things about poets. In the *Apology*, after the jury has returned its

---

[1] I give some illustrative references to Proclus. See further Sheppard 1980; Lamberton 1986: 162–232 and 1992; Kuisma 1996; Rangos 1999.

[2] Brittain 2008 is an excellent short introduction to the evolution of the Platonist tradition. Middle Platonism: Dillon 1977. Neoplatonism (i.e. developments under Plotinus' influence): Remes 2008.

death sentence, Socrates looks forward to conversations with Homer and other ancient poets (Orpheus, Musaeus and Hesiod) in the underworld (41a). In the *Ion*, when talking to a rhapsode, Socrates declares himself envious of a man who devotes himself to the works of Homer and needs to understand all Homer's thoughts (530b). About to embark on a myth which he maintains is a truthful account, Socrates invokes the support of something Homer says (*Grg.* 523a). Elsewhere he introduces illustrative or corroborative citations from Homer (e.g. *Phd.* 94d–e), or from Pindar 'and other divine poets' (*Meno* 81a–c), into his conversation. According to the Athenian Stranger in *Laws*, Homer and Hesiod are admired by older men – that is, by those whose mature judgement is to be trusted (2, 658a–9c). In *Symposium*, Socrates reports the wise priestess Diotima, who taught him the true nature of love, as saying that Homer and Hesiod have earned immortal fame for their wisdom and virtue (209c–d); she has already declared that poets (among others) are begetters of wisdom and the rest of virtue (208e–9a).

How might we explain remarks which seem so far removed from the harsh criticism of these poets in the *Republic*? There are various possible answers.[3] One is that, though positive and respectful things are said about poets in these passages, it is not Plato who says them. Since Plato never speaks in his own voice, he is never committed to what is said by the characters in his dialogues (§2.1). Perhaps he uses the dialogues to explore ideas or stimulate thought. On this view, the passages just mentioned offer us one way of thinking about poetry, while the *Republic* shows us another possibility; it is our responsibility to consider which view is nearer to the truth. Socrates' explicit invitation to defences of imitative poetry (*Rep.* 10, 607b–e) suggests that the questions raised by the critique are not presented as being closed.

A second possibility is that what is said in these passages only *seems* to be positive and respectful. Socrates had a reputation for hiding his own opinions, so that he can trip people up by questioning them; he pretends to be ignorant; he toys with people and is not serious (*Rep.* 1, 336e–7a; *Grg.* 489d–e; *Smp.* 216e; Xen. *Mem.* 4.4.9). Perhaps, then, Plato (or Plato's Socrates) is being ironical. Consider his claim to envy the rhapsode Ion: the first enviable thing mentioned is the smart clothes the rhapsode wears in performance (*Ion* 530b: cf. *Hi. Maj.* 291a–b). Can Socrates be serious?

---

[3] I stress 'possible': in what follows I express no opinion on how – or whether – the Platonic material introduced in this chapter should be integrated with the critique in the *Republic*. See Chapter 2 n.3.

Or is he making fun of Ion? Ion, pompous and not very bright, is an ideal target for such treatment. On the other hand, contextual cues to irony are harder to find when Diotima says that Homer, Hesiod and other good poets are enviable for the 'offspring' that have earned them undying fame (*Smp.* 209d). Unlike Socrates, Diotima is not a notorious ironist.

A third possibility is that Plato changed his mind about poetry over the course of his career. Consider the passage from *Symposium*: Diotima says that poets are envied for the offspring of their wisdom and virtue, as are great legislators like Lycurgus and Solon (209d). This does not mean that the poets' achievements are equal to those of legislators: she has already said that running cities is the greatest wisdom (209a). Even so, poets and statesmen are associated in a positive way. By contrast, in *Republic* part of Socrates' argument against the poets' claims to wisdom is that they only create imitations: unlike statesmen and legislators, they have no real achievements of their own (10, 599c–d). This, it has been suggested, is a deliberate correction of what was said in *Symposium*.[4] It is even possible to conjecture an explanation for Plato's change of mind. Accounts of the development of his thought generally argue that Plato's earliest work presents a unitary psychology; the tripartite soul makes it first appearances relatively late, in *Republic* 4 (§2.5) and *Phaedrus*. Perhaps, once Plato had started to develop his psychological theories along these lines, it prompted a re-assessment of poetry, and he only then realised how serious and deep a threat imitative poetry posed.

The later Platonists did not look for development in Plato's thinking. They took a unitarian approach to his writings, convinced that the whole body of Platonic texts (including some that modern scholars do not regard as authentic) was informed by a single, consistent philosophical position. They also read Platonic texts doctrinally: that is, they thought that Plato had positive doctrines to convey, and that authority figures in the dialogues, like Socrates or the Athenian Stranger, spoke on his behalf. But they were not unintelligent or careless readers. They could see that different dialogues had different interests and different approaches. No single dialogue says everything there is to be said; each offers a distinct angle on part of the truth. Some dialogues are aporetic: Socrates tackles (for example) an ethical question without reaching any stable conclusion. Though such dialogues may implicitly point towards a solution, they do not explicitly advance any positive doctrine; readers are left to reflect on

---

[4] Asmis 1992: 354–5. Janaway 1995: 78 points out the verbal echo of *Smp.* 212a4–5 in *Rep.* 10, 600e5–6.

the implications themselves. The later Platonists could see, too, that Plato often communicates obliquely – for example, using images (such as the Sun, Line and Cave in *Republic* 6–7) and myths. So Plato's meaning is not always evident at a superficial level: we may have to look beneath the surface to see what he is hinting at. And they did not overlook the fact that Plato sometimes appears to say different things in different places about the same subject. Since they started from unitarian premises, and understood that Plato sometimes communicates indirectly, they were inclined to take these apparent contradictions as a stimulus to look beneath the surface to discover the consistent set of claims that he is guiding us towards. In a sense, modern interpreters who appeal to irony are following the same strategy: they, too, aim to achieve a consistent interpretation by looking beneath the surface of what Plato says. Taking Socrates' criticisms at face value, they discount the surface meaning of seemingly positive statements about poetry by interpreting them ironically. By contrast, the later Platonists took these positive statements at face value, and concluded that it is the apparently hostile passages whose meaning does not lie on the surface.

The later Platonists, then, were looking for consistency in Plato. If Plato is willing to praise Homer, his criticisms cannot be taken at face value. They also looked for consistency in Homer. Homer says things that seem to give a bad (and therefore false) impression of the gods: for example, he shows the gods fighting each other. On the other hand, he also describes the gods as living a life of uninterrupted bliss. If that is what Homer really believes about the gods, the stories about gods fighting cannot be taken at face value. If we make each of these authors consistent with himself, the later Platonists maintain, we will find that they are also consistent with each other.[5]

The fundamental problem with imitative poetry identified in *Republic* 10 is that the poets, including and especially Homer, are ignorant of the truth (§2.7). But does ignorance necessarily discredit them? Socrates famously insisted on his own ignorance.[6] In the *Apology*, he explains that a friend had asked the Delphic oracle whether there was anyone wiser than Socrates (20e–21a); since he did not count himself wise he was puzzled by the oracle's answer, that there was no one wiser than him. In order to discover what the god meant, he made it his business to question people

---

[5] Consistency: Proclus *in Remp.* 1.70.1–71.2 (Plato), 87.4–28 (Homer, quoting *Od.* 6.46), 155.1–25 (quoting *Phd.* 95a to show that Plato places self-contradiction and disagreement with Homer on the same level).

[6] Socratic ignorance: Bett 2011.

with a reputation for wisdom, such as politicians (21b–22a) and poets (22a–c). These people proved unable to explain or justify the things they said; they were not really wise, though they thought they were. Socrates lays no claim to superiority in wisdom over the victims of his interrogations, except in this respect: he does not think he knows what he does not know (23a–b).

The poets whose interrogation is reported in the *Apology* had a reputation for wisdom because of the fine things they said. The discovery that they do not understand their fine sayings does not make the things they say less fine: it only makes us wonder how these people manage to say them. The conclusion Socrates claims to have reached is that poets are like inspired prophets and oracle-singers: they, too, can say 'many fine things' about subjects of which they have no knowledge (22b–c).

The idea that poets are inspired has deep roots in Greek tradition (§1.1). Hesiod claims that the Muses met him and taught him to sing; Homer invokes the Muses at the start of both the *Iliad* and the *Odyssey*, and before the Catalogue of Ships he appeals to them for information about things of which reliable knowledge is not otherwise available (*Il.* 2.484–92). But there is no suggestion in such passages that the inspired poet is in a state of possession or frenzy, is not in his right mind, or is indeed mad, which is the picture that Plato paints. In the *Ion*, when Socrates proposes that poets are possessed, inspired and not in their right minds (533d–5a), Ion – a rhapsode – raises no objection (535a); but he is decidedly uncomfortable when Socrates extends the idea to rhapsodes (535e–6d). To Ion, clearly, this does not feel like a flattering description. Perhaps, then, we should read the concept of poetic inspiration ironically.[7]

On the other hand, Ion is not a man with deep philosophical insight: his qualms may simply reflect his limited understanding. In the *Phaedrus*, Socrates appeals to ancient evidence (in the form of an etymology: §4.4) to establish a connection between madness (*mania*) and inspired prophecy (*mantikē*), claiming that madness is the greatest good fortune – provided that it is a divine gift (244a–5c). Philosophy itself arises from a kind of madness, the best of all forms of possession (249d–e). So the description of inspiration as madness is not, as such, disparaging. It is true that inspired poets, though superior to merely technical poets (245a), are on a much lower level than the philosopher. In fact, poets come strikingly low in a ranking of souls in the *Phaedrus* – sixth out of nine (248c–e).

---

[7] Plato on inspiration: Murray 1981; 1995, 235–8; Tigerstedt 1969. Against irony: Büttner 2011. *Ion*: Stern-Gillet 2004.

They rank below philosophers (of course), but also below constitutional monarchs and military leaders; politicians, household managers and businessmen; athletic trainers and doctors; and prophets and practitioners of religious rites. They come just above craftsmen and farmers; sophists and demagogues; and tyrants. So, while inspiration is respectable, inspired poetry is not held in exceptionally high esteem. On the other hand, it is acknowledged that inspired poets have a positive function: by 'adorning' the deeds of the ancients they educate posterity (245a). We may recall the encomia of good men retained in the *Republic*.

If the picture of the inspired poet seems to flicker, that may be because inspiration is an inherently double-edged concept. Its explanation of how people who lack understanding are able to say fine things is also an explanation of why people who say fine things are unable to explain and justify what they have said. Their fine sayings are not the product of their own wisdom, but come from outside them. They are therefore beyond the poets' control. If poets do not have reliable access to a source of wisdom,[8] it is no surprise if the good things in poetry are scattered about among much that is bad (cf. *Laws* 7, 811b). Poetry's content therefore needs to be evaluated. Even if some poets seem sometimes to be inspired, if the good is to be disentangled from the bad, their poetry must be subjected to assessment by people who do have some understanding of the truth: that is, by philosophers.

Plato frequently examines ideas from the poets, and in doing so often exposes poetry's inadequacy as a source of wisdom. Polemarchus quotes Simonides in *Republic* 1, but when Socrates tests the quotation it turns out to be either false, or else a typically poetic riddle (1, 332b–c: see §2.2). Something similar happens in *Lysis* (213e–4d): a poetic quotation is introduced with what seems to be a flattering reference to poets' wisdom ('they are as it were our fathers in wisdom and guides'), but under closer scrutiny it is found to be problematic; Socrates concludes that its proponents are talking in riddles. The fact that poetry often seems to be either wrong or riddling poses a problem, since we cannot ask dead poets what they mean,[9] and we cannot reach agreement on their meaning (*Prt.* 347e; *Hi. Min.* 365c–d). If poetry resists interpretation, the wisdom it supposedly

---

[8] That formulation is importantly different from Hesiod's claim to have access to a source of wisdom that cannot be relied on (§1.1).

[9] Unless one asks them in the underworld: near the end of the *Apology* (41a), Socrates remarks that, if there is an afterlife, he has lots of interesting conversations to look forward to: 'How much would any of you give to meet Orpheus and Musaeus, Hesiod and Homer?' But his intention even then is to examine them to test *whether* they are wise (41b).

contains is of no use to us; we are left to find the truth for ourselves.[10] Discussing poetry is a waste of time: we would do better to leave the poets aside, therefore and investigate the truth for ourselves through discussion (*Prt.* 347c–8a).[11]

But the objection to imitative poetry in *Republic* 10 is not simply that the poets are ignorant. Ignorance is consistent with saying fine things; and Socratic ignorance is a form of wisdom. The ignorance that Plato is concerned with in *Republic* 10 goes deeper. The claim is not that the poets have true opinions about the gods and morality that they cannot explain, but that they have false opinions about the gods and morality. If the poets say 'many fine things' (cf. *Ap.* 22c; *Ion* 534b; *Meno* 99c–d), inspiration might explain how they manage to do so despite their ignorance. But if the things they say are bad, how can they be inspired?

What above all shows that the imitative poets say many bad things is that their narratives misrepresent gods and morality. This argument relies on the premise that Homer is an imitator, a maker of likenesses. If that assumption is granted, then the conclusion is inescapable: the gods are not like that, so Homer's representation of the gods is false. But we have already established that Plato's meaning cannot always be read off the surface of what he says. Suppose, then, that Plato's aim in *Republic* 10 is not to tell us what view we ought to take of poets, but to provoke us into thinking about the issue for ourselves. Plato shows us that if Homer is read as an imitator, he has to be condemned as a bad imitator. It does not follow that Homer has to be condemned as a bad imitator: an alternative conclusion is that he should not be read as an imitator. Perhaps Homer is not producing imitations of the gods, but *symbolic* images (§4.6). Then the question we need to ask is not 'is this image an accurate likeness of the gods?' but 'is there a mediating concept that links this image to the truth about the gods?' In that case, Plato's critique misses the point – or, at least, it will appear to do so if we read him superficially. But it may be that in reading him in this way we are the ones who are missing the point. By confronting us with the shocking consequences of reading Homer as an imitator, Plato aims to jolt us into recognising for ourselves that we must abandon a superficial approach to Homer that prevents us from discovering the deeper truths.

---

[10] Compare Plutarch's recommendation that young people should be taught to introduce truths into their reading of poetry, because it cannot be relied upon to furnish them with truths (§4.1).

[11] That does not mean that the poets can be completely ignored. When Socrates enters into discussion with people whose outlook has already been influenced by poetry, he has to provide philosophically informed correctives to the poets' errors.

It should not seem strange that Homer's meaning does not lie open on the surface of his narrative. When Plato repeatedly tells us that poetry is riddling (*Rep.* 1, 332b and *Lys.* 214d above; cf. *Tht.* 194c; *Phdr.* 252b), he points towards the necessity of reading Homer at a deeper level. True, we have seen that the riddling nature of poetry can be framed as a problem: if we cannot be sure that we have correctly unravelled poetry's riddles, it does not provide us with a reliable source of insight. But this problem is not exclusive to poetry. In the *Phaedrus*, Socrates maintains that written texts in general are unable to defend themselves (275c–6c), and should be treated at best as amusements and reminders for those who already know – learning is only possible in live discussion (276d–8a). Plato's dialogues are not a transparent source of truths. But we should not conclude that reading Plato is a waste of time, and that we would do better to ignore him and investigate the truth for ourselves. Interpreting Plato is not equivalent to thinking philosophically, but nor are they mutually exclusive; interpreting Plato is an aid to thinking philosophically. There is no reason in principle why the same should not apply to the riddling utterances of poets.

Let us suppose that Plato was telling the truth, however obliquely. Even if we think that we understand what Plato meant, we will not have understood the truth we think we have found in Plato until we have understood *why* it is true. But until we have understood that, we cannot be sure that what we have found in Plato is a *truth* – or, therefore, that we have in fact understood what Plato meant. Can we be sure even then? Recall the problem of self-authorisation (§1.2): what grounds do we have for trusting the results of our philosophical thinking, when we know that our thinking is fallible? We have some grounds for reassurance if our attempts to philosophise and our attempts to understand Plato can be brought into agreement: each gives support to the other. This incipient structure of mutually supporting components is extended and strengthened if agreement can be found between Plato and Homer. That procedure may seem methodologically problematic, since it involves finding hidden meanings in each of them: we might worry that this allows too much latitude for accommodating each to the other, and both to our own opinions (this was Porphyry's criticism of Cronius' reading of Homer: §4.7). But the problem is eased to the extent that each of them supplies overt indications of the meaning that is sometimes hidden. For example, the co-existence in Homer of apparently obnoxious theology with explicit acknowledgements of the perfection of divine bliss presents us with a forced choice: either we must look beneath the seemingly objectionable surface of Homer's narratives of the gods, or we must write him off as an entertainer indifferent to consistency and truth. The latter was, as we have seen, an available option in the ancient world. But for later Platonists, the convergence between Plato's positive comments on poetry and the conclusions they drew from reflecting on the latent implications of his critique of Homer gave reason for confidence that they had drawn the right conclusions, and thus encouraged their belief that they were right to read beneath the surface of Homer, too.

It might be thought that the appeal to symbolic meaning is precisely the kind of defence that Plato pre-empted when he commented on allegorical interpretation, making Socrates object that children are unable to see past the surface to the deeper truth (2, 378d–e). But consider what he said just before that: Hesiod's Succession Myth should not be told, even if true, *except* under tightly controlled conditions (2, 378a). That might be read as a hint that, though such stories are unsuitable for educating young people and should be concealed from the masses, they could be revealed in secret to the philosophically enlightened few who could be trusted to understand them correctly.[12] In actual societies, there is no possibility of restricting access in this way. But Plato's comments, here and elsewhere, could be read as leaving open the possibility of an acceptable use of allegory with a restricted audience – and the fact that the allegorical texts have leaked out to a wider audience is no reason why the few should forego the benefit to be gained from them.

The hypothesis, then, is that Plato's aim in confronting us so forcefully with the shocking implications of a superficial reading of Homer is to shock us out of that superficiality. The conclusion we should draw is that Homer's poetry expresses deep philosophical truths in a symbolic mode. This does not necessarily mean that Homer himself had reached insight into those truths by philosophical thinking, or that he could have explained or justified them in the face of a Socratic interrogation. Rather, those truths came to him from outside, through divine inspiration – as, indeed, Plato has told us explicitly elsewhere.

Can we take it seriously when a philosopher appeals to irrational sources of insight? Let us return to Socrates, and remind ourselves how deeply indebted he was to the supernatural. The nature of Socratic wisdom is not the only message conveyed by the story Socrates tells in the *Apology*: it also shows that he was willing to organise his whole way of life on the basis of an oracle – a communication from a divine source

---

[12] See Proclus *in Remp.* 1.80.13–81.21.

that he could not understand when he first received it.[13] Indeed, he did not see at first how it could possibly be true; yet he took the riddle as a guide for the conduct of his life. Later in the *Apology* Socrates explains that he had been the recipient of many other divine promptings ('oracles and dreams', 33c),[14] and habitually also of a prophetic supernatural sign that frequently restrained him from doing anything that would be bad (40a–c). In particular, this supernatural sign (his *daimonion*) prevented him from engaging in politics (31d–e). Socrates speaks of this sign as 'a voice' (*Ap.* 31d; *Phdr.* 242b–c; cf. *Tht.* 151a; *Euthd.* 272e), and says that it is pretty well unique to him (*Rep.* 6, 496c). This sign was a matter of public knowledge, and contributed to the accusation of religious innovation that was brought against him (*Ap.* 31c–d; *Euthphr.* 3b).[15]

The prompting of this sign led Socrates to a philosophical vocation. His commitment to a rational search for understanding is one crucial difference between him and poets, politicians or prophets. But even if one lacks philosophical understanding, it is a good and useful thing to have true opinions and communicate them. In the ideal city, the education of the Auxiliaries is designed to give them true opinions and a good character, and to ensure that these are stable, but they do not come to a rational understanding of them (*Rep.* 6, 503b–d); only a small minority will become Guardians in the strict sense and study philosophy.

Socrates, then, is willing to rely on prophecies, and thinks of his own supernatural sign as prophetic. The Greeks took prophecy seriously. But they knew that some prophets were charlatans, and that it was necessary to exercise judgement to determine which prophecies should be believed (e.g. *Rep.* 2, 364b–c; *Laws* 11, 908d). Judgement was also needed to determine the meaning of a prophecy, even if it came with convincing credentials. It was not obvious that the Delphic oracle's famous advice to the Athenians during the Persian invasion, to trust in the wooden wall (Herodotus 7.170–4), referred to the navy. Socrates realised that the correct interpretation of the oracle's testimony to his wisdom did not lie on the surface. Prophecies, like poetry, are riddling and in need of interpretation. But genuine prophecies, correctly understood, tell you something you could not know otherwise. So why should we not be willing to attach

[13] Consultation of oracles is prescribed at *Rep.* 4, 427b–c; *Laws* 5, 738b–e; 6, 759c–d; 8, 828a–b; 9, 871b–d; 12, 947d.

[14] Dreams: *Crito* 43d–44b; *Phd.* 60d–61b; cf. *Rep.* 9, 571d–2a; *Tim.* 70d–72. See Büttner 2011: 121–5.

[15] Socrates himself maintains that he is a divine gift to Athens: *Ap.* 30e–31b; for his god-given mission cf. *Tht.* 150c–e. Socrates' religion: Bussanich 2006; Long 2006; McPherran 2011.

positive value to inspired poetry that communicates truths in a symbolic, and therefore not transparent, form?

The hypothesis stated above needs further refinement: to say that the truths in inspired poetry come to the poet from outside is not the whole story. In *Republic* 5 we met the 'sightseers', who think that the many beautiful things in the world of their experience are all there is and give no thought to beauty itself (§2.5). This is the common pattern: most people are so absorbed in things they encounter in the embodied world that they give no thought to the Forms. But a few people search for a deeper reality. What is it that motivates their search? And how is it possible for them to recognise the goal of their search? Socrates suggests a solution to the latter problem in the *Meno* by arguing that the soul is immortal: it survives the death of the body, and will be reincarnated in another body (81a–d, 85b–6c). Between the periods of embodiment, our discarnate intellect has direct acquaintance with the reality of Justice, Beauty, Goodness and so forth. That acquaintance with the Forms is not lost when we are born into a new body: truth is still there, latent within us (86b). That truth is not easily retrieved; but when recollection occurs, the fact that we become aware of something that we already (in some sense) know (85c–d) explains our ability to recognise what we were looking for.

This conception of immortality and reincarnation is developed more fully in *Phaedo* (72e–77a) and *Phaedrus* (245c–250c), and is implicit in *Symposium*. In *Phaedrus* and *Symposium* it provides an explanation of the motivation of the search for reality. The experience of embodied beauty is for most people a distraction from the reality of beauty, but for some it acts as a trigger for the recovery of their latent acquaintance with beauty. Embodied beauty provides the impetus to a philosophical search for beauty itself. It is in this sense that Plato can describe philosophy as a kind of madness: philosophical madness is the madness of love (*Phdr.* 249d–e, 265a–b; *Smp.* 201d–2a). But that madness is a divine gift (*Phdr.* 244a). The divine fortune that preserves a few philosophical souls in a corrupt society (*Rep.* 1, 492a) and would be necessary to bring about the establishment of an ideal city (9, 599c); the divine inspiration (*epipnoia*) that might make rulers fall in love with philosophy (6, 499c); the divine allotment (*moira*) that guided Socrates (*Ap.* 33c; *Phd.* 58e), that can produce virtue in unexpected places (*Laws* 1, 642c; *Meno* 99e, 100b) and that can inspire poetry (*Ion* 534c, 535a, 536c–d, 542a) – these are not things at our command. We cannot predict or fully understand their occurrence in one place or another.

What are the implications of this cluster of ideas? First, we have an answer to one question raised by Plato's critique. The basic problem, for Plato, is that imitators are full of ignorant misconceptions. Even if we take them to be creating symbolic images rather than imitations, what reason is there to suppose that they have any knowledge of the truth? Where would that insight come from? If the theory of recollection is right, we all have truth within us already. Retrieving it is not easy: but the possibility of inspiration and of other sources of non-rational insight means that influences coming from outside may help us to an insight that we would not have reached otherwise. We are not wholly dependent on our own resources.

Secondly, when Plato talks about non-rational forms of insight, the insight is non-rational only in the sense that it has not been reached by a process of reasoning and argument. When the insight comes to us, we may have no understanding of it. But the insight is rational, in the sense that it is insight into an intelligible reality. It is our intellect that has become acquainted with that reality when not embodied, and it will be by the exercise of intellect that we achieve understanding of the insight that has come to us by non-rational means. Non-rational insight, like prophecy, gives us access to truths that we could not have reached by our own resources alone, but leaves us with the task of understanding why they are true. Something latent within the rational part of our soul is brought to awareness; reaching a rational understanding of it is a further step.

Thirdly, the theory of recollection postulates a latent potential for knowledge that is not necessarily expressed in actual belief. In this respect, it does the same work as Epicurean and Stoic pre-conceptions (§4.4; cf. Alcin. *Did.* 4.6),[16] though the way in which that latent potential has been acquired makes it plausible to attribute a much richer content to it. Given such a theory, wisdom and insight into the gods and virtue cannot be regarded as the exclusive possession of a sophisticated civilisation or a single cultural tradition. We might be inclined to think of philosophical insight as something that needs an advanced civilisation (as Aristotle does), and perhaps (therefore) as the product of one, or at most a few, highly developed cultural traditions. But if all human beings have been acquainted with the Forms between their embodied lives, and have this memory latent within themselves, then these insights are in principle accessible to people of every period in history and of every nation. Socrates advises Cebes to seek the truth about the immortality of the

---

[16] Recollection and pre-conceptions: Boys-Stones 2005; Brittain 2008: 544–6.

soul among Greeks and non-Greeks alike (*Phd.* 78a). The participants in
the discussion of divine images shared (in varying degrees) a willingness
to treat the thought of non-Greek peoples with respect (§4.6). The concept of recollection confirms that they were right to do, explaining why
the expectation of a single common wisdom to be found across many
different cultures is a reasonable one (cf. §4.4). The diversity of different cultures, like the endemic disagreements among philosophers, shows
that we have deviated from that common heritage. But it may be possible
to recover the primitive universal wisdom by studying the traces it has
left across many different cultures. That, in turn, opens up the possibility
of a further layer of confirmatory convergence. The mutually supportive
structure produced by the agreement of our best attempts to think philosophically with our readings both of Plato and of the ancient wisdom of
our own culture (and where would we look for that, if not in its oldest
and most revered poets?) is strengthened if we can show that it agrees also
with the universal wisdom of humanity.[17]

2 MAXIMUS OF TYRE

The previous section surveyed some Platonic resources from which a positive account of poetry, or at least of Homer, could be developed, but did
not analyse how any one later Platonist exploited those resources. In the
rest of the chapter we move from the abstract to the concrete in a series of
case studies. We begin by returning to Maximus of Tyre (§4.6), to consider his reflections on the relationship between poetry and philosophy
and his diagnosis of the breakdown of that relationship. Though there is
no reason to regard Maximus as an original or creative thinker, that may
be an advantage, if it means that he is representative of this stage of the
Platonist tradition.[18] But there are obstacles, too. Because he is writing
short essays or lectures designed for a non-specialist audience, Maximus
adopts a style that would be accessible and appealing to educated listen-
ers, avoiding philosophical technicalities. This can make it hard to pin
his meaning down. His heavily ornamented prose, full of images and
allusions, does not lend itself to precise statement. Moreover, the short

---

[17] On later Platonism's response to the sceptical argument from disagreement see Boys-Stones
2001: 123–50: the hypothesis that Plato was right is the only hope of overcoming the fragmentation of later philosophy and finding the truth (134); see also 99–122 on the authority of Plato and
primitive wisdom.

[18] See Trapp 1997a: xvi–xxxii, on Maximus as a philosopher, and a Platonist. More generally:
Trapp 1997b, 2007.

essay format means that he approaches topics in an unsystematic way. Synthesising ideas from different essays to discern the underlying coherence of his thought requires some effort.

Is that effort warranted? If Maximus is simply promoting derivative ideas to a non-specialist audience in an attractive but imprecise and unsystematic form, he may be philosophically shallow, and efforts to find underlying coherence in his thought may simply import it. Yet Maximus is not lacking in subtlety. If one were to read his discussion of divine images on a surface level, its repeated references to memory, remembrance and recollection will be understood in terms of ordinary remembering. But philosophically informed readers will realise that a deeper meaning is in play. If those with strong memories 'reach out for heaven with their soul and encounter the divine', then the images which provide the rest of us with 'as it were a guide and path to recollection' (2.2) are doing more than prompting us not to be negligent of our religious duties. The comparison of the use of images in worship to the pleasure that lovers take in things that remind them of their absent partners (2.10) is a clear allusion to Plato's account of recollection in the *Phaedo* (73dc–e: §5.1). We know that Maximus accepted the theory of recollection, which he discusses in *Oration* 10 (see especially 10.3; cf. 21.7–8). The concluding exhortation of his essay on images must therefore be read in the light of this doctrine: 'let men know the race of gods – let them only know it! If Greeks are aroused to the memory of God by Pheidias' art, and Egyptians by the honour paid to animals, and a river or fire arouses others, I have no objection to that diversity. Let them only know God, let them only love him, let them remember him!' (2.10). It is worth noting how in this passage a conception of human knowledge of the divine as recollection is linked both to an acknowledgement of the unity underlying the diversity of human religious practice, and to a tolerant attitude to that diversity.

Maximus is therefore not attributing an outlandish eccentricity to Homer and Plato when he maintains that they communicate on a deeper as well as on a surface level: this is part of his own communicative practice. Moreover, it is a practice which he is able to justify: as we shall see, he attaches significance to the fact that, if we are to understand and value the truth, we must seek it out ourselves. If we encounter what appear to be gaps, loose ends and inconsistencies in Maximus, we should at least consider the possibility that they were put there to make us think.

Poetry is at the centre of three of Maximus' essays: *Oration* 4, on the treatment of the gods in poetry and philosophy; *Oration* 17, on the expulsion of Homer from Plato's *Republic*; and *Oration* 26, on Homer's philosophy.

At the beginning of *Oration* 4, Maximus declares that poetry and philosophy are basically the same thing (4.1):

It is something double in name, but a single thing in reality, differing within itself in the same way that someone might think day is something other than the sun's light falling on the earth, or the sun in its course above the earth something other than day. That is how poetry stands in relation to philosophy. What is poetry if not philosophy, ancient in time, metrical in composition, mythological in thought? What is philosophy, if not poetry, more modern in time, less formal in composition, more lucid in thought?

The headline claim is an overstatement. For one thing, it does not embrace all poetry and all philosophy. For reasons that will become apparent, the poets that Maximus takes seriously are ancient poets – primarily Homer, but also Hesiod and Orpheus (4.2; 17.3). On the philosophical side, he disapproves of Epicureanism (4.4, 8–9; cf. 26.2). That is not surprising. The Epicurean claim that the gods, though they exist, have no interest in or involvement in the world was unacceptable to other schools of philosophy: denying divine providence is tantamount to atheism, even if you admit that gods exist.[19] Maximus ends this essay by denouncing Epicurus' leaderless universe as a genuinely incredible myth; Homer's gods, by contrast, correspond to philosophical conceptions of the divine (4.8–9).

It might seem that Maximus is setting himself up in opposition to Plato when he claims that ancient poetry, including Homer, is philosophy. That is not how Maximus sees it. He is aware that Plato *appears* to attack Homer and other poets, and that many take this appearance at face value. In the first of a series of addresses on the use by Plato's Socrates of erotic desire as an image for the philosophical desire of truth and beauty, he initially gives the impression of endorsing this reading himself (18.5):

What did these clever remarks mean for Socrates, whether riddling or ironical? Let someone answer to us on behalf of Socrates – Plato or Xenophon or Aeschines or someone else who speaks the same language as him. For my part, I am astonished and shocked by the way he expelled Homer's poetry from his wonderful republic and the education of young people, and Homer himself, crowning the poet and anointing him with myrrh, but objecting to the frankness of his verse, because he portrayed Zeus making love with Hera on Ida ... and all the other things in addition to these that Homer spoke in riddles and that Socrates found

---

[19] Stoic theology was unacceptable to Platonists for its materialist identification of God with the corporeal cosmos, but the Stoics did not deny that the universe is a rationally ordered one.

fault with. And yet Socrates himself, the lover of wisdom, conqueror of poverty, enemy of pleasure, and friend of truth, mixed such risky and dangerous stories into his conversations that Homer's riddles seem far removed from criticism by comparison!

It is only when this attack has run its course that Maximus reveals that he has not been speaking in his own voice: 'That is what I think Thrasymachus would have said, or Callicles or Polus, or anyone else hostile to Socrates' philosophy.' He has therefore not committed himself to condemning Socrates' erotic imagery (he goes on to defend it); nor is he committed to the premise that Socrates' attack on Homer is what it appears to be.

In *Oration* 17, where he directly confronts the fact that Plato bans Homer from his ideal city, he is emphatic that the two are not in conflict: 'it is possible both to honour Plato and to admire Homer' (17.3). Maximus recognises that Plato and Homer were widely thought to be at odds with each other, and that the critique in *Republic* was the source of that view. His task is to show why that is the wrong conclusion to draw. He begins with a lengthy introduction illustrating with many examples the principle that different communities have different customs and laws. The customs and laws appropriate to each community depend on local circumstances, so it is not surprising if Plato's state has distinctive customs, adapted to its particular circumstances (17.1–2). This, without being explicit, sets the basic strategy of Maximus' argument: he seeks to drive a wedge between the purely theoretical ideal city of the *Republic* and cities that actually exist, and maintains that Plato's arguments refer exclusively to the ideal city, and do not generalise to real cities. In other cities, Homer (along with other early poets) has a useful function (17.3): poetry is able to enchant and guide young people, because it combines truth with pleasure. But Plato's city is an idealisation, not designed to be realised in practice. Sculptors can produce idealised images of human beings that could not exist in reality. Maximus proposes a thought-experiment: suppose that it were possible to produce ideal living humans by artificial means. Since they are physically perfect, they will not fall ill and will not need doctors. If a doctor were to present himself, the creator of these ideal humans could not sensibly be accused of denigrating the art of medicine if he said that 'they ought to crown the man with wool and anoint him with myrrh before sending him off to others, to gain a reputation where there was a demand for his art because of illness'. The application to the farewell to the versatile imitator – who is clearly Homer – in *Republic* 3 (398a–b) is obvious: it makes no more sense to read it as denigrating Homer.

Though Maximus does not make the point explicitly, one might argue that on his interpretation the marks of honour with which Homer is sent away make better sense: Homer is sent to another city with accreditation, because his poetry will be positively beneficial there.[20] Homer's poetry is of value in that other city because it is both useful and pleasant (17.4). The usefulness resides in the truth it contains, which has an educational influence on young people – it 'guides' them.[21] The pleasure is what 'enchants' them, and makes them receptive to that guidance. This combination of usefulness and pleasure satisfies the requirement that a successful defence of pleasurable poetry should show that it is beneficial as well as enjoyable (*Rep.* 10, 607c–e). But that, Maximus maintains, applies only in actual cities. In Plato's ideal city, Homer's poetry would have no value (17.4–5). It cannot be educationally beneficial in a city whose citizens have had a flawless upbringing and do not need remedial treatment. If Homer were admitted to the ideal city, it would only be because he is enjoyable; but giving priority to pleasure is the first step towards moral degeneration (cf. *Rep.* 10, 607a, and recall how the ideal City of Pigs degenerates when it admits unnecessary luxuries). Where there is no useful function to be served, seeking pleasure for its own sake is dangerous; but when pleasure is instrumental in supporting a genuinely useful function, the combination of usefulness and pleasure is appropriate. In Plato's city, Homer serves no useful function: so the pleasure he gives is also unwanted.

In *Oration* 17, Maximus concentrates on the contrast between the ideal and the actual. In *Orations* 4 and 26, the important contrast is between old and new. *Oration* 4 contrasts ancient times, when souls were uncomplicated and naïve and could be guided by myths as children are guided by stories in the nursery, with modern times, when souls have become shrewder, more questioning, and less willing to take stories seriously. This straightforward opposition fits the context: the oration begins by declaring the identity of poetry and philosophy, and Maximus wants to give a clear image of two ways of doing what we now associate with philosophy – one using the 'riddling' form of myth, the other stripped bare. Yet, realistically, the change from one form to the other must have come about gradually, and a transitional stage is hinted at even in this oration: Plato

---

[20] Cf. Proclus *in Remp.* 1.42.5–10, 47.20–48.26.

[21] By contrast, Proclus insists that Homer is not suitable for the education of young people (e.g. *in Remp.* 1.76.17–77.12, 79.5–80.13, 140.6–16); hence, as Socrates says (*Rep.* 2, 378a), access to some myths should be restricted (see n.12 above). Proclus marks his own discussion of Plato and poetry as something that can legitimately be transmitted from teacher to pupils (as he received it from Syrianus), but is not to be spoken of to outsiders (*in Remp.* 1.205.12–14).

and certain of his predecessors use myths and riddles in their philosophy (4.4–5).[22] They are not poets, but have not gone the whole way in turning philosophy into bare doctrine.

This transitional stage is presented explicitly in *Oration* 26, where Maximus offers another (but complementary) account of the history of poetry and philosophy. If philosophy is defined as 'detailed knowledge of matters divine and human, the source of virtue and fine thoughts and a harmonious way of life and intelligent occupations', then Homer must be a philosopher (26.1). In the past, philosophy offered its guidance in a number of different guises: through religious rites and rituals, myth, the arts (*mousikē*, including poetry), and prophecy (26.2; cf. Pl. *Prt.* 316d–e: §3.3). But in time people's 'wisdom' made them behave 'yobbishly'. Philosophy was stripped of its coverings, left naked, insulted, available to everyone. The result is that the inspired poetry of ancient times is no longer taken seriously: it is regarded as nothing but myths. People enjoy the stories and the poetic style, but treat it as having no more content than instrumental music; no one thinks that it has anything to do with virtue. 'And Homer is exiled from philosophy – Homer, who was the leader of that tribe.'[23] There was, however, a period when Homer's poetry still had some influence, and produced 'noble, genuine and legitimate offspring of philosophy' – above all, Plato (26.3). Plato lived in a transitional period, when Homer's philosophical influence had not been entirely suppressed by modern attitudes, and he was willing to follow his leader. Maximus emphasises that Plato's debt to Homer extends to his thought, not just his literary technique.[24] But he acknowledges that Plato says things that give the impression that he is not following Homer's lead: 'even if he abjures his teacher, I see the characteristic features and recognise the signs … I, for one, would go so far as to say that Plato bears more resemblance to Homer than to Socrates, even if he shuns Homer and runs after Socrates.' Plato is an unruly follower, who puts on a show of rebellion even though he really is in agreement with the leader.[25]

---

[22] Here, and sometimes elsewhere, Trapp 1997a translates *ainigma* ('riddle'), and even *eikōn* ('image'), as 'allegory'. That is potentially misleading: Maximus never uses *allēgoria* or *huponoia*.

[23] Echoing *Rep.* 10, 598d, where Homer is the leader (*hēgemōn*) of *tragedy*. Cf. (less concisely) Proclus *in Remp.* 1.158.12–17, 195.21–6.13: tragedians followed Homer, but only on the lowest (eikastic, i.e. appearance-rendering, imitative) level of poetry.

[24] Plato's philosophical, as well as literary, debt to Homer: Proclus *in Remp.* 1.163.13–172.30.

[25] Compare Longinus (§5.4), who speaks of Plato's emulation of Homer 'showing perhaps too much love of contention and breaking a lance with him, as it were: but the contest for primacy was not without its use' (*Subl.* 13.4).

Plato's philosophy resembles ancient poetic philosophy because of its use of 'riddles' (4.5): that is, it communicates indirectly, rather than making everything plain and explicit. Maximus includes certain earlier thinkers among the transitional figures for the same reason: Pherecydes of Syros, who wrote about the gods in prose (cf. Ar. *Met.* 14.4, 1091b8–10),[26] and the presocratic Heraclitus, whose cryptic and riddling style was notorious. So there are riddles in poetry but also in philosophy – that is, in some older, transitional philosophers. In Plato's case, that is most obviously true of his use of myth; Maximus mentions the myths in *Phaedrus*, *Symposium*, *Phaedo* and *Republic* 10 (4.4; 26.7). But consider also this assessment of the overall strategy of the *Republic* (37.1):

Socrates, conversing in the Peiraeus with men versed in public life, fashions in argument, as if in a play, an image of a good city and constitution, and passes laws and raises children and protectors for his city, entrusting to intellectual and physical training the bodies of his citizens and their souls; providing good teachers in both disciplines, selected, like the leaders of a herd, calling the leaders 'Guardians'. It was as a dream, not as a waking reality (as one of the less cultivated might suppose), that he constituted the city. But this was the manner of ancient philosophy, resembling oracles.

Maximus compares Plato to ancient philosophy in oracular form (prophecy was one of the vehicles of ancient philosophy in 26.32), because the construction of an ideal city is not, as some people imagine, intended to be a blueprint for a realisable political structure: it is a kind of image, not meant literally. As we have seen, in *Oration* 17 a sharp distinction between real societies and the theoretical ideal city of the *Republic* is crucial to the interpretation of Plato's critique of Homer.

Maximus credits Homer with an inspired nature, penetrating intelligence, and very wide-ranging experience (26.4; cf. 26.1); these were the advantages with which he applied himself to philosophy. Though the external form is mythological narrative, the real content of his poetry is theology, politics and ethics. Maximus takes up those three subjects in the latter part of the oration, illustrating Homer's ethical teaching (26.5–6); his treatment of the gods, and its agreement with Plato (26.7–8); and his portrayal of different kinds of community (26.9).

Maximus introduces this survey by inviting us to imagine a philosophically minded painter, who possesses both artistic skill and virtue (26.5):

By his art he preserves a resemblance to the truth in his shapes and colours; by his virtue he produces an imitation of true beauty from the grace of his brushwork.

---

[26] Pherecydes: Granger 2007b.

Think of Homer's poetry in that way, as a twofold phenomenon, as poetry set in the form of myth, but as philosophy organised to promote the pursuit of virtue and knowledge of truth.

This passage illustrates Maximus' view of what is important in Homer's poetry, but the reference to a *resemblance* (*homoiotēs*) to the truth might suggest that he thinks of poetry and painting as forms of imitation. That would raise the question of how he deals with Plato's critique of imitative poetry. Yet, despite its prominence in *Republic* 3 and 10, Maximus never directly addresses the issue of poetic imitation. Indeed, the word 'imitation' occurs only once in his discussions of poetry – at 17.3, where it is applied, not to poetry, but to sculpture (idealised statues of humans). In 26.5, similarly, it is a painter who produces a resemblance; and in 2.3, anthropomorphic images of gods have a human resemblance. Maximus might simply be evading an embarrassing problem. It is more probable, however, that he neglects the issue of poetic imitation because he takes for granted a perspective in which it has ceased to seem important. Artistic skill enables visual artists to produce imitations or likenesses of visible things: what, then, does their virtue contribute? Presumably, it enables them to discern what visible things they should make likenesses of in order to have a beneficial effect on those who view their paintings. That is consistent with painters selecting subjects because they have an appropriate *symbolic* meaning. In poetry, Maximus attaches less importance to the element of imitation or likeness, and places greater emphasis on the symbolic element through his references to the riddling nature of the poet's narrative.[27] He refers to the description of Zeus's nod (*Il.* 1.158), the passage that was thought to lie behind Pheidias' famous statue of Zeus (§4.6), to illustrate Homer's doctrine of divine providence (26.5). In Maximus' essay on the problem of reconciling the existence of evil with a theology in which God is the source only of good, an enthusiastic account of Zeus as beneficent provider reaches a climax with Zeus's nod as the doctrine's symbolic ('riddling') expression (41.2):

Whose mind, irrefragable and unwearying, reaching every part of nature with amazing speed, like the glance of an eye, brings order to everything it touches, just as the sun's rays, falling on the earth, light up every part they reach. What is the manner of this touch, I cannot say; but Homer gives it riddling expression: 'the son of Cronos spoke, and nodded his dark brows' (*Il.* 1.528). At Zeus's nod

---

[27] For Proclus, imitation (the lowest level of poetry: n.23) is incidental (*hōsper parergon*) to Homer (*in Remp.* 1.201.4–8, cf. 195.13–21), whose poetry is predominantly symbolic; since symbolic communication can work through opposites, symbols *qua* symbols are not imitations (198.13–19).

the earth took form, and all the nurslings of the earth, and the sea took form, and all the offspring of the sea, and the air took form, and all that is borne in the air, and the heavens took form, and all that moves in heaven. These are the work of Zeus's nods. Thus far I have no need of an oracle: I believe Homer, place my trust in Plato, and pity Epicurus.

In *Oration* 4 Maximus insists that the contrast between ancient and modern does not necessarily mean that one is better than the other. Consider the difference between ancient and modern medicine (4.2). Since modern medicine has a more varied range of treatments available to it, one might suppose that it is more effective. In fact, Maximus argues, the greater sophistication of modern medicine is a symptom of the decadence of modern life. Ancient medicine was perfectly adequate in dealing with the medical problems that arose when people had a simple and healthy lifestyle. But the varied and decadent modern lifestyle has created more varied and complex medical problems, and medical practice has had to adapt itself to the changes in physical constitution that have resulted from changes in diet and lifestyle (cf. *Rep.* 3, 405c–6a, 407c–8b). So it is not that modern medicine has improved on ancient medicine: each is appropriate to the conditions in its own time. The same applies to dealing with people's souls (4.3).[28] The greater sophistication of later philosophy does not mean that it has improved on ancient thought: it is simply an adaptation to changed conditions.

It is clear, even so, that Maximus believes that things have changed for the worse. Just as medicine changed because it had to deal with the physical effects of a degenerate lifestyle, so the spiritual changes that have forced philosophy to develop are equally deplorable. In ancient times, people were more straightforward, more responsive to the arts, gentler; they could be guided by story-telling (*muthologia*), just as children are guided by the stories their nurses tell them. But modern people are sophisticated, unwilling to take things on trust, unscrupulous. So they examine myths, and refuse to accept 'riddles'. They have stripped philosophy of its adornments, and use plain language (4.3). We have already seen in *Oration* 26 that the 'yobbish' behaviour (26.2) which the unscrupulous and untrusting modern cast of mind incites has had bad effects on philosophy and poetry alike. Poetry is no longer taken seriously: it is regarded as mere entertainment. This, we may reflect, must have had an effect on the way poetry was composed. It would be a mistake to look

---

[28] Therapeutic conceptions of philosophy had long been current in antiquity: Nussbaum, 1994, esp. chapter 1.

for hidden wisdom in the work of poets writing for an audience that demanded entertaining stories and a pleasant style. Maximus therefore has good reason to distinguish Homer and the ancient poets from their later successors. Philosophy, for its part, having been stripped naked is left 'open to insult, common property easily available to everyone and anyone to consort with, a fine pursuit reduced to a bare name, lost among wretched sophistries' (26.2).

Maximus' analysis of the modern misunderstanding and maltreatment of poetry must be borne in mind when reading his account of how poetry works. Poetry is unlikely to work as it should on people who see poetry as philosophically irrelevant entertainment. We must remember, too, that even when poetry did work as it should, its effect was remedial; as we have seen, there is no place for this effect in an ideal city. What Maximus describes, therefore, is how poetry *would* work in its proper environment, not how it *does* work in every case. He is describing the kind of susceptibility to poetry that we must recover if poetry is to have the remedial effect that is the justifying benefit of its presence in any society which lacks a perfect educational regime.

Here, then, is one description of the psychological effect that poetry has in such societies – or would have, if it were properly respected (17.4):

> That is what a poet's words can do when they fall on ears that have been badly brought up: they echo around within them, leaving them no leisure to put their trust in stories bandied about at random, but they are forced to realise that all poetry is riddling, and to interpret the riddles with the grandeur that befits the gods.

You cannot get the poet's words out of your head. They establish a monopoly on your attention,[29] making it impossible for you to pass them over as merely entertaining stories. But the more you think about them, the more you realise that the poetry makes no sense if taken literally. So you are forced to conclude that it must be 'riddling': it hints at something that it does not say. That prompts you to look for a deeper meaning that treats the gods in a proper way.[30] Poetic myths, 'less clear than explicit doctrine, yet more lucid than a riddle', are at once enjoyable, winning our trust, and a challenge to our expectations because of what they seem to say; and that makes us mistrustful. By putting us in that contradictory position myths 'guide the soul to search for truth and to enquire more deeply'

---

[29] Maximus alludes to Pl. *Crito* 54d, where Socrates says that the *Laws'* words echo within him, making him unable to attend to any others, and compares the effect to that of the music which induced an ecstatic state in corybantic ritual.

[30] Cf. Proclus *in Remp.* 1.85.16–26.

(4.6). This is how Homer is able 'to add a suitable grandeur to existing opinions about the gods, and to raise the souls of the populace from lowly imaginings to a sense of awe' (17.4).

Maximus sees numerous advantages in this poetic mode. One is the grandeur it lends to theology. Raising our souls above the 'lowly imaginings' of the masses is only a part of that: it is also, and more fundamentally, a matter of reverence for truths that transcend human understanding (cf. 2.10; 11.11). Philosophy that tries to explain these truths in plain language creates a misleading impression of complete understanding: 'things that, because of human frailty, cannot be seen clearly and distinctly are most fittingly expressed by myth' (4.5). Modern philosophers, Maximus suggests, should be congratulated if they have genuinely achieved deeper insights; but if they have done no more than translate age-old insights into plain words (*muthoi*),[31] it is as if they had revealed the secrets of a mystery religion (4.5).

A related advantage is that the element of concealment confers increased subjective value on the content. It is a psychological fact that what is easily accessible is not valued (4.5; cf. 26.2): we attach more value to something if we have to work for it. That is what myth does: it forces us to look for the truth behind the riddles. Poetic myths attract us, but also puzzle us, and therefore provoke us to search (4.6). If our search is frustrated, that simply increases our desire to find the answer; and when we discover something for ourselves, we feel a genuine commitment to it (4.5).

Thirdly, concealment also allowed the poets to camouflage their designs on the audience's attention. Poetry is philosophy by stealth, and thus avoids the hostility that philosophy tends to excite when it works openly. People react badly to philosophy, because they resent its posture of superior virtue and dislike being lectured openly about their moral shortcomings. When the teaching is clothed in poetic form, they find it easy to listen to and do not realise that they are being taught; so the fact that poetry is teaching virtue escapes notice, and does not provoke resentment. Ancient philosophy used myths and metre in the same way that doctors use pleasant-tasting food to conceal the bitterness of beneficial medicines (4.6).

Poetry's effect therefore depends on our being responsive to its stimulus. If we are not puzzled by the surface meaning, or if our puzzlement

---

[31] The paradox is calculated. Philosophers' inevitably failed attempts to articulate the ineffable in plain words are myths in the pejorative sense: they lack truth and credibility. Poetic myths that convey the truth obliquely, through symbols, are more authentically philosophical. Compare the critique of Epicurean cosmology in § 4.9 (above).

does not make us reflect more deeply, then we gain nothing. We can perhaps imagine people who swallow poetic myths as literal truth: they would be trapped in profound ignorance, like the prisoners in Plato's Cave. But we can also imagine people who regard the literal meaning as obviously absurd, but who are not puzzled or moved to deeper reflection because they are convinced that poetry has nothing to do with philosophy, and has no more to offer than entertaining stories (26.2). In such an environment, only a minority are likely to respond to poetry in the right way – for example, those who are convinced by Platonist arguments to abandon the prevailing outlook of the times.[32]

The philosophy that has made poetry ineffective and displaced it is, in Maximus' eyes, an inferior substitute in every respect except for its being better adapted to 'yobbish' attitudes. But that contextual strength is also the source of its intrinsic faults. It exposes what should be approached with reverence and reticence to public view; it tries to reduce the transcendent to intelligible formulae; it furnishes ready-made answers which, because they are not the fruit of our own search for understanding, are not valued or internalised. Moreover, the attitudes which produced this development and have been reinforced by it are responsible for the fragmentation of philosophy into innumerable warring camps. Philosophy has become a matter of the words and whispered slanders of conflicting sophists – words which no one puts into practice: 'the "Good" that is talked about so much, over which the Greek world has divided and split into hostile factions, is nowhere to be seen' (26.2; cf. 29.7).

Maximus began his essay on the gods in poetry and philosophy by saying that poetry and philosophy are one (4.1): but now philosophy itself has splintered, and is many things. He maintains that the difference in form between poetry and modern philosophy does not imply a difference in philosophical substance: the earlier doctrine about the gods has continued through the later history of philosophy (4.3). There is, indeed, an illusion of substantive disagreement if Homer's mythological way of speaking about the gods is taken literally, but that (Maximus implies) would be absurd – just as it would be absurd if Plato's myths about the gods were taken literally (4.4–5). Yet the fragmented philosophical sects do not speak about the gods with a single voice, so they cannot all have preserved the theology of Homer intact. The Epicureans, admittedly, may

[32] Maximus cannot literally mean that no one in modern times thinks of poetry as philosophy: that is precisely what he thinks himself. It is an exaggerated statement of a true generalisation: most people think this way. Maximus is aware that he is advancing a controversial view of poetry that most of his contemporaries would reject. Cf. Proclus *in Remp.* 1.79.23–6.

be dismissed as a singular aberration: 'Epicurus I exclude from consideration both as a poet and as a philosopher, but all others have adhered to one and the same course' (4.4). Maximus' policy of avoiding overt sectarian controversy means that other philosophies escape direct criticism.[33] But there is no doubt that Plato, who still followed Homer's lead and had not gone all the way along the path to philosophy's later and inferior state, is the one to whom we must return if we are to find our way back to the philosophy he shares with Homer.

3 PLOTINUS

Unlike Maximus, Plotinus does not give focused attention to questions of poetics. But he does have things to say that are relevant to our theme: as well as sporadic allusions to the symbolic meanings that can be found in poetry and (more often) in myth and ritual, and more specific references to the visual arts, he expresses views on aesthetics and the arts in general (though it must be remembered that *tekhnē* embraces all forms of productive expertise, including but not only what we would call 'the arts').[34]

For Plotinus, philosophical enquiry starts with a presumption that some of the 'ancient and blessed philosophers' found the truth. But simply assembling what the ancients said on any subject does not resolve our problems: we have to investigate which of them had the best grasp of truth, and how we too can achieve understanding of the issues (3.7.1). We know, broadly speaking, where the truth is to be found: but we have still to locate it precisely, and come to an appreciation of its truth for ourselves. Plotinus can call on Plato for evidence that the things he is saying 'are not novelties, and have not been said just now, but long ago, though not set out openly, and what we are saying now is an interpretation of those things' (5.1.8.10–14). Since Plotinus goes on to confirm this claim with a survey of philosophers even older than Plato, it is clear that the evidence of antiquity that Plato provides is indirect: if Plato says something, that is evidence that the thought is of even greater antiquity. Plato did not discover new insights, but articulated more clearly insights that were older than him. How much older? Though Plotinus speaks of ancient philosophers, it is clear that he also believes that these insights were already embodied in symbolic ('riddling') form in mystery rituals,

---

[33] Trapp 1997a : xxiii–xxv.
[34] Plotinus' aesthetics: Kuisma 2003. O'Meara 1993 is an accessible general introduction to Plotinus; see also Gerson 1994; 1996.

the pronouncements of their prophets and priests, myths, cult-titles, and religious architecture and iconography.³⁵ We should aim to reach agreement, or at least to avoid conflict, with ancient philosophers (6.4.16.4–7), but oracles and religious practice can also provide support for the conclusions reached by philosophical demonstration (4.7.15). They do not constitute proof, but the convergence has corroborative force.

The 'riddling' form does not set these traditional sources apart from philosophers, down to and including Plato. Plotinus explains the myths of *Phaedrus* (248c) and *Symposium* (180d–e, 203b–c) alongside pictures of Eros and Psyche (6.9.9.20–38). He has a conception of the continuity between early philosophy and its antecedents parallel to what we found in Maximus (§5.2), and gives what is in essence the same explanation of why an oblique mode of exposition is philosophically appropriate (4.8.1). Heraclitus' neglect of clarity was perhaps a deliberate ploy: it forces us to recapitulate for ourselves his own process of search and discovery. Empedocles and the Pythagoreans are also unclear, having expressed themselves in 'riddles'. We might hope to find clarity in Plato, who said 'many fine things' [!] about the soul; but then we discover that he does not say the same thing everywhere, which makes it hard to catch his meaning. When we try to learn something from Plato about our own soul, we are forced into a general enquiry about the soul (4.8.2.1–3). Plato expresses himself in scattered and seemingly inconsistent statements, so as to force us to seek for ourselves the overall understanding that he has withheld. His writings help us towards an understanding of the truths he has grasped, but we must achieve that understanding ourselves: otherwise, it would not be understanding.

We have seen that it was possible to draw a distinction between religious tradition and the poets' elaborations and distortions of myth (§4.4), and also possible to shift the boundary so as to include Homer and other ancient poets among the sources of wisdom (§4.7). Plotinus was certainly familiar with the work of philosophers who took the latter path: Cronius and Numenius were among the authors studied in his seminar (Porph. *Plot.* 14.10–14). But none of the evidence considered so far suggests that he shared their view, and his substantive references to poetry are so infrequent as to raise doubts. When he cites the myth of Prometheus and Pandora (4.3.14) and the Succession Myth

³⁵ E.g. 1.6.6.1–6; 1.6.8.10–12; 3.5.2.14–17; 3.6.19.25–30; 4.3.11.1–8 (Egyptian); 5.1.7.31–7; 5.8.4.25–7; 6.9.11. The argument against atomism at 3.1.3.13–17 presupposes the reality of divination, both technical and by inspiration (cf. 5.3.14.8–13; 5.8.10.39–43); magic is assumed at 4.4.26.1–4; 4.4.40; 4.9.3.5–7 (cf. Porph. *Plot.* 10).

(5.8.12–13; 5.5.3.16–24)[36] he shows a degree of indifference to the details of Hesiod's text that might be taken to show that he is looking beyond particular poetic retellings of the myths to hypothetical authentic original versions.[37] Similarly, when he invokes the *Odyssey* (1.6.8.16–18), he shows more interest in the basic story-pattern of wandering and return than the details of Homer's narrative – though he does attribute symbolic ('riddling') significance to Calypso and Circe. It is perhaps only in his treatment of Homer's lines on Heracles in the underworld (*Od.* 11.601–2) that Plotinus unmistakably reveals an expectation that philosophical insights, or adumbrations of them, may lie beneath the surface of Homer's text (1.1.12.31–2, cf. 4.3.27.7–14).[38]

It would be reasonable to expect such latent insights if artists had direct access to the Forms. Plotinus has often been reported as holding that they do have such direct access – a striking departure from Plato's critique of imitative art. In fact, the passage on which that interpretation is based makes no mention of the Forms (5.8.1.32–8):

> If anyone denigrates the arts because they produce by imitating nature, first one must say that even natural entities are imitations of other things. Then one must realise that they [i.e. the arts] do not straightforwardly imitate what they see, but they have recourse to the *logoi* from which nature is. Then also that they do a great deal by themselves, making additions where something is deficient, since they possess beauty.

The arts, then, do not simply reproduce a perceptible model. However, the *logoi* to which they have recourse instead are not Plato's Forms. They are entities which mediate, epistemologically and ontologically, between the Forms and embodied thoughts and objects.[39] In Plotinus' (controversial) view, the Forms are internal to (and, indeed, are) the second hypostasis, Intellect (5.5). He distinguishes these transcendent *logoi* from the *logoi* that, although they can be thought in abstraction from their embodiments, exist inseparably from the material entities they inform (2.7.3.8–15, cf. 1.8.8.13–16). The *logoi* to which the arts have recourse are therefore not the transcendent Forms themselves but the inseparably

---

[36] 5.8 and 5.5 were originally successive components of a larger anti-gnostic treatise, which Porphyry dismembered into four separate parts (3.8, 5.8, 5.5, 2.9) when he edited the *Enneads*. On Plotinus' interpretation of the Succession Myth see Hadot 1981.

[37] Plotinus does not insist on the details of his own interpretation, though he is confident of a core significance (4.3.14.15–17; cf. 5.5.5.14–6.1 on etymologies).

[38] Plotinus and Homer: Lamberton 1986: 90–107. Plotinus complemented Porphyry as 'at once poet, philosopher and hierophant', on hearing his mystical poem on the Sacred Marriage (Porph. *VP* 15.1–6: §4.7 n.45).

[39] On incarnate thinking and *logoi* see Gerson 1994: 170–84; Remes 2007: 59–91.

embodied intelligible structures of material entities, and their correlates in understanding.

In mediating between the intelligible and the empirical, Plotinus' *logoi* explain the possibility of understanding. Plato secured that possibility through the theory of reincarnation and recollection. Myth, as Plotinus notes, typically translates synchronic structures into a narrative sequence (3.5.9.24–9, in an interpretation of the Eros myth in *Symposium*). Accordingly, Plotinus can be seen as translating Plato's myth-like narrative explanation of embodied human cognition into an analysis of its synchronic structure. He argued (again, controversially) that the soul does not descend into the body completely: 'not even our soul descends in its entirety, but there is something of it in the intelligible world always' (4.8.8.1–3). Thus we are always in contact with the Forms, though we are not always aware of what we grasp through the undescended intellect (cf. 1.4.9–10). If the part of the soul that has descended into the world of sense-perception is thrown into confusion by its embodiment, that prevents awareness of what is contemplated by the part of the soul that remains above: 'for not all that happens to any one part of the soul is known to us until it reaches the whole soul' (4.8.8.3–9; cf. 4.4.17).

Though the *logoi* explain the possibility of understanding, therefore, they do not guarantee it, any more than Plato's discarnate encounter with the Forms guarantees understanding in embodied existence. Plato maintains that most people have an incomplete and distorted understanding of reality, and Plotinus would agree. The *logoi* can be imperfectly realised in understanding, as they can in the embodied entities they inform.[40] Plato maintains that poetry may be, and in practice generally is, composed by (and for) people whose understanding of reality is indeed incomplete and distorted; there is no reason to suppose that Plotinus would disagree. In the context of an argument against 'those who believe the universe and its maker are evil',[41] Plotinus defends artistic imitation against an extremist attack. He does so, not by developing a theory of art, but by alluding to a theory of human cognition in general: once we understand the human cognitive relationship to the intelligible world, we understand why imitation need not be restricted to mere reproduction of appearances. But we can also understand why it often is just that.

---

[40] Cf. 5.9.10.4–6, using lameness as an example of imperfect realisation of *logos* in a material entity. Hence the deficiencies mentioned in 5.8.1.32–8 (above). Even more strikingly, see 2.3.16.27–9 on the degeneration of the human race over time.

[41] The alternative title of 2.9, the concluding part of the treatise against the gnostics (see n.36), in Porph. *Plot.* 24.56–7.

Plotinus, like Plato, believes that a profound moral and intellectual reorientation is needed to escape from our incomplete and distorted understanding of reality. Since what is accessible to the senses is able to redirect our attention towards the intelligible world, the arts can play a role in initiating this reorientation. That can happen when people look at paintings: 'recognising an imitation [*mimēma*] in the perceptible of what lies in understanding, they are as it were thrown into confusion and come to recollection of the truth. This is the experience which gives rise to love' (2.9.16.43–8; cf. Pl. *Phdr.* 251a). But, again, Plotinus' argument is based, not on a theory of art, but on a theory of human cognition in general. The whole of the perceptible world – a beautiful face and the starry heavens above – can raise our thoughts to a reality beyond the senses (2.9.16.48–56; cf. 5.3.9.28–35).

Despite this recognition that the products of art may contribute to our reorientation towards the intelligible world, Plotinus' willingness to defend the arts against denigration by extreme anti-materialists must be balanced against the relatively disparaging way in which he himself speaks of the arts elsewhere. In protreptic contexts, his emphasis is on inner self-cultivation. Odysseus' return to his native land is symbolic of a turning away from material, perceptible beauty towards intelligible reality (1.6.8). In reorienting ourselves, we must look at beautiful 'works' (*erga*): but these are not the products of art – they are the deeds of good men (1.6.9.1–6; cf. 1.6.4–6 on virtue's beauty). We must look within ourselves, and sculpt our inner statue (1.6.9.6–15; cf. 4.7.10). Though not an extreme anti-materialist, Plotinus does not celebrate the materiality of art. The beauty of an artistic product, such as a statue of a god or idealised human being, does not derive from the material object but from the form or shape that was imposed on it by the artist. That beauty was in the sculptor's mind before it was in the stone; and it was in the sculptor, not because he possessed sense-perception and an ability to work on matter, but because in some degree he was in possession of the art. It is therefore in the art that the beauty resides. The beauty in the art is prior and superior to the beauty realised by art in stone; the latter, constrained by the stone's materiality, is derivative and imperfect (5.8.1.1–32). In the same way, the beauty of the beautiful natural objects that the arts imitate is also derivative and imperfect, inferior to the beauty of the intelligible *logos* that informs them (5.8.2).

Artistic imitation is not limited to reproducing the appearance of particular material objects. It can idealise by combining elements from many models (5.8.1.10–11),[42] and can supplement the deficiencies of particular models by drawing on the artist's grasp of their *logoi* (5.8.1.34–8). Nevertheless, the result is inevitably less satisfactory than the antecedent *logos*, since artistic imitation is limited to reproducing externally, in matter. Soul's natural inner activity and spontaneous external effects are always superior to the products of art: 'dim, weak imitations, playthings of little value, employing many contrivances to produce an image [*eidōlon*] of nature' (4.3.10.13–19). External activity is a 'shadow' of inner contemplation, to which humans turn when they are incapable of contemplation; no one who could contemplate true reality would be satisfied with its images (*eidōlon*, 3.8.4.31–47).

Plotinus illustrates his point about artistic recourse to the *logoi* with a familiar example (5.8.1.38–40):

> For example, Pheidias made his Zeus without reference to any perceptible object, but conceived what Zeus would be like if he should wish to be manifest to us in visible form.

That conditional clause has caused less astonishment than, in a Platonist, it ought. Recall Plato's condemnation of poetic accounts of deceptive divine appearances and divine self-transformations (*Rep.* 2, 380d–1e). Plotinus acknowledges the existence of supernatural beings who manifest themselves visibly to humans (5.8.2.11–14; 6.5.12.29–36), but they are lower-level entities, sharply distinguished from any being to which Plotinus would apply the name 'Zeus'. There is nothing that Zeus would be like if he wished to make himself visible. This is not a quibbling objection. Can you imagine what a centaur would look like? You have probably seen centaurs in drawings, paintings or cinematic special effects. But problems arise as soon as you start to think about the centaur as a viable entity. From a physiological point of view, the centaur is a nonsense (how, for example, could human dentition supply the needs of an equine digestive system?). If centaurs are physically impossible, there can be nothing that a centaur would look like. To suppose that it is possible to portray what a centaur would look like if it existed would simply show that you are ignorant of, or do not care about, zoological truth. Similarly, if you suppose that it is possible to portray what Zeus would look like if he chose to make himself visible, then you are demonstrating an equivalent ignorance or

---

[42] Cf. Xen. *Mem.* 3.10.2; Ar. *Pol.* 3.11, 1281b12–15. See also Pl. *Rep.* 4, 487e–8a (imaginary, rather than idealised, objects).

indifference to theological truth – a far more serious error, with profound psychological and ethical consequences.

It is understandable that Plotinus has expressed himself imprecisely in what is no more than a passing reminder of a familiar, even clichéd, example. Does our knowledge of previous discussions of the example (§4.6) help us to unpack the thought compressed into this allusion? Though he does not mention the anecdote which traces Pheidias' inspiration to Homer, he must have been aware of it.[43] Elsewhere, he is willing to apply verbal descriptions to Zeus, such as 'king', 'leader' (cf. Pl. *Phdr.* 246e) and 'father' (4.3.12.8–9; 3.5.8.6–14; 4.4.9.1–6; 5.5.3.6–24). This suggests the possibility that, as in Dio, the relationship of the statue to the god is understood symbolically. When Plotinus speaks of Zeus making himself visible, he tacitly presupposes that the gods' epithets provide the mediating concepts which determine the nature of the visual image. The inner *logos* that is our understanding of the god's intelligible nature is translated into a material representation with the aid of the externalised *logos* that gives expression to that understanding.[44]

Plotinus contrasts imitative arts (painting, sculpture, dance, mime), which produce likenesses of perceptible models in matter, with arts such as music, which is akin to mathematics in its engagement with the intelligible proportions of rhythm and harmony (5.9.11.1–13). But the contrast is not absolute: Plotinus mentions two ways in which the imitative arts stand in a relationship to the intelligible world. First, these imitative practices are included in the intelligible *logos* of being human, insofar as they are natural human activities (5.9.11.6; cf. 5.9.14.18–19). Secondly, but more cryptically, they may proceed from the proportion (*summetria*) of (individual?) living things to that of living things in general, and as such 'it would be a part of the capacity that considers and contemplates proportion universally in the intelligible world' (5.9.11.7–10). The artist's recourse to intelligible *logoi* to supplement or correct the deficiencies of individual perceptible models may illustrate the movement from particular to

---

[43] Proclus *in Tim.* 1.265.18–22 does make the connection (on *Tim.* 28a–b): 'For example, Pheidias, who made the statue of Zeus, did not look to any generated being, but managed to reach the conception of Zeus in Homer. If he could have extended his reach to the intellective [*noeros*] god himself, clearly he would have made his work more beautiful.' In Proclus' bewilderingly complex theology, the universal demiurge is the intellective Zeus, but there is another Zeus at each of two lower levels. See Opsomer 2003.

[44] Plotinus' ideal, however, would be for symbols not to be mediated by discursive expression: see 5.8.6, on Egyptian ideograms (with Emilsson 2007: 177–9). *Logos* in speech is an imitation (*mimēma*) of *logos* in the soul (cf. Pl. *Rep.* 2, 382b–c: §2.7), as *logos* in the soul is of *logos* in Intellect (1.2.3.27–30); and every imitation is inferior to its model.

universal that Plotinus has in mind. In addition, if (some) visual art is understood as symbolic, intelligible *logos* is also implicated by the element of conceptual mediation. So Plotinus has various resources for a positive account of the relation of visual art to intelligible reality. He also, clearly, acknowledges the relation of music to intelligible reality. When he recognises that music's affinity to mathematics fits it to function as a preparation for philosophy (1.3.1–3), he follows an idea that Plato embraced (*Rep.* 7, 530d–1c), and that persisted in the Platonist tradition (e.g. Alcin. *Did.* 7.4). It is noteworthy, however, that Plotinus' survey omits the literary arts. The one exception is rhetoric, but that is grouped with generalship and kingship: that is, it is not treated as one of 'the arts' (in our sense), but as one of the technical instrumentalities of practical politics, which have a part in the intelligible world to the extent that they impart excellence to actions (5.9.11.21–4). What does that omission imply about Plotinus' views on the differences between the discursive, visual and musical arts? Before addressing this question, it will be helpful to gather comparative material from one of Plotinus' contemporaries.

4 LONGINUS

Cassius Longinus was a third-century philosopher, literary scholar and rhetorician of immense erudition: 'a living library, and a research institute on legs' in the words of Eunapius, who testifies to his continuing high reputation in the fourth century (*VS* 4.1.1–6). He engaged in philosophical dispute with his contemporary Plotinus, contesting in particular the thesis that the Forms are internal to Intellect. Porphyry, who studied with Longinus before joining Plotinus and (after some resistance) accepting his thesis about the Forms, reports that on reading one of Longinus' contributions to this debate Plotinus described him as 'a literary scholar [*philologos*] but not a philosopher [*philosophos*]'. We should not, of course, assume that an opponent's neat (if unoriginal)[45] epigram represents an objective assessment of Longinus' philosophical standing.[46]

We have fragments of Longinus across the whole breadth of his intellectual interests – literary and rhetorical, as well as philosophical. We also

---

[45] Whittaker 1987: 120 (and n.150) has references.
[46] On Longinus' account of the Forms see Frede 1990; Menn 2001 discusses his dispute with Plotinus. Longinus could be criticised for making the Forms analogous to Stoic *lekta* (F18 = Syrianus *in Met.* 105.25–30). But there is nothing abnormal about the presence of Stoic elements in Platonists of this period: Porphyry found latent Stoic and Peripatetic doctrine in Plotinus (*Plot.* 14: cf. Brittain 2008: 539).

have the treatise *On Sublimity*, which used to be attributed to Longinus on the basis of an (admittedly equivocal) manuscript ascription. Since the early nineteenth century, the scholarly consensus has rejected that attribution, primarily on the grounds that the final chapter presupposes political circumstances inconsistent with a third-century date; the early first century is the most widely favoured alternative. I find the arguments against a third-century date entirely unconvincing, and there is much to be said in favour of the attribution to Cassius Longinus. In particular, we know from the fragments that he was interested in sublimity, and that the works of Caecilius (the predecessor whose work on sublimity is criticised in the treatise) were read in his intellectual circle. I therefore think it is reasonable to take Longinus' authorship, not as a certainty, but as the most plausible working hypothesis. In this section, I shall assume that the fragments of Longinus and *On Sublimity* are a single person's work, and read them in a third-century philosophical context. Readers will judge for themselves how fruitful this experiment proves to be.[47]

On Sublimity does not define sublimity, but offers a variety of oblique characterisations (1.3–4): it is 'a certain pinnacle and excellence of discourse'; it is the one thing that secures the pre-eminence and enduring fame of all the greatest writers of poetry and prose; it produces an ecstatic effect, astounding (not merely persuading) the audience, which it irresistibly compels; it is a local rather than a global effect, coming at a single stroke, like lightning. This last point should not mislead us: sublimity does not always depend on Demosthenic thunderbolts: Cicero's inexorably expanding conflagration also achieves it, as does the smooth, silent flow of Plato's grandeur (12.3–13.1). It can be found in Sappho's lyric poetry, too (10.1–3). The diversity of the forms which sublimity takes is one of Longinus' central themes; another is the existence of deviations from true sublimity which (as is often the case with faults) have the same origin as the real thing (3–5). Definition would therefore be of little practical use for anyone without 'a pure understanding and appreciation of true sublimity'. But that is hard to acquire: 'literary judgement is the final fruition of much experience' (6). Longinus' aim in *On Sublimity* is to help his readers develop their critical ability through its richly illustrated analysis of sublimity's five sources. If he succeeds, Longinus will have rectified the complete failure of his predecessor Caecilius to fulfil the most important

---

[47] Defence of a third-century date: Heath 1999. For a more detailed analysis of the treatise's overall argument, with less attention to the philosophical context, see Heath 2012. Background to rhetoric in later Platonism: Heath 2009b.

function of 'technical discourse', which is 'to show the methods by which it can be achieved' (1.1). The professed purpose of the treatise, therefore, is the practical one of helping 'political men' (1.2: in rhetorical theory, this includes anyone who uses skilled discourse to persuade in public contexts) to acquire the requisite judgement so that they can exercise it in their own composition.

How would Plotinus have viewed this project? Two pertinent points emerge from the discussion in the previous section. First, Plotinus acknowledges the value of rhetoric: it has a stake in the intelligible world to the extent that it promotes virtuous action (5.9.11.21–4). There is no conflict with Longinus in this respect: although *On Sublimity* is primarily a contribution to rhetorical technography, it has a substantial ethical strand – and needs one, since the concept of a discursive effect that irresistibly compels the audience raises obvious ethical concerns. (We shall return to this point shortly.) Secondly, we have also seen that for Plotinus the turn to external activity and production is in itself evidence of limited capacity for or commitment to contemplation (3.8.4). It does not follow that Longinus' rhetorical interests are condemned. As in Aristotle, while the best human life is one structured round philosophical *theōria*, the political life is a secondary but still genuine expression of human excellence (*NE* 10.7–8). Even so, the turn to rhetoric is a decline from the life of contemplation, and Longinus has settled for a second best.[48] Plotinus' epigram does not simply assess Longinus' philosophical achievement as limited, but also explains its limitations.

Plotinus' belief that spontaneous natural production is superior to deliberated technical production (3.8.4; 4.3.10) is relevant to a debate within contemporary Platonism about Plato's literary artistry. Plato is one of the 'heroes' of *On Sublimity* (4.4), a supremely great writer, though one who often falls into error (4.6; 29.1; 32.8; 35.1–2; 36.2). More precisely, he often falls into error *because* he is a supremely great writer: sublimity is inherently risky, and Longinus argues at length that great achievement with its attendant lapses is superior to risk-free mediocrity (33.1–36.4). In the fragments, too, we find admiring comment on Plato's style alongside a willingness to recognise lapses in judgement. A particularly noteworthy example of admiration is the analysis of the opening sentence of *Timaeus*, which shows how variation in the syntax, vocabulary and imagery of its three cola achieves sublimity (F24 Patillon-Brisson = Proclus *in Tim.*

---

[48] Plotinus tried to discourage the political interests of his associate Zethus, and praised Rogatianus' withdrawal from public life as an example for philosophers (Porph. *Plot.* 7.17–21, 32–46).

1.14.7–20). This effect depends entirely on figures, diction and composition: there is nothing sublime in the thought. But in this respect the analysis is no different from the discussion of Demosthenes' Marathon Oath in *On Sublimity* (16.2–4). Demosthenes' use of figuration creates a stunning effect of sublimity, but the 'natural', unfigured, formulation has no sublimity; so there is no thought capable of achieving sublimity independently of the way Demosthenes has expressed it. Longinus also comments appreciatively on the techniques which Plato used to achieve stylistic beauty in *Timaeus* 19b (F28 = Proclus *in Tim.* 1.59.10–60.1), and on an elegant lexical variation in *Timaeus* 21a (F33 = 1.86.17–25). On the other hand, Plato's fallibility is recognised when the adaptation of a Homeric idiom in *Timaeus* 19e is described as 'utterly bizarre' (F31 = 1.68.3–12). Since Longinus admired Plato for being the first and best to transfer the weightiness of Homer to prose (F50.9), this fault is a side-effect of the risky aspiration that makes Plato's greatness possible. Longinus, like Maximus, holds that Plato's philosophy, as well as his style, was shaped by his emulation of Homer (*Subl.* 13.4: cf. §5.2 n.25).

In these comments, Longinus takes issue with those Platonists who maintained that Plato's style was spontaneous rather than being the product of artistic care (F28, 1.59.12–14). He argues that Plato's choice of vocabulary was carefully considered, not random. Even if someone should claim that his vocabulary conformed to the standard usage of his day, Plato put a great deal of forethought into the arrangement of his words: this is universally admired, even if some criticise his use of metaphors (cf. *Subl.* 32.7–8). That this success should result from random placement of words is even more improbable than the random motion of Epicurus' atoms producing an ordered universe. To clinch the argument, there is Plato's habitual use of language that is made beautiful so as to charm the listener (1.59.14–31). The philosopher Origen[49] conceded that Plato had taken care to write charmingly in the passage in question, but denied that he was aiming to please and persuade his readers: Plato's style expressed what he felt (F9 Weber = Proclus *in Tim.* 1. 60.1–4). Another fragment of Origen maintains, not only that Plato was not aiming at pleasure, but that the stylistic effect was spontaneous, 'as is fitting for an educated man' (F14 = Proclus *in Tim.* 1.86.25–30). Proclus, who takes the opportunity to quote Plotinus' epigram about Longinus (1.86.24–5), agrees with Iamblichus that preoccupation with style is unworthy of Plato (1.87.6–15). Plotinus' belief

---

[49] Not the Christian theologian, but a Platonist philosopher: he had been a fellow-student of Ammonius Saccas with Plotinus; Longinus had spent time with him (Porph. *Plot.* 3, 20).

that spontaneous natural production is superior to deliberated technical production suggests one reason why some Platonists thought it important to insist that Plato's artistry was spontaneous: technical contrivance would evidence a turn to external activity and production, and therefore a turning away from contemplation.

The theoretical underpinning of Longinus' dissent from this view can be found in the sustained argument developed in *On Sublimity* about the relationship between nature and art. This argument is proximately a defence of his project against a challenge to rhetorical technography (2.1):

Some think that those who reduce such matters to technical precepts are wholly deceived. Greatness, it is said, is innate; it does not come about by teaching, and the one 'art' that produces it is to be born. The works of nature, so they suppose, are rendered utterly feeble when technical discourse has reduced them to skeletons.

The argument that there is no need of art if we aim to compose in accordance with nature is familiar from responses in the rhetorical literature (e.g. Quint. 2.11–13). But Longinus' response has much wider implications. His argument has two strands. First, he maintains the complementarity of art and nature. Some of the sources of sublimity are *largely* endogenous; others are *also* through art (8.1) – none, therefore, are entirely independent of either art or nature. There is no neat division between what is owed to nature and what to art, and the two are always implicated with each other. Art is most perfect when it appears to be natural; nature is most successful when it contains latent art (22.1). Art is able to assess nature's spontaneous products and (if necessary) correct them. This corrective function is especially important in view of the inherent riskiness of sublimity. Since erratic excellence is the product of a great nature, and art produces correctness, art should come to nature's aid: 'their reciprocity would perhaps be perfection' (36.4).

The second strand of Longinus' argument questions his opponents' premise that nature is a fixed endowment ('greatness … is innate … and the one "art" that produces it is to be born'). At the very outset, the question for technography is 'in what manner we might be able to advance our own natures to a certain degree of greatness' (1.1). Even if 'greatness of nature', the most important of the sources of sublimity, 'is more a gift than an acquisition, nevertheless we must train our souls towards great things' (9.1). Longinus' point goes further than a denial that nature is fixed at birth. In the final chapter he stages a discussion with 'one of the philosophers', who poses the question why 'sublime and exceptionally great natures no longer arise, or only rarely' (44.1). The philosopher, at a loss to explain this, falls back on what he himself describes as a 'cliché': great oratory begins and ends with democracy. Freedom and political competition stimulate ambition, and therefore achievement; enslavement stunts spiritual growth (44.2–5). The philosopher shares Longinus' developmentalist view of nature, but his political explanation has a determinist slant incompatible with the conviction that we can and should develop our own natures to achieve sublimity. In reply, Longinus shifts the debate from politics to ethics: 'It is easy, and characteristically human, to find fault with the current state of affairs. But perhaps it is not world peace that is destroying great natures, so much as this unlimited war that holds our desires in its grip' (44.6). In describing imperial autocracy negatively, as a loss of freedom, rather than positively, as a guarantor of peace, the philosopher has fallen into the moral error of focusing on the bad rather than the good which Longinus has criticised in another context (33.3). Moreover, the philosopher's explanation is self-servingly evasive of personal responsibility: making the destruction of great natures an automatic product of political circumstance places it beyond the individual's responsibility. By shifting the focus from world peace to inner strife, Longinus returns the discussion to the issue of individual responsibility. Even if the social environment is unfavourable, achieving greatness is within our power.

The argument of the final chapter therefore reassures us that greatness is, in principle, within our power to achieve. It also, implicitly, offers another kind of reassurance. Longinus distinguishes persuasion, which generally depends on the listener, from sublimity, the effects of which 'exerting irresistible power and force, have the upper hand over every listener' (1.4). Do we, then, have no control over, or responsibility for, the effects that sublimity has on us? Worse: if technography can teach us how to achieve sublimity, does that put the means of irresistible psychological control into the hands of those who might use it manipulatively and amorally? In reality, sublimity is beyond the reach of anyone who would wish to abuse it, since achieving it requires, not merely mastery of technique, but also the ethical development of our nature. Thus Longinus' technography is fundamentally ethical. We cannot achieve the pinnacle of literary excellence without ethical development; striving for that pinnacle – cultivating an appreciation of sublime authors, and imitating them – is a way for us to escape from the moral trap of a corrupt society. Put into practice by 'political men', we might also expect the art of sublimity to exercise a positive force in that society.

Applied to poetry, the implication that sublimity's compelling force cannot be abused has an important bearing on Longinus' discussion of Homer's representation of gods (9.5–10). Longinus approves unreservedly when the divine is presented as 'something truly undefiled and great and pure', as in Homer's description of Poseidon at *Iliad* 13.18–29 or the opening of the creation myth in Genesis – a famous citation, which we should not be surprised to find in an intellectual context that was interested in non-Greek religious thought. Numenius, with whose work Longinus was familiar, cited Genesis 1.2; Porphyry cited Genesis 2.7 in an essay on embryology.[50] Longinus recognises that Homer conveys the greatness of divinity elsewhere (*Il.* 5.770–2); even the images conjured up in the battle of the gods are outstanding (*Il.* 21.388; 20.61–5). Yet these passages, though awe-inspiring, are 'completely irreligious and improper' unless they are interpreted allegorically. Longinus does not say outright that they are to be interpreted allegorically, but an author who did, in fact, compose passages that are 'completely irreligious' could not have satisfied the ethical requirements for achieving sublimity. The implication must therefore be that these passages do have allegorical meaning.[51] That is consistent with a preference for passages in which the sublime effect is achieved without raising theological objections at the surface level: Longinus goes on to acknowledge that Homer does not always sustain his highest level of achievement (9.11–15).

The question of Homer's status is also raised by Socrates' claim in *Timaeus* 19c–e that poets, both ancient and contemporary, share his own inability to give an adequate encomium of the ideal city in action: 'I mean no disrespect to the poetic race, but it is obvious that the imitative tribe will imitate most easily and best what one has been brought up in, and that what is outside each person's upbringing is hard to imitate in action, and even harder in words.' Proclus reports that, while the application to poets contemporary with Plato goes without saying, Longinus and Origen found it problematic that Homer and the ancient poets should be included (Proclus *in Tim.* 1.63.24–9). Longinus was puzzled about the reason Socrates gives for the alleged inability (F30 = 1.66.14–23), since it would apply equally to Critias and Hermocrates, who are called on to fill

[50] Numenius F30 (= Porph. *Cave of the Nymphs* 10); Porph. *Gaur.* 11.1 (48.18 Kalbfleisch).
[51] Tarrant 2007: 75, 227 n.551, suggests that Proclus *in Tim.* 1.129.11–23 derives from Longinus. If this attractive conjecture is correct, Longinus denies that Plato uses a 'riddling' style of communication like Pherecydes – which puts him at odds with (for example) Maximus; but we cannot extrapolate Longinus' Homeric hermeneutics from his view of Plato. He also thinks that allegorical interpretation of Homer can be taken to excess: but that would not commit him to denying that anything in Homer is allegorical.

the gap. If, on the other hand, the problem is that imitators lack knowledge (cf. *Rep.* 10), why should they not apply their imitative capacity in accordance with guidelines supplied by those who do have knowledge (cf. *Rep.* 2, 379a etc)? Origen was unable to see how Homer could fail to be adequate to portraying virtuous action: 'who is more magniloquent than Homer, who when he puts the gods themselves into strife and combat does not fall short of the imitation, but is equal to the nature of the events in the sublimity of his language?' (F10 = Proclus *in Tim.* 1.63.29–64.6). Porphyry defends Homer's inclusion in Socrates' critique: 'Homer is capable of conferring grandeur and sublimity on emotions, and giving imaginative weightiness to actions, but he cannot convey intellectual freedom from passion and activities of a philosophical life' (1.64.7–11); there are inherent limitations on every kind of imitation: painters cannot imitate midday light; the life of an ideal city exceeds the capacity of poets (1.66.29–32). Proclus raises Longinus' point against Porphyry: how are Critias and Hermocrates able to do what Homer cannot? His own solution to the problem (1.64.1–65.3) is that Plato assumes a distinction between inspired and technical poetry (cf. *Phdr.* 245a). The magniloquence and sublimity of inspired poetry is owed to the gods, as in the case of oracles; only poetry that depends on human art lacks the capacity to praise the ideal city: 'Socrates needs an encomiast who displays spontaneous sublimity and has a magniloquence that is unforced and pure.' Socrates' insistence that he means no disrespect to poets shows that he is not rejecting poetry in its entirety (Proclus cites *Laws* 3, 682a for Plato's approval of divinely inspired poetry), but only technical poetry – and even that only when it has been brought up on bad customs and laws.

Longinus, too, can speak of poetic inspiration. In a fragment summing up his critique of the Stoic doctrine of the soul (F20 BP = Eusebius *Praep. Evang.* 15.21) he claims that a materialist account cannot succeed, and in a final gesture extends his attack to Stoic theology. He speaks of poets who 'although they have no accurate knowledge of the gods nevertheless partly from the common conception [*epinoia*] of humankind, partly from the inspiration [*epipnoia*] of the Muses, which by its nature moves them to these things, have spoken of them with more reverence [sc., than the Stoics]'.[52]

---

[52] *On Sublimity* attributes inspiration to oracles (13.2), but otherwise uses the concept only metaphorically – not surprisingly, since he is speaking of orators and modern emulators of the classics (8.4; 13.2–3; 16.2). See Maximus *Or.* 13 for the complementarity of human intellect and divine prophecy.

In arguing for the superiority of authors who achieve greatness but are sometimes faulty to those who are faultless but fail to achieve greatness, Longinus distinguishes between products of nature, admired for their grandeur, and products of art, admired for precision (36.3–4). Humans possess *logos* (rationality and discourse) by nature (36.3). Discursive arts are therefore at their best when the natural capacity for *logos* furnishes greatness, with art playing a corrective and perfecting role – the complementarity which we noted earlier. At the beginning of the treatise sublimity is characterised as 'a certain pinnacle and excellence of *discourse*' (1.3), already implying that it is not to be found in non-discursive arts, but also that it is not to be found in the non-discursive products of nature, either. Our admiration is aroused by great natural phenomena – mighty rivers and the Ocean, the heavenly bodies, volcanic eruptions (35.3–5). But their grandeur is not in itself sublime. They certainly cannot provide one of the markers of sublimity, that 'the soul … is filled with joy and exultation, as if it was itself the source of what it heard' (7.2), and Longinus contrasts the greatness of natural phenomena with greatness in discourse: natural phenomena, however awe-inspiring, are of no benefit to us, while greatness in discourse is inseparable from benefit (36.1). To be sublime, therefore, natural grandeur would have to become the subject of human discourse.

Discourse is a product of human rational nature, and if it achieves greatness is admired (like any product of nature) for its greatness; by contrast, the visual arts are admired on technical grounds, for precision rather than greatness (36.3–4). Maximus, too, distinguishes Pheidias' statues from Homer's poetry: both give pleasure, but while we praise the statues for their art, Homer's poetry is praised for more serious qualities (25.7). This pattern of privileging discursive over visual arts might make sense of the omission of discursive arts from Plotinus' survey (5.9.11.1–13: see §5.3). But Longinus makes a more uncompromising distinction than Plotinus, who does (as we saw) accord a place to the visual arts in human nature, and has ways to connect them with *logos*. It might, indeed, be objected against Longinus' argument that *tekhnē* itself is a product of human rationality: humans are rational, and therefore also technical, by nature.[53] But Longinus could reasonably maintain that *logos*, which is a direct expression of rational nature, has precedence over any derivative manifestation of rational nature.

---

[53] Cf. Plot. 5.9.12.1–2, 14.18–19.

The privileged status of discourse leads Longinus to give it priority over the musical, as well as the visual, arts. The psychological effects of music might seem to have some similarity to the effects of the sublime: melody and rhythm are a natural source of grandeur and emotion (39.1), and instrumental music exercises a compelling force on the audience (39.2). Nevertheless, it gives rise only to 'images [*eidōla*] and bastard imitations [*mimēmata*] of persuasion, not authentic activities of human nature' (39.3). In context, the emphasis on music's psychological force is designed only to highlight the much greater force of melody and rhythm in discourse: sublimity reappears when melody and rhythm are applied to '*logoi* that are natural to humans and to the soul itself, not just the ear' (39.3). Maximus again provides a parallel. Instrumental music provides pleasure, but has 'no meaning, no *logos*, no voice'; *logos* provides solid food, while the instrumental accompaniment is like an aroma – attractive, but not nourishing (22.3). According to Maximus, the respect that is due to music is not given to purely instrumental music, 'entering the soul without *logos* and valued for the pleasure it gives to the ear'. But the passion for this pleasure has led to music being 'bastardised', leaving us (though we do not realise it) with only a false image (*eidōlon*) of music. The simple improvised music of ancient times has turned into this modern bastard, Maximus suggests, because people have been seduced by its appeal to the ear (37.4). The implication is that it was the absence of discursive content that exposed this music, innocent in itself, to corruption. The true music, which is that of the ancient poets – Homer, Hesiod and Orpheus – is, of course, identical to philosophy (1.2). In the light of this contrast, the tendency to treat the inspired poetry of ancient times as having no more content than instrumental music, which Maximus deplores in another context (26.2), is even more shocking than we realised when we first met it (§5.2). Plotinus has a potentially stronger basis for appreciation of the non-verbal dimension of music, since he emphasises its contact with the intelligible world (5.9.11.10–12). Admittedly, it would be possible to value the study of abstract mathematical patterns in music as a preparation for dialectic (1.3.1.21–35, cf. Pl. *Rep.* 7, 522a–b, 530d–1c) while placing little value on audible music (for the contrast see 1.6.3.28–33). But Plotinus is not in fact as dismissive of musical performance as that: he says that a musician who 'sees' melody in the intelligible world cannot help but be stirred when he hears them in perceptible sounds (2.9.16.39–41). Nevertheless, as we saw in our discussion of his views on visual art, Plotinus' interest is primarily in the capacity of the perceptible to initiate our reorientation towards intelligible reality.

In privileging discourse and rationality, Longinus acknowledges what had long been seen as a defining characteristic of humanity. More than that: in distinguishing humans from other animals, rationality makes humans godlike. Assimilation to the divine was identified as the goal of human life by a strong philosophical tradition.[54] Longinus adumbrated this theme at the beginning of the treatise, when he quoted with approval the saying that we resemble the gods in beneficence and truth (1.2): the pairing captures the link between ethical and discursive excellence that we have found to be fundamental to his conception of sublimity. For Longinus, therefore, the striving for the highest level of greatness achievable by human rational nature is also a striving to maximise godlikeness. This, ultimately, is the reason why he values flawed greatness more than mediocre correctness. While the latter never raises us above mere humanity, the former may do so: if it does so only intermittently, the attendant failures are a small price to pay for such a prize. 'What, then', Longinus asks, 'was the vision of those equals of the gods [*isotheoi*] who, aspiring to the greatest things in writing, despised precision in every detail?' (35.2). Adapting an old and much-used image,[55] he compares the role to which humans are assigned by nature to that of spectators (*theatai*) and ambitious athletes competing in a festival – but the festival venue is the whole universe. Hence nature has inspired our souls with an invincible passion for what is great and more divine than ourselves: so much so that even the limits of the universe do not constrain our intellectual vision (*theōria*, 35.2–3). Longinus' answer to his question about those godlike writers is that in rejecting flawlessness they were able to transcend their mortality: 'other things prove that they are human, but sublimity raises them near to the greatness of the mind of god' (36.1).

---

[54] E.g. Pl. *Tht.* 176a–b; *Rep.* 6, 500c–d; *Laws* 4, 716c–d; Arist. *NE* 10.8, 1178b25–7; Cic. *ND* 2.153; *Tusc.* 5.70; Epict. 2.14.11–13; Plut. *de sera* 500c–d; Alcin. *Did.* 28; Plot. 1.2.1–3; Porph. *Sent.* 32 (25.9 Lamberz).

[55] See Heraclides of Pontus F85 Schütrumpf (= F88 Wehrli = Cic. *Tusc.* 5.9); cf. Iamb. *VP* 58. The image lies behind the passage of Aristotle's *Protrepticus* discussed in §3.7.

Bibliography

Abbreviations for ancient authors and their works generally follow the conventions of Liddell and Scott's *Greek Lexicon* and the *Oxford Latin Dictionary*, though I have sometimes modified them to be less cryptic or more transparent to English readers (e.g. *Rep.*, not *R.* or *Resp.*, for *Republic*; *NE*, not *EN*, for *Nicomachean Ethics*; *WD*, not *Op.*, for *Works and Days*).

TEXTS AND TRANSLATIONS

Translations in the text and notes are my own (though I have, of course, been unable to escape the influence of existing versions). Readers will, I hope, want to explore the ancient sources more extensively for themselves: hence the following notes on texts and translations of the authors discussed in the book. The recommendations have been made with a view to maximising accessibility to non-specialist readers, so far as possible; but in some cases, regrettably, there is no genuinely accessible version.

Two useful anthologies of translated extracts are D. A. Russell and M. Winterbottom, *Ancient Literary Criticism* (Oxford University Press, 1972); O. V. Bychkov and A. Sheppard, *Greek and Roman Aesthetics* (Cambridge University Press, 2010).

Alcinous: Text: J. Whittaker, *Alcinoos: Enseignement des doctrines de Platon* (Paris: Belles Lettres, 1990). Translation and commentary: J. Dillon, *Alcinous: The Handbook of Platonism* (Oxford: Clarendon Press, 1993).

Aristotle: References are by book and chapter, with the conventional Bekker page, column and line numbers (printed in the margins of most texts and translations) for precise references. J. Barnes (ed.), *The Complete Works of Aristotle* (Princeton University Press, 1984) is a convenient two-volume translation of the complete works. The edition of the *Poetics* by R. Kassel is reprinted with a commentary in D. W. Lucas, *Aristotle's Poetics* (Oxford: Clarendon Press, 1968). There is a text with translation by S. Halliwell, in Halliwell *et al.* 1995; my own translation of the *Poetics* for Penguin Classics is in Heath 1996. References to fragments use the numbering in V. Rose, *Aristotelis qui ferebantur librorum fragmenta* (Leipzig: Teubner, 1886) and O. Gigon, *Librorum deperditorum fragmenta* (Berlin: de Gruyter, 1987). Fragments of the *Protrepticus* are numbered according to I. Düring, *Der Protreptikos des Aristoteles* (Frankfurt: Klostermann, 1969), with a reference to the passage in Iamblichus' *Protrepticus* (see below) in which the fragment is preserved.

Athenaeus: Text and translation: S. D. Olson. *Athenaeus: The Learned Banqueters* (Cambridge, MA: Harvard University Press, 2006–11).

Cicero: Text and translation of the works cited can be found in H. Rackham, *Cicero: De natura deorum. Academica* (Cambridge, MA: Harvard University Press, 1933). J. E. King, *Tusculan Disputations* (Cambridge, MA: Harvard University Press, 1927); H. Rackham, *De finibus bonorum et malorum* (London: Heinemann, 1914).

Cornutus: References are by chapter, with page and line in C. Lang, *Cornuti theologiae graecae compendium* (Leipzig: Teubner, 1881). No English translation is yet available.

Derveni commentary: Text, translation and commentary: T. Kouremenos, G. M. Parássoglou and K. Tsantsanoglou, *The Derveni Papyrus* (Florence: Olschki, 2006). There is also a text and translation in Betegh 2004.

Dio Chrysostom: Text and translation: J. W. Cohoon, *Dio Chrysostom* (Cambridge, MA: Harvard University Press, 1932–51). The *Olympic Oration* is in vol. II.

Diogenes of Apollonia (see Presocratics): A. Laks, *Diogène d'Apollonie: La dernière cosmologie présocratique* (Presses universitaires de Lille, 1983).

Diogenes Laertius: Text and translation: R. D. Hicks, *Diogenes Laertius: Lives of Eminent Philosophers* (Cambridge, MA: Harvard University Press, 1925).

Epicurus: References to fragments use the numbering in H. Usener, *Epicurea* (Leipzig: Teubner, 1887) and G. Arrighetti, *Opere di Epicuro* (Turin: Einaudi, 1973). Translation: B. Inwood and L. P. Gerson, *The Epicurus Reader: Selected Writings and Testimonia* (Indianapolis: Hackett, 1994).

Gorgias (see Presocratics): Text, translation and commentary on B11: D. M. MacDowell, *Gorgias: Encomium of Helen* (Bristol Classical Press, 1982).

Heraclides of Pontus: Text and translation of the fragments: E. Schütrumpf, P. Stork, J. van Ophuijsen and S. Prince, *Heraclides of Pontus* (New Brunswick, NJ: Transaction, 2008).

Heraclitus (see Presocratics): Text and translation with commentary: Robinson 1987.

Heraclitus (Homeric allegorist): Text and translation: D. A. Russell and D. Konstan, *Heraclitus: Homeric Problems* (Atlanta: Society of Biblical Literature, 2005).

Hesiod: Text and translation: G. Most, *Hesiod I: Theogony, Works and Days, Testimonia* (Cambridge, MA: Harvard University Press, 2006).

Iamblichus: References are by page and line numbers in H. Pistelli, *Iamblichi Protrepticus* (Leipzig: Teubner, 1888). Text and French translation: É. des Places, *Jamblique: Protreptique* (Paris: Les Belles Lettres, 1989)

Longinus: Text and translation by D. A. Russell in Halliwell *et al.* (1995). Text and commentary: D. A. Russell, *'Longinus' On the Sublime* (Oxford University Press, 1964). Text and translation of the fragments: M. Patillon and L. Brisson, *Longin. Fragments. Art Rhétorique. Rufus. Art Rhétorique* (Paris: Les Belles Lettres, 2001).

Maximus of Tyre: Text: M. Trapp, *Maximus Tyrius: Dissertationes* (Stuttgart and Leipzig: Teubner, 1994). Translation: Trapp 1997a.

Numenius: Text and French translation of the fragments: É. des Places, *Numénius: Fragments* (Paris: Les Belles Lettres, 1973).

Parmenides (see Presocratics): Text and translation with commentary: Coxon 2009; Palmer 2009.

Pherecydes: Text, translation and analysis in H. S. Schibli, *Pherekydes of Syros* (Oxford: Clarendon Press, 1990).

Philodemus: Two volumes of the Philodemus Translation Project's edition of Philodemus' aesthetic works have appeared to date: R. Janko, *Philodemus: On Poems Book I* (Oxford University Press, 2000), and *Philodemus: On Poems Books Three and Four* (Oxford University Press, 2011): the edition of the fragments of Aristotle *On Poets* included in the latter is extremely unreliable. Text of *On Poems* Book 5: C. Mangoni, *Filodemo: Il quinto libro della poetica: PHerc. 1425 e 1538* (Napoli: Bibliopolis, 1993); translation by D. Armstrong in Obbink 1995b: 255–69. Only the first part of the edition of Philodemus *On Piety* by D. Obbink has yet appeared (Oxford University Press, 1996). Pending a new edition of *On Rhetoric*, the passage cited is to be found in S. Sudhaus, *Philodemi volumina rhetorica* (Leipzig: Teubner, 1892–6), translated in H. M. Hubbell, 'The *Rhetorica* of Philodemus', *Transactions of the Connecticut Academy of Arts and Sciences* 23 (1920), 243–382.

Philostratus: Text and translation: C. P. Jones, *Philostratus: The Life of Apollonius of Tyana* (Cambridge, MA: Harvard University Press, 2005).

Plato: References use the conventional Stephanus page numbers (printed in the margins of most texts and translations); book numbers are given for *Republic* and *Laws*. J. M. Cooper (ed.), *Plato: Complete Works* (Indianapolis: Hackett, 1997), is recommended as a convenient one-volume translation of the complete works. (Waterfield's translation of the *Republic*, despite some felicitous turns of phrase, blurs crucial detail too often to be satisfactory.) Halliwell 1988 has a text, translation and commentary on *Rep.* 10; Murray 1995 provides a text and commentary on *Ion* and relevant sections of *Republic* 2–3 and 10.

Plotinus: Text and translation: A. H. Armstrong, *Plotinus* (Cambridge, MA: Harvard University Press, 1966–88). Porphyry divided Plotinus' works into six groups of nine treatises (hence *Enneads*): references are by ennead, treatise, chapter and lines.

Plutarch: References are by chapter, with the conventional Stephanus page numbers. Text and translation of all the works cited here can be found in the Loeb Classical Library edition of the *Moralia* (Cambridge, MA: Harvard University Press, 1927–76). *How to Read Poetry* is in vol. I (F. C. Babbitt); *On Isis and Osiris* in vol. v (F. C. Babbitt); the anti-Epicurean *Non posse suaviter* ('Living a pleasant life in conformity with Epicurus is not possible') is in vol. xiv (B. Einarson and P. H. De Lacy); the fragments are in vol. xv (F. H. Sandbach). Text and commentary on *How to Read Poetry*: Hunter and Russell 2011. Text, translation and commentary of *On Isis and Osiris*: Griffiths 1970.

Porphyry: Fragments are cited from A. Smith, *Porphyrii philosophi fragmenta* (Stuttgart: Teubner, 1993). For fragments of *On Images* see also J. Bidez, *Vie de Porphyre, le philosophe néo-platonicien: Avec les fragments des traités Περὶ ἀγαλμάτων et De regressu animae* (Université de Gand, 1913). Text and translation of *On the Cave of the Nymphs*: Seminar Classics 609, *Porphyry: The Cave of the Nymphs in the Odyssey* (Buffalo, NY: State University of New York, Department of Classics, 1969): translation: R. Lamberton, *Porphyry: On the Cave of the Nymphs* (Barrytown, NY: Station Hill Press, 1983). The first book of the *Homeric Questions* has been edited by A. R. Sodano, *Porphyrii quaestionum homericarum liber I* (Naples: Giannini, 1970), and translated by R. R. Schlunk, *Porphyry: The Homeric Questions* (New York, 1993). The rest of the work is preserved only in fragments scattered through the Homeric scholia: text and translation of those related to the *Iliad* in J. A. MacPhail, *Porphyry's Homeric Questions on the Iliad* (Berlin: de Gruyter, 2011). *Life of Plotinus*: text and translation in vol. I of Armstrong's edition of Plotinus.

Presocratics: References to Diogenes of Apollonia, Gorgias, Heraclitus, Parmenides and Xenophanes use the numbering in H. Diels and W. Kranz, *Die Fragmente der Vorsokratiker* (6th edition, Berlin: Weidmann, 1951–2): the numbers for testimonia and fragments are distinguished by the prefix A and B respectively. Translations with commentary: R. D. McKirahan, *Philosophy before Socrates: An Introduction with Texts and Commentary* (Indianapolis: Hackett, 1994). See also under individual authors.

Proclus: The commentary on the *Republic* is cited by volume, page and line in W. Kroll, *Procli diadochi in Platonis Rem publicam commentarii* (Leipzig: Teubner, 1899–1901). French translation: A. J. Festugière, *Proclus: Commentaire sur la République* (Paris: Vrin, 1970). The commentary on the *Timaeus* is cited by volume, page and line of E. Diehl, *Procli diadochi in Platonis Timaeum commentaria* (Leipzig: Teubner, 1903–6). A multi-volume English translation is in progress: Tarrant 2007 was the first instalment.

Sextus Empiricus: Text and translation: R. G. Bury (Cambridge, MA: Harvard University Press, 1933–49, revised 1953–9). Translation and commentary on *Against the Grammarians*: Blank 1998.

Xenophanes (see Presocratics): Text and translation with commentary: Lesher 1992.

SECONDARY LITERATURE

Ahbel-Rappe, S. and Kamtekar, R. (eds.) (2006) *A Companion to Socrates.* London: Blackwell.

Algra, K. (2009) 'Stoic philosophical theology and Graeco-Roman religion', in R. Salles (ed.), *God and Cosmos in Stoicism*, Oxford University Press, 224–51.

Allen, J. (2005) 'The Stoics on the origin of language and the foundations of etymology', in Frede and Inwood 2005: 14–35.

Anagnostopoulos, G. (ed.) (2009) *A Companion to Aristotle.* Oxford: Wiley-Blackwell.

Andersen, Ø. and Haarberg, J. (eds.) (2001) *Making Sense of Aristotle: Essays in Poetics.* London: Duckworth.

Asmis, E. (1991) 'Philodemus' poetic theory and *On the Good King According to Homer*', *Classical Antiquity* 10: 1–45.

  (1992) 'Plato on poetic creativity', in Kraut 1992: 338–64.

  (1993) 'Epicurean poetics', *Proceedings of the Boston Area Colloquium in Ancient Philosophy* 7: 63–93; revised in Obbink 1995b: 15–34; reprinted in Laird 2006: 237–66.

  (1995) 'Philodemus on censorship, moral utility, and formalism in poetry', in Obbink 1995b: 148–77.

Barber, E. J. W. (1992) 'The *peplos* of Athena', in J. Neils (ed.), *Goddess and Polis: The Panathenaic Festival in Ancient Athens*, Princeton University Press, 103–17.

Barnes, J. (1995a) *The Toils of Scepticism.* Oxford University Press.

Barnes, J. (ed.) (1995b) *The Cambridge Companion to Aristotle.* Cambridge University Press.

Barney, R. (2001) *Names and Nature in Plato's Cratylus.* London: Routledge.

Baxter, T. M. S. (1992) *The Cratylus: Plato's Critique of Naming.* Leiden: Brill.

Belfiore, E. (1983) 'Plato's greatest accusation against poetry', *Canadian Journal of Philosophy* Suppl. 9: 39–62.

  (1984) 'A theory of imitation in Plato's *Republic*', *Transactions of the American Philological Association* 114: 121–46, reprinted in Laird 2006: 87–114.

  (1985) 'Lies unlike the truth: Plato on Hesiod, *Theogony* 27', *Transactions of the American Philological Association* 115: 47–57.

  (1992) *Tragic Pleasures: Aristotle on Plot and Emotion.* Princeton University Press.

Benson, H. H. (ed.) (2006) *A Companion to Plato.* Wiley-Blackwell.

Bernabé, A. (2007) 'The *Derveni* theogony: Many questions and some answers', *Harvard Studies in Classical Philology* 103: 99–133.

Betegh, G. (2004) *The Derveni Papyrus: Cosmology, Theology and Interpretation.* Cambridge University Press.

Bett, R. (2011) 'Socratic ignorance', in Morrison 2011: 215–36.

Blank, D. (1998) *Sextus Empiricus: Against the Grammarians.* Oxford University Press.

  (2009) '*Philosophia* and *technē*: Epicureans on the arts', in Warren 2009: 216–33.

Bowie, E. L. (1993) 'Lies, fiction and slander in early Greek poetry', in C. Gill and T. P. Wiseman (eds.), *Lies and Fiction in the Ancient World*, Exeter University Press, 1993, 1–37.

Boys-Stones, G. (2001) *Post-Hellenistic Philosophy: A Study of its Development from the Stoics to Origen*. Oxford University Press.

(2003) 'The Stoics' two types of allegory', in G. Boys-Stones (ed.), *Metaphor, Allegory, and the Classical Tradition: Ancient Thought and Modern Revisions*, Oxford University Press, 189–216.

(2005) 'Alcinous, *Didaskalikos* 4: In defence of dogmatism', in M. Bonazzi and V. Celluprica (eds.), *L'eredità platonica: Studi sul platonismo da Arcesilao a Proclo*, Naples: Bibliopolis, 201–34.

Boys-Stones, G. and Haubold, J. (eds.) (2009) *Plato and Hesiod*. Oxford University Press.

Brisson, L. (2004) *How Philosophers Saved Myths: Allegorical Interpretation and Classical Mythology*. University of Chicago Press.

Brittain, C. (2008) 'Plato and Platonism', in Fine 2008: 526–52.

Broadie, S. (2007) 'Why no Platonistic ideas of artefacts?', in D. Scott (ed.), *Maieusis: Essays in Ancient Philosophy in Honour of Myles Burnyeat*, Oxford University Press, 135–50.

Burnyeat, M. (1999) 'Culture and society in Plato's *Republic*', *Tanner Lectures in Human Values* 20: 215–324.

Bussanich, J. (2006) 'Socrates and religious experience', in Ahbel-Rappe and Kamtekar 2006: 200–13.

Büttner, S. (2011) 'Inspiration and inspired poets in Plato's dialogues', in Destrée and Herrmann 2011: 111–29.

Chroust, A. H. (1973a) 'The great deluge in Aristotle's *On Philosophy*', *Antiquité Classique* 42: 113–22.

(1973b) *Aristotle: New Light on His Life and on Some of His Lost Works*. London: Routledge.

Coxon, A. H. (2009) *The Fragments of Parmenides*. Revised edition. Las Vegas: Parmenides Publishing.

Curd, P. and Graham, D. W. (eds.) (2008) *The Oxford Handbook of Presocratic Philosophy*. Oxford University Press.

Curzer, H. (2005) 'How good people do bad things: Aristotle on the misdeeds of the virtuous', *Oxford Studies in Ancient Philosophy* 28: 233–56.

Destrée, P. (2003) 'Education morale et catharsis tragique', *Les Études Philosophiques*: 518–35.

Destrée, P. and Herrmann, F.-G. (eds.) (2011) *Plato and the Poets*. Leiden: Brill.

Dillon, J. (1977) *The Middle Platonists: A Study of Platonism 80 BC to AD 220*. London: Duckworth.

Dyson, H. (2009) *Prolepsis and Ennoia in the Early Stoa*. Berlin: de Gruyter.

Edwards, M. J. (2000) 'In defense of Euthyphro', *American Journal of Philology* 121: 213–24.

Else, G. (1986) *Plato and Aristotle on Poetry*. Chapel Hill: University of North Carolina Press.

Emilsson, E. K. (2007) *Plotinus on Intellect*. Oxford University Press.

Ferrari, G. R. F. (1989) 'Plato and poetry', in G. A. Kennedy (ed.), *The Cambridge History of Literary Criticism, I: Classical Criticism*, Cambridge University Press, 92–128.

(1999) 'Aristotle's literary aesthetics', *Phronesis* 44: 181–98.

Ferrari, G. R. F. (ed.) (2007) *The Cambridge Companion to Plato's Republic*. Cambridge University Press.

Fine, G. (ed.) (2008) *The Oxford Handbook of Plato*. Oxford University Press.

Finkelberg, M. (1998) *The Birth of Literary Fiction in Ancient Greece*. Oxford University Press.

Fitch, W. T., von Graevenitz, A. and Nicolas, A. (2009) 'Bio-aesthetics and the aesthetic trajectory: A dynamic cognitive and cultural perspective', in M. Skov and O. Vartanian (eds.), *Neuroaesthetics*, Amityville, NY: Baywood, 59–101.

Ford, A. (2004) 'Catharsis: The power of music in Aristotle's *Politics*', in P. Murray and P. Wilson (eds.), *Music and the Muses*, Oxford University Press, 309–36.

Frede, M. (1987) 'Numenius', *Aufstieg und Niedergang der Römishen Welt* II 36.2: 1034–75.

(1990) 'La teoría de las ideas de Longino', *Methexis* 3: 85–98.

(1992) 'Plato's argument and the dialogue form', in Klagge and Smith 1992: 201–19.

(2007) 'On the unity and the aim of the Derveni text', *Rhizai* 4: 9–33.

Frede, D. and Inwood, B. (ed.) (2005) *Language and Learning: Philosophy of Language in the Hellenistic Age*. Cambridge University Press.

Freeland, C. A. (1996) 'Aristotle's *Poetics* in relation to the ethical treatises', in W. Wians (ed.), *Aristotle's Philosophical Development: Problems and Prospects*, Lanham, MD: Rowman and Littlefield, 327–45.

Furley, W. D. (1985) 'The figure of Euthyphro in Plato's dialogue', *Phronesis* 30: 201–8.

Gemelli Marciano, M. L. (2008) 'Images and experience: At the roots of Parmenides' *Aletheia*', *Ancient Philosophy* 28: 21–48.

Gerson, L. P. (1994) *Plotinus*. London: Routledge.

Gerson, L.P. (ed.) (1996) *The Cambridge Companion to Plotinus*. Cambridge University Press.

Gill, C. (2009) 'The Platonic dialogue', in M. L. Gill and P. Pellegrin (eds.), *A Companion to Ancient Philosophy*, Oxford: Wiley-Blackwell, 136–50.

Goulet, R. (2005) 'La méthode allégorique chez les stoïciens', in G. Romeyer Dherbey and J.-B. Gourinat (eds.), *Les stoïciens*, Paris: Vrin, 93–119.

Granger, H. (2004) 'Heraclitus' quarrel with polymathy and ἱστορίη', *Transactions of the American Philological Association* 134: 235–61.

(2007a) 'Poetry and prose: Xenophanes of Colophon', *Transactions of the American Philological Association* 137: 403–33.

(2007b) 'The theologian Pherecydes of Syros and the early days of natural philosophy', *Harvard Studies in Classical Philology* 103: 135–64.

(2008) 'The proem of Parmenides' poem', *Ancient Philosophy* 28: 1–20.

Griffiths, J. G. (1970) *Plutarch's De Iside et Osiride*. Cardiff: University of Wales Press.

Hadot, P. (1981) 'Ouranos, Kronos, and Zeus in Plotinus' treatise against the Gnostics', in H. J. Blumenthal and R. A. Markus (eds.), *Neoplatonism and Early Christian Thought: Essays in Honour of A. H. Armstrong*, London: Variorum, 124–37.

Halliwell, S. (1986) *Aristotle's Poetics*. London: Duckworth.

(1988) *Plato: Republic 10*. Warminster: Aris & Phillips.

(2000) 'The subjection of *muthos* to *logos*: Plato's citations of the poets', *The Classical Quarterly* 50: 94–112.

(2002) *The Aesthetics of Mimesis: Ancient Texts and Modern Problems*. Princeton University Press.

(2003) 'La psychologie morale de la catharsis: Un essai de reconstruction', *Les Études Philosophiques*, 67: 499–517.

(2008) *Greek Laughter: A Study of Cultural Psychology from Homer to Early Christianity*. Cambridge University Press.

(2011) *Between Ecstasy and Truth: Interpretations of Greek Poetics from Homer to Longinus*. Oxford University Press.

Halliwell, S., Russell, D. A. and Innes, D. I. (1995) *Aristotle, Poetics: Longinus, On the Sublime. Demetrius, On Style*. Cambridge, MA: Harvard University Press.

Hardie, P. R. (1992) 'Plutarch and the interpretation of myth', *Aufstieg und Niedergang der Römishen Welt* II 33.6: 4743–87.

Harte, V. (2010) '*Republic* 10 and the role of the audience in art', *Oxford Studies in Ancient Philosophy* 38: 69–96.

Heath, M. (1985) 'Hesiod's didactic poetry', *The Classical Quarterly* 35: 245–63.

(1989a) 'Aristotelian comedy', *The Classical Quarterly* 39: 344–54.

(1989b) *Unity in Greek Poetics*. Oxford University Press.

(1996) *Aristotle: Poetics*. Harmondsworth: Penguin.

(1999) 'Longinus *On Sublimity*', *Proceedings of the Cambridge Philological Society* 45: 43–74.

(2001) 'Aristotle and the pleasures of tragedy', in Andersen and Haarberg 2001: 7–23.

(2002) *Interpreting Classical Texts*. London: Duckworth.

(2008) 'Aristotle on natural slavery', *Phronesis* 53: 243–70.

(2009a) 'Heraclides of Pontus on Homer', in W. W. Fortenbaugh and E. E. Pender (eds.), *Heraclides of Pontus: Discussion*, New Brunswick NJ: Transaction, 251–72.

(2009b) 'Platonists and the teaching of rhetoric in late antiquity', in P. Vassilopoulou and S. R. L. Clark (eds.), *Late Antique Epistemology: Other Ways to Truth*, London: Palgrave Macmillan, 143–59.

(2009c) 'Cognition in Aristotle's *Poetics*', *Mnemosyne* 62: 51–75.

(2009d) 'Should there have been a *polis* in Aristotle's *Poetics*?', *The Classical Quarterly* 59: 468–85.

(2011) 'Aristotle and Homer', in M. Finkelberg (ed.), *Homer Encyclopaedia*, Oxford: Wiley-Blackwell, 93–6.

(2012) 'Longinus and the ancient sublime', in T. M. Costelloe (ed.), *The Sublime: From Antiquity to the Present*, Cambridge University Press, 11–23.

(in preparation) 'Aristotle on the best kind of tragic plot: *Poetics* 13–14'.

Helmig, C. (2008) 'Plutarch of Chaeronea and Porphyry on transmigration: Who is the author of Stobaeus I 445.14–448.3 (W.-H.)?', *The Classical Quarterly* 58: 250–5.

Hunter, R. and Russell, D. (2011) *Plutarch: How to Study Poetry (De audiendis poetis)*. Cambridge University Press.

Hurley, S. (2004) 'Imitation, media violence and freedom of speech', *Philosophical Studies* 117, 165–218.

Hurley, S. and Chater, N. (ed.) (2005) *Perspectives on Imitation: From Neuroscience to Social Science*. Cambridge, MA: MIT Press.

Hutchinson, D. S. and Johnson, M. R. (2005) 'Authenticating Aristotle's *Protrepticus*', *Oxford Studies of Ancient Philosophy* 29, 193–294.

Inwood, B. (ed.) (2003) *The Cambridge Companion to the Stoics*. Cambridge University Press.

Janaway, C. (1995) *Images of Excellence: Plato's Critique of the Arts*. Oxford University Press.

Janko, R. (1984) *Aristotle on Comedy: Towards a Reconstruction of Poetics II*. London: Duckworth.

(2001) 'Aristotle on comedy, Aristophanes and some new evidence from Herculaneum', in Andersen and Haarberg 2001: 51–71.

Johansen, T. K. (1999) 'Myth and logos in Aristotle', in R. Buxton (ed.), *From Myth to Reason? Studies in the Development of Greek Thought*, Oxford University Press, 279–91.

Kahn, C. H. (1997) 'Was Euthyphro the author of the Derveni papyrus?', in Laks and Most 1997: 55–63.

(1998) *Plato and the Socratic Dialogue: The Philosophical Use of a Literary Form*. Cambridge University Press.

Kingsley, P. (1995) *Ancient Philosophy, Mystery, and Magic: Empedocles and the Pythagorean Tradition*. Oxford University Press.

Klagge, J. C. and Smith, N. D. (eds.) (1992) *Methods of Interpreting Plato and His Dialogues*. Oxford University Press.

Konstan, D. (2004) '"The birth of the reader": Plutarch as a literary critic', *Scholia* 13: 3–27.

Kosman, L. A. (1992) 'Silence and imitation in the Platonic dialogue', in Klagge and Smith 1992: 73–92.

Kraut, R. (ed.) (1992) *The Cambridge Companion to Plato*. Cambridge University Press.

Kuisma, O. (1996) *Proclus' Defence of Homer*. Helsinki: Societas Scientiarum Fennica.

(2003) *Art or Experience: A Study on Plotinus' Aesthetics*. Helsinki: Societas Scientiarum Fennica.

Laird, A. (ed.) (2006) *Oxford Readings in Ancient Literary Criticism*. Oxford University Press.

Laks, A. (2008) 'Speculating about Diogenes of Apollonia', in Curd and Graham 2008: 353–64.

Laks, A. and Most, G. W. (eds.) (1997) *Studies on the Derveni Papyrus*. Oxford University Press.

Lamberton, R. (1986) *Homer the Theologian: Neoplatonist Allegorical Reading and the Growth of the Epic Tradition.* Berkeley: University of California Press.

(1992) 'The Neoplatonists and the spiritualisation of Homer', in Lamberton and Keaney 1992: 115–33.

Lamberton, R. and Keaney, J. J. (eds.) (1992) *Homer's Ancient Readers.* Princeton University Press.

Lesher, J. H. (1992) *Xenophanes of Colophon: Fragments: A Text and Translation with a Commentary.* Toronto University Press.

Lloyd, G. E. R. (1996) *Aristotelian Explorations.* Cambridge University Press.

Long, A. A. (1992) 'Stoic readings of Homer', in Lamberton and Keaney 1992: 41–66; reprinted in *Stoic Studies*, Cambridge University Press, 1999: 58–84, and in Laird 2006: 211–37.

(2005) 'Stoic linguistics, Plato's *Cratylus*, and Augustine's *De Dialectica*', in Frede and Inwood 2005: 37–55.

(2006) 'How does Socrates' divine sign communicate with him?', in Ahbel-Rappe and Kamtekar 2006: 63–92.

Long, A. A. (ed.) (1999) *The Cambridge Companion to Early Greek Philosophy.* Cambridge University Press.

Lorenz, H. (2006) *The Brute Within: Appetitive Desire in Plato and Aristotle.* Oxford University Press.

McCabe, M. M. (2008) 'Plato's ways of writing', in Fine 2008: 88–113.

McPherran, M. (2011) 'Socratic religion', in Morrison 2011: 111–37.

Mason, A. S. (2010) *Plato.* Durham: Acumen.

Mayhew, R. (2008) *Plato: Laws 10.* Oxford University Press.

Menn, S. (2001) 'Longinus on Plotinus', *Dionysius* 19: 113–23.

Moravcsik, J. and Temko, P. (eds.) (1982) *Plato on Beauty, Wisdom, and the Arts.* Totowa, NJ: Rowman and Littlefield.

Morgan, K. (2000) *Myth and Philosophy from the Presocratics to Plato.* Cambridge University Press.

Morrison, D. (2007) 'The utopian character of Plato's ideal city', in Ferrari 2007: 232–54.

Morrison, D. (ed.) (2011) *The Cambridge Companion to Socrates.* Cambridge University Press.

Moss, J. (2006) 'Pleasure and illusion in Plato', *Philosophy and Phenomenological Research* 72: 503–53.

(2007) 'What is imitative poetry and why is it bad?', in Ferrari 2007: 415–44.

(2008) 'Appearances and calculations: Plato's division of the soul', *Oxford Studies of Ancient Philosophy* 34: 35–68.

Most, G. (1980) 'Cornutus and Stoic allegoresis', *Aufstieg und Niedergang der Römishen Welt* II 36.3, 2014–65.

(1999) 'Poetics of early Greek philosophy', in Long 1999: 332–62.

Murray, P. (1981) 'Poetic inspiration in early Greece', *Journal of Hellenic Studies* 101: 87–100; reprinted in Laird 2006: 37–61.

(1995) *Plato on Poetry.* Cambridge University Press.

Naddaf, G. (2009) 'Allegory and the origins of philosophy', in W. Wians (ed.), *Logos and Muthos: Philosophical Essays in Greek Literature*, Albany: SUNY Press, 99–131.

Nussbaum, M. (1993) 'Poetry and the passions: Two Stoic views', in J. Brunschwig and M. Nussbaum (eds.), *Passions and Perceptions: Studies in Hellenistic Philosophy of Mind*, Cambridge University Press, 97–149.

(1994) *The Therapy of Desire: Theory and Practice in Hellenistic Ethics*. Princeton University Press.

Obbink, D. (1992) '"What all men believe – must be true": Common conceptions and *consensio omnium* in Aristotle and Hellenistic philosophy', *Oxford Studies of Ancient Philosophy* 10: 193–232.

(1995a) 'How to read poetry about gods', in Obbink 1995b: 188–209.

Obbink, D. (ed.) (1995b) *Philodemus and Poetry: Poetic Theory and Practice in Lucretius, Philodemus, and Horace*. Oxford University Press.

O'Keefe, T. (2010) *Epicureanism*. Durham: Acumen.

O'Meara, D. J. (1993) *Plotinus: An Introduction to the Enneads*. Oxford University Press.

Opsomer, J. (2003) 'La démiurgie des jeunes dieux selon Proclus', *Les Études Classiques* 71: 5–49.

Palmer, J. (2000) 'Aristotle on the ancient theologians', *Apeiron* 33: 181–205.

(2009) *Parmenides and Presocratic Philosophy*. Oxford University Press.

Pappas, N. (2003) *Plato and the Republic*. Second edition, London: Routledge.

Pemberton, G. (1976) 'A note on *skiagraphia*', *American Journal of Archaeology* 80: 82–4.

Pender, E. E. (2007) 'Sappho and Anacreon in Plato's *Phaedrus*', *Leeds International Classical Studies* 6.4.

(2009) 'Chaos corrected: The creation myths of Plato and Hesiod', in Boys-Stones and Haubold 2009: 219–45.

Pépin, J. (1965) 'Porphyre: Exégète d' Homère', *Entretiens sur l'Antiquité Classique* 12: 229–72.

Platt, V. (2009) 'Virtual visions: *Phantasia* and the perception of the divine in *The Life of Apollonius of Tyana*', in E. L. Bowie and J. Elsner (eds.), *Philostratus*, Cambridge University Press, 131–54.

Rangos, S. (1999) 'Proclus on poetic mimesis, symbolism, and truth', *Oxford Studies of Ancient Philosophy* 17: 249–77.

(2007) 'Latent meaning and manifest content in the Derveni Papyrus', *Rhizai* 4: 35–75.

Remes, P. (2007) *Plotinus on Self: The Philosophy of the 'We'*. Cambridge University Press.

(2008) *Neoplatonism*. Stocksfield: Acumen.

Richardson Lear, G. (2011) 'Mimesis and psychological change in *Republic* III', in Destrée and Herrmann 2011: 195–216.

Robinson, T. M. (1987) *Heraclitus of Ephesus: Fragments*. University of Toronto Press.

Rorty, A. O. (ed.) (1992) *Essays on Aristotle's Poetics*. Berkeley: University of California Press.

Rotstein, A. (2009) *The Idea of Iambos*. Oxford University Press.

Rowe, C. J. (2006) 'Interpreting Plato', in Benson 2006: 13–24.

Russell, D. A. (1992) *Dio Chrysostom: Orations 7, 12 and 36*. Cambridge University Press.

Saunders, T. J. (1991) *Plato's Penal Code: Tradition, Controversy, and Reform in Greek Penology*. Oxford University Press.

Schenkeveld, D. M. (1982) 'The structure of Plutarch's *De audiendis poetis*', *Mnemosyne* 35: 60–71; reprinted in Laird 2006: 313–24.

Schofield, M. (2006) *Plato: Political Philosophy*. Oxford University Press.

(2007) 'The noble lie', in Ferrari 2007: 138–64.

Scott, D. (1999) 'Platonic pessimism and moral education', *Oxford Studies of Ancient Philosophy* 17: 15–36.

Schütrumpf, E. (1989) 'Traditional elements in the concept of *hamartia* in Aristotle's *Poetics*', *Harvard Studies in Classical Philology* 92: 137–56.

Searle, J. (1975) 'The logical status of fictional discourse', *New Literary History* 6: 319–32; reprinted in *Expression and Meaning: Studies in the Theory of Speech Acts*, Cambridge University Press, 1979, 58–75.

Sedley, D. (2003) *Plato's Cratylus*. Cambridge University Press.

Sellars, J. (2006) *Stoicism*. Chesham: Acumen.

Sheppard, A. D. R. (1980) *Studies in the Fifth and Sixth Essays of Proclus' Commentary on the Republic*. Göttingen: Vandenhoeck & Ruprecht.

Sherman, N. (1992) '*Hamartia* and virtue', in Rorty 1992: 177–96.

Slater, W. J. (1982) 'Aristophanes of Byzantium and problem-solving in the museum', *The Classical Quarterly* 32: 336–49.

Smith, A. (1987) 'Porphyrian studies since 1913', *Aufstieg und Niedergang der Römishen Welt* II 36.2: 717–73.

Sorabji, R. (1980) *Necessity, Cause and Blame*. London: Duckworth.

(2000) *Emotion and Peace of Mind: From Stoic Agitation to Christian Temptation*. Oxford University Press.

Stalley, R. (1994) 'Persuasion in Plato's *Laws*', *History of Political Thought* 15: 157–77.

Stern-Gillet, S. (2004) 'On (mis)interpreting Plato's *Ion*', *Phronesis* 49, 169–99.

Stinton, T. C. W. (1975) '*Hamartia* in Aristotle and Greek tragedy', *The Classical Quarterly* 25: 221–54; reprinted in *Collected Papers on Greek Tragedy*, Oxford University Press, 1990, 143–85.

Struck, P. T. (2004) *Birth of the Symbol: Ancient Readers at the Limits of Their Texts*. Princeton University Press.

Tarrant, H. (trans.) (2007) *Proclus: Commentary on Plato's Timaeus I*. Cambridge University Press.

Tigerstedt, E. N. (1969) *Plato's Idea of Poetical Inspiration*. Helsinki: Societas Scientiarum Fennica.

Todd, R. B. (1973) 'Common notions', *Symbolae Osloenses* 48: 47–75.

Trapp, M. (trans.) (1997a) *Maximus of Tyre*. Oxford University Press.

(1997b) 'Philosophical sermons: The *Dialexeis* of Maximus of Tyre', *Aufstieg und Niedergang der Römishen Welt* II 34.3, 1945–76.

(2007) 'Apuleius of Madauros and Maximus of Tyre', in R. Sorabji and R. W. Sharples (eds.), *Greek and Roman Philosophy, 100BC–200AD*, London: Institute of Classical Studies, 467–82.

van der Stockt, L. (1992) *Twinkling and Twilight: Plutarch's Reflections on Literature*. Brussels: Akademie voor Wetenschappen, Letteren en Schone Kunsten van Belgie.

Vasiliou, I. (2008) *Aiming at Virtue in Plato*. Cambridge University Press.

Walsh, G. B. (1984) *The Varieties of Enchantment: Early Greek Views of the Nature and Function of Poetry*. Chapel Hill: University of North Carolina Press.

Warren, J. (2007) *Presocratics*. Stocksfield: Acumen.

Warren, J. (ed.) (2009) *The Cambridge Companion to Epicureanism*. Cambridge University Press.

Watson, G. (1994) 'The concept of "phantasia" from the late Hellenistic period to early Neoplatonism', *Aufstieg und Niedergang der Römishen Welt* II 36.7, 4765–810.

West, M. L. (2003) *Homeric Hymns. Homeric Apocrypha. Lives of Homer*. Cambridge, MA: Harvard University Press.

White, S. (2001) '*Principes sapientiae*: Dicaearchus' biography of philosophy', in W. W. Fortenbaugh and E. Schütrumpf (eds.), *Dicaearchus of Messana*, New Brunswick NJ: Transaction, 195–236.

Whittaker, J. (1987) 'Platonic philosophy in the early centuries of the Empire', *Aufstieg und Niedergang der Römishen Welt* II 36.1: 81–123.

Woolf, R. (2009) 'Truth as a value in Plato's *Republic*', *Phronesis* 54: 9–39.

Zadorojnyi, A. (2002) 'Safe drugs for the good boys: Platonism and pedagogy in Plutarch's *De audiendis poetis*', in P. A. Stadter and L. van der Stockt (eds.), *Sage and Emperor: Plutarch, Greek Intellectuals, and Roman Power in the Time of Trajan, 98–117 AD*, Leuven University Press, 297–314.

Index

References in **bold** type indicate the principal discussions of individual philosophers or philosophical traditions.

Printed in the United States
by Baker & Taylor Publisher Services